Critical Inve

General Editor: John Scha_
University of Lancaster

"a creative intellectual enterprise as rare as it is necessary in an academy which is now over-institutionalised and deadened by bureaucracy."
Jonathan Dollimore

PUBLISHED

GIVEN: 1° Art   2° Crime
Modernity, Murder and Mass Culture
Jean-Michel Rabaté

Heidegger's Bicycle
Interfering with Victorian Texts
Roger Ebbatson

Someone Called Derrida
An Oxford Mystery
John Schad

The English Question; or, Academic Freedoms
Thomas Docherty

FORTHCOMING

The Prodigal Sign
Kevin Mills

Rapture: Literature, Secrecy, Addiction
David Punter

The Habits of Distraction
Michael Wood

John Schad is Professor of Modern Literature at the University of Lancaster. He is the author of *The Reader in the Dickensian Mirrors* and *Victorians in Theory*, the editor of *Dickens Refigured*, Thomas Hardy's *A Laodicean*, and *Writing the Bodies of Christ*; and co-editor of *life.after.theory*. His latest work, *Queer Fish: Christian Unreason from Darwin to Derrida*, was published by Sussex Academic in 2004.

In memory of
Theresa McTaggart

THE ENGLISH QUESTION

QUESTION

OR ACADEMIC FREEDOMS

Thomas Docherty

sussex
ACADEMIC
PRESS

BRIGHTON • PORTLAND

Copyright © Thomas Docherty, 2008

The right of Thomas Docherty to be identified as Author of this work has been asserted in accordance with the Copyright, Designs and Patents Act 1988.
2 4 6 8 10 9 7 5 3

First published 2008 in Great Britain by
SUSSEX ACADEMIC PRESS
PO Box 139
Eastbourne BN24 9BP

and in the United States of America by
SUSSEX ACADEMIC PRESS
920 NE 58th Ave   Suite 300
Portland, Oregon 97213-3786

All rights reserved. Except for the quotation of short passages for the purposes of criticism and review, no part of this publication may be reproduced, stored in a retrieval system, or transmitted, in any form or by any means, electronic, mechanical, photocopying, recording or otherwise, without the prior permission of the publisher.

British Library Cataloguing in Publication Data
A CIP catalogue record for this book is available from the British Library.

Library of Congress Cataloging-in-Publication Data
Docherty, Thomas.
    The English question, or academic freedoms / Thomas
    Docherty.
    p. cm. — (Critical inventions)
    Includes bibliographical references and index.
    ISBN 978-1-84519-132-0 (acid-free paper) —
    ISBN 978-1-84519-133-7 (pbk. : acid-free paper)
    1. Great Britain—Civilization. 2. English literature—
History and criticism. 3. Academic freedom. I. Title.

    DA566.4.D585 2008
    378.1'2130941—dc22

                                                    2007021206

Typeset and designed by SAP, Brighton & Eastbourne
Printed by TJ International, Padstow, Cornwall
This book is printed on acid-free paper.

Contents

Series Editor's Preface

Be warned: whenever you read a real book you run a risk, the risk of never being quite the same again – and that's the whole point of books; or, at least, so argues Thomas Docherty in this particular book. To put it another way, *The English Question* might easily be called 'The English Imperative' since, for Docherty, to read literature is to be confronted with something so radically other that sameness, or remaining the same, is not an option. In fact, Docherty will argue that 'before art there is no hiding place for the human' and thus, like Rilke before the sculpture of Apollo, all we ever hear is the injunction: 'You must change your life!' So, be prepared for talk not only of critics but converts, or those who are both such as Newman and Augustine; be prepared too for rumours of grace as Docherty goes off in pursuit of a vision of reading that might yet blast open the outcomes-driven model of English Studies so beloved of the managerialist academy that surrounds us on every side.

If this monster is 'the official university' then Docherty calls us to join forces with what he calls the 'clandestine university' and thus to fight a war of resistance, from within occupied territory. Make no mistake, it is freedom that is at stake, for Docherty espies a link between the freedom to which literature summons us and the freedom involved in becoming a citizen rather than just a consumer. Such freedom is so precious as to call for the rhetoric of war, and Docherty (almost without knowing it) responds to the call, first glancing over his shoulder at such war-times thinkers as F. R. Leavis and I. A. Richards and then echoing Lyotard's famous battle-cry – the one that goes: 'let us wage a war on totality; let us be witnesses to the unpresentable . . . and [let us] save the honour of the name.'

For Docherty, the name is, of course, the name of 'English' which turns out to have many better or rather other names – names like: negative capability; undecidabilty; eloquence; humility; becoming; even dying; and (strangest of all) Scotland. Look out for this last, as the English Question suddenly and brilliantly gives rise to the Scottish Answer, or at least to the non-answer which is the potentiality that is contemporary Scotland – a nation devolved but not-yet-independent.

So, as you can see, there are surprises here – as we might expect (if that is not a contradiction) of a book that assures us that to read is always 'to read in the dark', or (if you like) that to read is not so much to know or understand as to encounter. But don't worry; if reading is an encounter with other-ness then, says Docherty, 'we are not in crisis but in love'. And if that seems funny, or even laughable then Docherty may yet prove right to believe, as he does, that 'laughter is . . . at the very core of a possible university'.

This may not sound like any university you know, or of which you could dream, but Docherty would suggest that is because you don't spend enough time failing to understand books that you love. Yes, 'love', a word literary critics rarely use, but a word toward which Docherty beckons those of us foolish enough to dream that the critic has agency, that he or she can ever *do* anything to a text. The trouble is, says Docherty, we literary critics suffer from the delusion that the text 'is there for us' whereas perhaps it 'is there' for an other, for someone else or something else, or even for . . . Well, I had better not say; you will need to read this book yourself. In the dark.

JOHN SCHAD, Series Editor

Preface and Acknowledgments

This book, as you know since you have picked it up, is called *The English Question*; and so it is actually about the relations between knowledge and freedom. The title is not a misnomer because I argue the case for a fundamental intimacy between knowledge of the questions that pertain to the 'English' on one hand and the establishment and articulation of emancipatory activity on the other. The hands – one side, other side – are joined: in an attitude of applause when the relation works, in an attitude of supplication when the intimacy is being broken. The book needs to be written, I fear, because the linking of the hands (my hand in my hand; your hand in mine; hers in hers and so on) is under immense pressure, to the point where the hoped-for intimacy between knowledge and freedom is close to becoming a fractured divorce.

The book is an attempt to refresh the case for what I would call a 'literate and humane University' institution, in and through which we can find what might be the possibilities for our humanity; and so, although my primary focus is on the subject and discipline of 'English', it pertains to all academic disciplines, including the social and so-called hard sciences as well. Such a literate and humane University is under particular threat, especially in the advanced economies; and what is threatened thereby, I claim in the pages that follow, is not only knowledge but also certain essential freedoms, freedoms that are essential to our becoming humane, even human.

The book has its roots in an experience of working in several Universities in a number of places; but if I am to find a particular moment when I felt that my thoughts on these matters needed to be collected and offered, it lies in a conversation that I had around two years ago. This is anecdotal, but I offer the terms of the conversation as revealing something fundamental about our contemporary predicaments. The conversation was with a colleague elsewhere whose work – and whose academic leadership – I have admired for a long time, but whose area is in the hard sciences. His career had taken him through numerous very senior positions in the various institutions where he had worked; and, as is sometimes the case, he also undertook a series of senior consultancies in the public domain beyond the academy as well. An extremely able leader of international standing in his subject, but with a profound interest in social sciences and a passion for the arts as well, the next obvious move for him to make in career terms was to a Vice-Chancellorship; but he opted, instead, to return to the lab for the final decade of his career.

It was with some resignation that he told me he had started to find it difficult to stand over some of the directives he was issuing, or being required to issue, in his senior role. The crunch had come with the introduction of so-called top-up fees in the UK sector which was, for him, a step too far: 'I really thought I could not stand over that, seriously, and still sleep comfortably at night.'

This is a man of some principle. The anecdote has more than local or biographical importance; for it reveals two things of more general applicability. First, there is an increasing division between actual everyday academic work and the governance of that daily routine within the University. Secondly, it raises the question of how many colleagues find themselves increasingly in the kind of 'bad faith' position, the pressure of which essentially arrested the leadership career of my friend.

These two things ghost this book in various ways: my fundamental contention is that the actual substance of study is under increasing threat; and there is an increasing requirement that people in the academy do things in which they have no belief – the response to which is sometimes, *1984*-style, that we do eventually agree with O'Brien just so that we can get on with things, and some Winstons among us even start to believe O'Brien's lies.

In some ways, I have been pondering the topic of this book ever since I entered the University profession – probably, indeed, ever since the days when I used to watch students collecting for charity in the streets of Glasgow as a child during rag-week. As those students ran around, in all sorts of hugely imaginative fancy dress, I had an image of them as exotic, alien, and quite extraordinarily seductive. I felt that they inhabited a world that was other than mine, that they were finding and thinking thoughts that were, at that time, unimaginable in my own philosophies, that they were open to all sorts of liberal and liberating possibility. It was frightening to think of their potential for disruption of the norms; and the carnival of rag-day gave me a thrilling and exhilarating glimpse of such freedoms.

Once I became a student, I was able to start asking more seriously what, then, is the purpose of a University? Within that, what is the purpose of reading literature? Indeed, what is the purpose of reading and study in this and other ostensibly non-productive or non-instrumentalist disciplines? To be briefly philosophical, what is the relation between what we do in English departments on one hand, and that exotically thrilling other world of the good, the true and the beautiful – we might even say the free – on the other?

This book examines the current conditions under which we read, study, and seek to enlarge freedom. It seeks to offer some suggestions as to how we might restore these activities – indeed all the activities of the intellectual associated with the University institution – to their proper domain in the public sphere. Yet more importantly, it argues for an intimate link between a certain attitude to humane study on one hand and the establishment and enlargement of human freedoms on the other. At various times, especially within the field of English literary studies, such a view has been associated with a certain self-aggrandisement. For example, in the heyday of 'theory', especially leftist theory, some academics assumed a rather grand importance for their work, seeing it as being continuous and contiguous with political struggles across the world: Nicaragua in the classroom, as it were. This is certainly not what I am arguing for here; and, indeed, the reader will see that the book's trajectory takes us steadily towards a position that is characterised by a 'critical humility'.

The humility in question requires trust. Over the past three decades, the very shape of our academic institutions has been radically changed; and behind the change is a systematic eradication of trust. This has been damaging. People do not trust the academy; the 'masses' mistrust the 'intellectuals'; students, pupils and their parents mistrust teachers; teachers often think the wool is being pulled over their eyes by plagiarising students; the government encourages a generalised mistrust of academic activity by asking it always and everywhere to demonstrate immediate accountabilities in terms of financial reward and return; and so on. A generalised culture of mistrust – even of distrust – leads to a state of affairs in which it is believed that everything is kept under surveillance, or that it should be kept under surveillance, all the time. Paradoxically, this results in a state of affairs where there is eventually nothing left to be surveyed in the public domain, for anything of substance or of significance goes underground. We are Gertrude in *Hamlet*, in the presence of her ghostly husband, encouraged by Hamlet to see, and yet seeing 'Nothing at all, yet all that is I see'.

Surveillance usually goes under a different name, of course: we call it 'transparency', and, in the new pornography of our 'personal-financial-profit' norms of the social, we require that everything be revealed. Indeed, all can be revealed all the time, for there is no public sphere left in which to be embarrassed by our nakedness. Surveillance sounds rather like something that would hamper or harness freedom. The demand for transparency is part of the rhetoric of a political right, clearly; but more troubling is the fact that it has been picked up and embraced by a political left as well. If the left stands for anything, it surely stands for the pursuit of truth and of justice, but instead, 'transparency' is what we get. Transparency might be defined as that state of affairs in which we are denied access to truth and to justice, but where we are allowed full access to the workings of a justice system that is not only revealed, but that vaunts and flaunts itself: trial by and on TV, say, where the TV-effect is more important than the justice found. The humility I favour brings with it a certain modesty as well; and, in restoring the public sphere, it also thereby gives substance to the possibility of a private life, a life of aesthetic sensibilities.

Fundamentally, then, these reflections lie at the core of this book, and I have written it to explore more fully their consequences and purchase. In my own case, certainly, such reflections have been ongoing for a number of years. At least since the day I was offered my first Chair Professorship, in 1989, I saw it as my responsibility to try to take an overview of the entire domain of English studies; and it is that more general turn that has given the impetus for writing this study. I am not the first to ponder the English question, as the merest glimpse at the names in this book will show; but, if this book helps to create more dialogue on the topic, my success will be that I am far from the last.

Some of the work that appears here has already appeared in different form in various places. I am grateful to the editors of *Critical Quarterly, Comparative Criticism, The Cambridge Quarterly* and *boundary 2* for permission to re-use some material in its new forms and contexts. I am also grateful to Elizabeth Beaumont-Bissell and Manchester University Press for permission to revisit 'The Question concerning Literature' from *The Question of Literature*; to Paul Sheehan and to Greenwood Publishing for permission to use material from 'On Critical Humility' in *Becoming Human*; and to Gavin Miller and Eleanor Bell for permission to return to 'The Existence of Scotland' in their *Scotland and Theory*. Some of the material has been tried out on audiences in Canterbury, London, Edinburgh, Warwick, Rosario, Utrecht, Prague, Belfast, Brighton and (in passing debates) in various other places. I thank my audiences and many interlocutors for their splendid interventions, often setting me off on a better track than I had foreseen. Despite what may appear from the pages that follow, I have myself been more than fortunate in always finding a congenial and supportive atmosphere among my academic colleagues (and even with some VCs), especially in Kent and, now, also, in Warwick. Finally, but firstly as well, I want to thank John Schad who has encouraged me to offer this book, and Anthony Grahame who has helped edit it. Their remarkable patience and encouragement while I grappled with my daily duties as a Head of Department whilst trying also to get on with writing this material have been enormously helpful; and I remain flattered by their kind interest in this work.

As always, the two who support me most are Bridie Sullivan and Hamish Docherty. They know what the book has cost; and they know, more impor-

tantly, the substance and significance of the love, friendship and trust –
those determinants of becoming free – that permeate its core.

The Critical Inventions Series

Do I dare / Disturb the universe?
(T. S. Eliot, 'The Love Song of J. Alfred Prufrock', 1917)

In 1961 C. S. Lewis published *An Experiment in Criticism*; over forty years later, at the beginning of a new century, there is pressing need for a renewed sense of experiment, or invention in criticism. The energies unleashed by the theoretical movements of the 1970s and 1980s have been largely exhausted – many now say we are experiencing life after theory; some, indeed, say we are experiencing life after criticism. Criticism, we might say, is in crisis. But that is where it should be; the word 'criticism' comes, as we know, from the word 'crisis'.

Talk of crisis does not, though, fit easily within the well-managed contemporary academy; with its confident talk of 'scholarly excellence', there is a presumption that we all know, and are agreed upon, what scholarship and criticism is. However, to echo Paul de Man, 'we don't even know what reading is'; and what is, potentially, exciting about our present crisis is that now we really know that we don't know what reading is. It is, then, in a spirit of learned ignorance that we propose 'critical inventions', a series which will feature books that, in one way or another, push the generic conventions of literary criticism to breaking point. In so doing the very figure of the critic will shift and change. We shall, no doubt, glimpse something of what Oscar Wilde famously called 'the critic as artist', or what Terry Eagleton called 'the critic as clown'; we may even glimpse still more unfamiliar figures – the critic as, for example, autobiographer, novelist, mourner, poet, parodist, detective, dreamer, diarist, flaneûr, surrealist, priest, montagist, gambler, traveller, beggar, anarchist… or even amateur. In short, this series seeks the truly critical critic – or, to be paradoxical, the critic as critic; the critic who is a critic of criticism as conventionally understood, or misunderstood. He or she is the critic who will dare to disturb the universe, or at least the university – in particular, the institutionalisation of criticism that is professional, university English.

Establishment English is, though, a strange institution that is capable of disestablishing itself, if only because it houses the still stranger institution of literature – which, as Jacques Derrida once wrote, 'in principle allows us to say everything/ anything [tout dire]'. We, therefore, do not or cannot yet know of what criticism may yet be capable – capable of being, capable of doing. 'Critical inventions' will be a series that seeks to find out.

Read the text right and emancipate the world.
(Robert Browning, 'Bishop Bloughram's Apology', 1855)

JOHN SCHAD, Series Editor

PART I

Looking Back

CHAPTER **1**

The English Question

1 A back story

'This is clearly a critical time'. Let us begin from that rather banal statement. Several important issues dominate world affairs: the possibility of ecological disaster on a grand scale; the question of a quasi-democratised world terror whose violences and violations, in their anarchic randomness, implicate us all ostensibly equally; the struggle, fought with a fundamental religious intensity, for pre-eminence of certain identifiable political orders over each other. At stake in all of these questions is the future of what we might call a generalised possibility of and for freedom. Yet more specifically, some major nation states have recently been engaged in an ongoing war, whose degeneration into a troubling state of attrition threatens to implicate and involve more and more nation states: we are involved in a joint British–American invasion of foreign territories. Some of these invasions appeared recently to have been successful in their stated aims: for example, an evil foreign leader was arrested, and put on trial.

'This is clearly a critical time'. The time in question is 25 July 1943, and Mussolini has just been arrested by Italian soldiers; this in the wake of the Allied invasion, under Patton, of Palermo, and after the various military successes in North Africa. The man who has just said that 'This is clearly a critical time' is not I, but rather F. R. Leavis. When he wrote these words, in 1943, his attention was less on the war in Italy and more on what he saw as a more fundamental war: not a battle between civilisations but a battle, as a later Prime Minister would put it, for civilisation itself. Perhaps paradoxically, unlike Tony Blair who came to power in Britain in 1997 claiming that his three priorities would be 'education, education, and education', it is Leavis and not Blair who sees that at the centre of that battle 'for civilisation itself' is to be the University; and at the centre of the University for Leavis, a discipline of literary criticism that we will call 'English'. When he re-issued his 1943 text, *Education and the University* – after the war, after Auschwitz, after Hiroshima[1] – in 1948, he argued in the preface that 'It is still possible to say that "post-war reconstruction" represents opportunities as well as depressing possibilities'.

In this book, and in this not-quite post-war moment,[2] I want to look at some of the opportunities and depressing possibilities that shape and will shape our subject. In its most extreme form, the question that I am putting as 'The English Question' is one regarding the proper place of English – and more generally of literature – within a society. When Leavis asked the question, in 1943, he put it in terms of a conundrum: does the university replicate the society of which it is a part; or does it rather exist in order to counter the tendencies and drift of that society in some measure? In putting the conundrum in this way, he is thinking that there must be some fundamental 'mirroring' relation, a relation of reflection, that hinges society and institution together; and for him, essentially, the question is whether the mirror accurately reflects a pre-existing order or whether it exists as a critical mirror that distorts in order to prompt change in the existing order. In short, he thinks of the relation between university and society as being one founded and grounded in a question of *representation*. In what follows, I shall be exploring the limitations of that formulation of the relation. What Leavis needs, as it were, is the answer to the Snow White question: who is the fairest? Yet the stakes of the question are much more important than might be suggested by the Snow White analogy.

Leavis framed the question in this way because he was not content with the society in which he found himself, of course. Some fifteen years later, of course, another Snow, C. P. Snow, gave his famous 'Two Cultures' Rede Lecture; and it is in his response to this that Leavis was able to formulate more precisely the terms of his distaste for his contemporary world. Fundamentally, the Snow–Leavis controversy of the early 1960s concerned a difference of view about progress and tradition.[3] For Snow, progress was signalled by, among other things, the advances of science and of technology; it was high time that we acknowledged that fact and that we therefore concentrated on having more science and more scientists. This would serve two functions: it would help the society advance more generally in practical matters, and thereby remain at the forefront of world powers; and it would speak to the inmost possibilities of many young people skilled in technical and technological education (as opposed to the formalities of the humanistic classics, say) and their associated disciplines, and allow them to have a fulfilled life.[4] Against this railed Leavis, who would argue that such a position, in its perceived demotion of literature, would, at best, allow us to have a form of knowledge that was not 'lived', not actually 'felt' at the level of an inner intensity of sensibility. It would be, for Leavis, a triumph of the industrialisation of the human spirit. Paradoxically, therefore, he would have seen the Snow preferences as anti-progressive, for they essentially hearkened back to the great period of Oxbridge 'reforms' in the period between 1850 and 1870, reforms that were essentially driven by the demands of an industrialising society for instrumental and practically applicable knowledge.

In his plea for English, against what he saw as the incipient barbarism of Snow, Leavis argued that here was a subject that would allow an English student to acquire the tradition in his (at this time, still predominantly 'his', of course; 'her' comes later) bones, to feel it intimately, and – this above all – to judge of virtually all that mattered in general life by combining both sensibility and intelligence. He stigmatised Snow as one caught up in a bland advocacy of the primacy of intelligence *over* sensibility; and, for Leavis, that was not a *critical* intelligence – and therefore not really an intelligence – at all.

Put like this, of course, the Leavis position is recognisable within a broader history: essentially, he sees criticism here as being the site in which we regulate the competing demands of sense or reason and sensibility or feeling: he needs a position that reconciles Austen's Elinor *and* Marianne Dashwood, as it were (and, indeed, much of his own subsequent literary criticism focuses attention on precisely those writers where he finds this reconciliation).[5] What he adds to this very general aesthetic problem is a kind of ethnic dimension: this subject of 'English literary criticism' is concerned with a tradition of Englishness, with a national character of sorts, lived at its best.

It might be instructive, in this opening section, to advert a little to the history that pre-dates these and more recent contests of faculties; for these questions are of more than parochial interest. The matters that excited Leavis have, as we will see, something of a pre-history, and the percussions of that history can still be felt in the present condition of English and of the University as an institution.

Ever since Universities have existed, there have been debates about their function and their use. This book is not concerned directly with the pre-history of the modern institution; but it will nonetheless be useful to offer here some key elements of a very broad-brush sketch of the early formation of the University. Scholarship usually agrees that, in the period of an emergent modernity in Europe, some key elements coalesce to shape the inaugurating institutions from which our contemporary University draws its authority and identity. First, in the early modern moment, there is an 'importation' or domestication in Europe of learning from the Arabic countries and cultures: central to this is mathematics and medicine, both of which are essentially 'translated' into a European community that begins to identify itself as 'modern' precisely through what it sees as 'advances' or progress in these two disciplines. Along with this goes a further and rapidly spreading institutionalisation of a legal system, brought from Roman Law, across the key economic centres of the new Europe and its nascent nation states.

The new polity in Europe is one that positively highly valorises medicine, law, and number (which is clearly crucial for that new economic formation of society that eventually takes its shape around trade and capitalist forms of exchange). With this new polity taking shape, groups of itinerant scholars started to organise themselves very informally. Students keen to advance in the new conditions would gather for their learning around a magus figure, one who would 'profess' the knowledge that is now available – and that is potentially rather revolutionary in its liberating power and intellectual force. The liberation in question here is both sociopolitical and individual: my command of number regulates wealth; my command of law regulates social order and hierarchy, itself somewhat determined by that wealth; my command of medicine regulates the body itself and with it, therefore, the very possibilities of human interaction or social order, the ways in which bodies will interact (most immediately in sexualised love and in structured labour relations). All three fundamentals of the new society are interlinked; all are grounded in the new institution that is the University.

Gradually, these groups of scholars – communities who were peregrine by nature and sometimes of necessity – began to assert a kind of autonomy, and with it an identity – a group identity. As Murray G. Ross indicates in his 'anatomy of academe', the emerging universities or communities gained this autonomy and secured certain social privileges by two main methods: strike (or cessation of work), and migration (or readiness to move and relocate). When there are no buildings to worry about, groups of nomadic scholars could simply decamp into another community, who would then be in a position to threaten the community that the scholars had just left; and the threat came from the increased power – essentially tied to a notion of advance and therefore modernisation[6] – that their knowledge would bring to their new host community. 'By these means', wrote Ross, 'the universities were able to secure unusual privileges – exemption from local laws and taxes, for example – and make legal their separation from the daily life of society' (p. 10).

I focus on this particular aspect of University development because of its significance as the inauguration of an institutionalisation of the separation from the State that has come in some ways to dominate our thinking about 'academic freedom', a quasi-separation that persists to our own times.

Among the first of what we might call the 'proto-neo-cons', Daniel Bell took up this description of the University in the 1970s when he argued that there were essentially only two real models of the University. In the first or 'classical' model, the University is 'that institution in the society endowed with the special function (and the extraordinary immunity) of searching for truth and evaluating the culture of the times. In this sense, it is free to question everything – *in theory*'. This classical University has no practical function at all, but exists instead as an institution whose function remains purely theoretical and within the bounds of the freely speculative; its speculations remain non-financial, purely in the market of ideas. Against this is Bell's second model, the 'pragmatic' model as he calls it, in which 'the function of the university is primarily one of service to the society: service in training large numbers of persons, service in the application of knowledge, service of the members of the university in government and elsewhere' (Bell, 233). The pragmatic University operates within the realm of the financial market, and is designed for returns on investment in the form of *immediate* prosperity or gains in power.

This leaves us with a pretty clear, if somewhat crudely schematic, choice. As Bell puts it, 'If one chooses the first, then one is barred, in the role of scholar and researcher (though not as citizen) from political advocacy and active partisanship. If the second, the question becomes: "Who shall decide?" "Should the universities serve the military? Or the urban poor? Or the radicals? Should the criterion be national interest, social need, the command of money, the influence of power groups, or what?"' (Bell, 233). In the first position here, we have the University as an 'academic' institution: 'academic' here signalling impracticality; and in the second, we again have the University as an 'academic' institution: 'academic' here signalling blameworthiness, responsibility for crisis and for the shortcomings in the performativity or economic efficiency of a society. The former sees the University as essentially divorced from the social realities; the second sees it as integral to the social, but as purely instrumental or even incidental to the operations that matter, those operations that drive and govern the holding or maintenance of power by particular interested or partisan – social or political – groups.

Bell's schema is useful in laying bare the stakes of the University for the conservative tradition: the real point, for the conservative, is to see the University as being involved in a power struggle – essentially a power struggle in which intellectuals might disinterestedly contest the grounds of politicians – and therefore as an institution that needs to be divested of power in real terms. This, then, is a position that, in its innate suspicion of the power of intellection and thus also of the intellectual, is broadly recognisable for our times; and it is a position that still shapes the debate about the point of the University as a social institution. Is it to be divorced from society, as a kind of 'pagan' critical body whose members are essentially 'outside' of the social – in which case, it divests itself of political practice and social practicability?[7] Or is it to be seen as instrumental, as one more institution that is there essentially to advance competing versions of what will constitute human happiness in political and practical terms, in which case it becomes the site for interested political debate or controversy (i.e. not neutral or concerned with the disinterested pursuit of knowledge or truth); and, at the same time, an institution that politicians need to colonise for partial and interested ends (given that politics is essentially an argument about what it is that will contribute to the greater sum of human happiness).

So we might see here that the terms of 'representation' (that shaped the formulation of the key question for Leavis) might not be fully adequate to the predicament in which we find ourselves. To limit ourselves to the terms of representation that governed Leavis's formulation would be to keep ourselves constrained within the rather bourgeois 'Snow White' style question about the mediation between labour and intellect: not so much a 'two cultures' debate as a 'mind–body' dualism debate. As we will see, this latter dualism is of great significance. We perhaps need slightly different terms for our exploration of the real stakes of the argument: what is the relation of the University to a *freedom* that will be real, lived and felt; and, yet more specifically, what is the importance of English for this?

Our contemporary idea of 'academic freedom' is largely indebted to Karl Jaspers, in fact. He wrote his initial version of *The Idea of the University* during Weimar, in 1923; but it is the version that he revised and re-wrote in 1946 that really states the importance of this freedom established in and by the institution. In 1946, Jaspers had been installed as the Rector of Heidelberg University. His task was essentially a repetition of that given to Humboldt in 1810: to describe a University that is adequate to a specific political situation or predicament. For Humboldt, as we will see later, the problem to be faced was essentially the invention of a nation; for Jaspers, it is the re-invention of a nation after the tragic predicament brought about – with especial force in Germany – by the Second War. Central to both is the issue of an intellectual culture; and, for Jaspers, that culture now has to be one that is clearly differentiated from the immediately preceding Hitler years and that will be characterised by an emancipation of human potential.

Jaspers, we might say, is in the position of having to try to regulate the competing demands of what Daniel Bell was to call the classical and the pragmatic. His idea of academic freedom is essentially very close to the position in which the University scholar must have total freedom to pursue whatever line of inquiry is required by the disinterested pursuit of truth and knowledge; and must also have the total freedom to disseminate the knowledge that arises then through an unhindered teaching. Research and teaching are fully reconciled in this; the demonstration of the freedom in question is, in fact, the very teaching of the knowledge that has been discovered in the free pursuit of truth. That much we will recognise as 'classical'. Yet Jaspers is also profoundly aware of the context in which this idea of a University has to take root; and to that extent, he is aware of the relation of the University as an institution to the reconstruction of a social order; and this much is 'pragmatic'. In short, Jaspers is working in a situation where it becomes clear that the pragmatic and the classical cannot be separated, for the very establishment of the ideals of a classical institution has to occur within a practical situation where not everything will be possible. In this, the result is that the University becomes the institution that helps to identify the nature of the freedoms that will give the society (or the nation) its identity. There is, as it were, a dialectical relation between institution and society.

In the case of Jaspers, the resolution of the predicament is essentially a kind of blurring of the issue. On one hand, the principle of classical academic freedom is sacrosanct. On the other hand, the realisation of that freedom depends not just on research but also on the pedagogical dissemination of the knowledge that is discovered through the free research. In this, we have a kind of answer to Bell's 'Quis custodiet?' question: who will decide *what is to be done* in a given society, or who will decide what powers the University will serve? The answer implied in Jaspers is that it is the intellectuals themselves, in their role as *teachers*, who will decide; for teaching is itself the pragmatic aspect of the enunciation and articulation of the classical academic freedom that is to underpin the University.

In this way, Jaspers answers the predicament; and yet, of course, he also simultaneously evades the real substance of the predicament. In short, he simply displaces the problem onto another social level; for the question now posed is whether teaching – a teaching that is supposedly the enactment of freedom – itself has any actual and material social effect, or whether, given that it is happening *within the framework of a circumscribed institution*, it has no social effects at all. Teaching itself, it seems, becomes fully 'theoretical', in Bell's sense of the term.

To put this crudely, I am totally free not only to discover (say) the 'truth of Marxism', but also to teach it. My society, inimical to the demands of a Marxist analysis of its foundations, is nonetheless perfectly happy for me to teach this and will celebrate my freedom so to do. In permitting me to teach it, the society demonstrates that it permits my freedom to be faithful to the demands of knowledge, gained from my disinterested research. Yet, despite that teaching, the society remains inimical to a Marxist analysis (and to the corollary of revolution), for it has made my teaching a purely circumscribed – one might almost say 'ghettoised' – affair. Not only is the teaching something that happens in the abstract, and in a place that is artificially divorced from the body politic (as its decapitated head, the mind in the mind–body dualism that governs this idea); but it is also even *celebrated* – on condition that it remains a Marxism that relates to matters of (say) literary criticism, a 'Marxism' that describes the culture of my ghetto and identifies me within it. The initial position of 'disinterestedness' in the pursuit of truth through research permeates the whole. The freedom has become purely 'academic' freedom.

In this post-war idea of the University, we essentially reiterate the metaphor of the body politic, in which the materiality of culture is the domain of the worker-by-hand, as it were; and the matters of the intellect, far from being matters of a directing intelligence, become instead the domain in which we can describe, after the fact, what has happened in the social. We are now, as intellectuals, in the position of being able to do nothing about material conditions, while being in the best possible place for the analysis of how those material conditions arise and how they organise themselves into social and other kinds of formation. We can see and understand the world's predicaments, but we are unable to do anything whatsoever about them: the classic 'academic' predicament.[8] The head, as I suggested, is decapitated: the University as an architectural space, is removed from the centre of cities and placed on 'pagan' edge-of-town self-contained campuses. The civic centre is now identified with the fully and nakedly capitalistic: banks, finance houses, commercial centres – and the citizen, accordingly, identifies herself or himself in relation to these institutions, seeing the University and its attendant 'culture' as marginal to that civic identity. Universities now assume their place as a kind of 'peasant-class' in a culture that locates them as 'a striking triumph of the pastoral ideal'.[9]

Within this, we can also see that certain intellectual priorities have been set. I indicated earlier the essentially 'vocational' nature of the early University: it needed to place law, medicine, and number at the centre of things to allow us to regulate the social (politics), the corporal (the bio-cultural, essentially a matter of our regulating death, labour and sex), and the economic (which requires the abstraction of number to allow us to deal with the new forms of social exchange based on capital). Among these, it is number that triumphs over all else; and the centrality of number – of mathematics – as a foundation of disinterested knowledge becomes the key to the idea of 'academic freedom'. The appropriateness of number for this function derives essentially from its abstract nature: mathematics, in an odd sense, has no content at all, and in its purest state becomes pure form. There is 'nothing' to the number 2 or 5, or 17; and yet these signs are packed full of *abstract* significance: they can be applied to virtually anything and, so applied, can transform those things. 'Forty thousand' means not very much to me as the answer to an abstract question ('what is twenty thousand multiplied by two?' say); but it may mean a great deal when I am trying to negotiate a salary, for example. It is the very vacuous nature of the number in itself that gives it such power: applied to the right materials (pounds, euros or dollars; acres or hectares; lovers or companions; victims in wars, say), it transforms individuals and transforms the world. It is therefore a prime analogue of that version of the social or of the nation in which we consider the University to be an institution required to deal in knowledge as pure abstraction (disinterested in its very divorce from any material constraints); but that, at the same time, is profoundly aware of the potency of that knowledge when it is 'applied' to any given material conditions.

Two things follow from this observation or analysis. First, the modern University is a 'capitalist' institution, in that it is grounded in a social framework that puts the structures of capitalist exchange – and the abstraction that is number – at the centre of the conditions of life. Second, the University is complicit with that structure of thought or of feeling in which a primacy is given to abstract forms of knowledge over practical and experiential forms of knowledge.[10] The University starts to identify itself as an institution organised around a social polity in which there is not only a divorce of mind from body (and a constant struggle to heal that wound), but also a divorce of form from content (the University focused on abstract but understood forms, the social world focused on ill-understood content).

In what follows, I will be exploring the ramifications for freedom of a state of affairs in which 'experiential' knowledge is marginalized, giving place to abstract and theoretical knowledge.

Let us look at Europe around 1700.

Why 1700? Well, in 1699, Giambattista Vico became the Rector of the University of Naples; and at the start of each year until 1707, he gave a rectorial oration, a kind of 'keynote' lecture for the cohort of students, setting the tone for their education that year. In these orations, he prioritises reason above sense, acknowledging the obvious contest between rational thought about something and sensible perception of it, but preferring the move to reasoned abstraction. In this, then, we see precisely that spirit of abstraction that seems to marginalise the sensible and the experienced. Yet, in Vico, we have something different and more subtle: at the centre of the orations, he places *eloquence*. In 1707, he explicitly states that 'eloquence is the foundation of knowledge': not what you know simply, but how you state what you know.

This does two things: it states that *knowledge is intrinsically public*, a matter of shared language, never simply the possession of a single individual; it also states that the proper foundation of knowledge is poetry, or that knowledge, in a sense, is made *available* through poetry. Poetry grounds knowledge.

Put simply, these two facts, put together, place poetry at the centre of a civil society, even at the centre of a civilising society. However, as we all know, the following century in Europe is one where this kind of proposition is regarded increasingly as contentious. The incipient debates around aesthetics and aestheticism, starting essentially with Frances Hutcheson in 1725, focus on the centrality of rhetoric or grammar in all knowledge, and wonder about the rival claims of other, more abstract forms of knowledge. For example, if truth is to be regarded as essentially transpositional or universal, then for a statement to be true, it must be true regardless of the positionality – and also, therefore, regardless of the experience – of its speaker. Mathematics would seem to offer such a mode of truth: one cannot argue with number, precisely because number is governed by agreed laws; but one can argue with me, since I am just one voice among many, no matter how 'poetic' or seductive – how eloquent – my rhetoric. Indeed, we begin at this moment precisely to *distrust* any claim to knowledge that is based upon experience; and here, in Enlightenment, we begin that 'two cultures' contestation or legitimacy crisis that continues to dog us.

Something else happens in 1707 that is also of importance: a political union is established on the 'primary' anglophone island, bringing Scotland and England together. This is not entirely happy. When, half a century later, a man called Blair, Hugh Blair, is appointed as Professor of Rhetoric and Belles-Lettres (note the French title) in Edinburgh (in 1760), the repercussions of that union are strongly felt, and Blair's lectures on rhetoric can be seen to address directly our concerns. Famously, Blair makes a distinction insistently between speech and writing; equally insistently, he favours speech over writing. The reason he favours it is that it essentially gives the same content as writing, but it does so in all the lived immediacy and experience of the present voice. It takes the present moment of communication, and fills it with sensuous *content*; whereas writing abstracts that communication and essentially gives us the *forms* of knowledge without the specific content – a content that can be modified precisely because, in the speech-situation, the presence of the public is directly felt. Speech, in its shared and public dimension, is historical in ways that writing can never be; 'knowledge' or what constitutes knowledge depends on the experiencing of the public sphere and upon the conversation among speaking subjects that actually constructs the knowledge; knowledge is not simply a matter of 'information' that can be archived, literally 'abstracted', and then transmitted in writings. Behind this, and informing it, is a sense that behind the *political* union of voices that constitutes this new national entity there lies an essential *disunity* because we speak different languages or speak a shared language but in different ways or from different positions or experiences.

This comes to a head somewhat later, during the Romantic period, and specifically in the pages of the *Edinburgh Review* between July 1809 and April 1810. In these issues of the *Review*, there is a systematic questioning of English education by Scots who are arguing for the greater sense of purpose and utility in the Scottish system. Fundamentally, a series of articles and reviews damningly critical of the work of the Oxford classicists reveals what was mediated as 'basic incompetence' among the Oxonian scholars. Richard Payne Knight's devastating attack on the Oxford edition of Strabo's geography is used to advance a simple syllogistic formulation: classical education is the key to government and power; to demonstrate incompetence in the classics among the Oxfordian English is therefore also to demonstrate incompetence in English government and policy. Sydney Smith then follows this with a meditation on R. L. Edgeworth's *Essays on Professional Education* in which he attacks the narrowness of the extremely specialised education on offer in Oxbridge: one that concentrates exclusively on the classics, to the exclusion of the new sciences and more practical disciplines. Here we find the origins of those debates that have continued to the present time about the difference between a specialised and professionalist education in England and a more general and wide-ranging exposure to many disciplines and interdisciplinary practices that are the foundation of the much-vaunted Scottish 'democratic intellect'. Smith sees Oxford as a place that produces what he calls 'elegant imbecility': smooth self-presentation based on profound ignorance and uselessness. England is, in this, suave sweetness but no light: a style covering a basic malformation of culture.

This is as much as to say that there is an awareness here that modes of speaking can ground cultural authority and legitimacy. To put it baldly, those who speak English 'properly' or in a manner approved as legitimate *thereby* gain cultural and even political legitimacy: RP, 'received pronunciation', 'the Queen's English' – these are what ground a sovereign authority, regardless of the content of the speeches made in these styles. It is important to note that this is *not* a matter simply of 'accent'; rather, the claim is that some speakers have a closer approximation to an *abstract* form of English, for it is equally true – and more important for our present purposes – that there is no such substantive thing as a 'proper' way of speaking English: RP, 'Queen's English' and so on are mere formal abstractions – not even the Queen can speak 'the Queen's English'. In a sense, this abstraction exists in order quite simply to offer what Bourdieu called 'cultural capital' to some while excluding others from having socio-cultural and even socio-political authority, again regardless of the actual content of what these others might say. The complaint of the Scots in this historical moment is partly determined by this sense that people who identify themselves as English gain authority because, *ipso facto*, they have some kind of prior claim – however fatuous – upon the language and therefore upon the cultural authority that their voice has.[11]

Vico's 1707 celebration of rhetoric, and also Blair's 1760s celebration of speech above writing, then, both come under some pressure here. On one hand, we have the tendency to prioritise the immediacy of the spoken – the spoken as the site of a felt or lived history (what Leavis would later call 'felt life'); but at the same time, we have the necessity, in the University, of speaking many things, including the languages of sciences, which will ensure that what we are saying is in some sense, if not necessarily abstractly and transpositionally true, then at least *useful* or *practical* in a general fashion – having a general applicability – and not simply useful for single discrete occasions. This latter is what we have come, in recent times, to associate with the technical or, more precisely, the 'vocational', while the former is regarded as the 'academic'. Two things need to be said: first, the 'academic' is now as idealised and unreal as the 'Queen's English' and deals, therefore, *purely* with the realm of the idea; second, in this crude distinction, we often forget how 'vocational' subjects like medicine or law or economics might actually be.

Coincidentally with these arguments in the *Edinburgh Review*, in 1810, Humboldt is also opening the University of Berlin. This University will be what Bill Readings called a 'university of culture'. By this, Readings meant that the form and function of Berlin was one that was meant to provide a model of a new nation-state for the people to look up to, and at the same time to produce a people capable of living up to this new idea of the nation state. In this dialectical relation between institution and people, 'Germany' can be invented as a specific identity that emerges from a Prussia that can now be retrospectively characterised as vague and amorphous, lacking in specific cultural identity or – more politically useful – characterised by the *wrong* cultural identity. The institution gives a series of norms or models for what it might mean to be German; and the German people see themselves therefore represented more or less adequately by and in the institution that is the repository of their knowledge, their morals, their socio-political and cultural normativities.

It is clear from the foregoing that there is some ostensibly structural link that establishes an intimacy in the modern period between the nation state and its University institutions. Yet it is odd that that intimacy is not necessarily to be found where one might most expect it: in the national vernacular as studied through a national literature. It is odd that it might be abstract knowledge such as maths that constitutes the national identity of all peoples, when we might rather expect that, for England it might be English poetry; for Germany, German poetry and so on. Insofar as it may indeed be poetry that gives such intimacy, it is not the content of poetry but rather the abstraction of an imagined essential national voice – actually spoken by no particular individuals – that speaks the poetry which is thought to ground cultural authority and legitimacy. We used to call this the voice of the bard, of course. But essentially, the question now remains: what has happened to Viconian eloquence here?

This question of a national character has, in fact, been fundamental to the formation of the modern University institution. Further, it has been structurally tied to the very conception of knowledge itself. One important influence on Vico was Francis Bacon; and of particular importance for present purposes, Bacon's *Advancement of Learning*. This text was published in 1605, in the shadow of a major political event in which a group of individuals, claiming the right to represent a substantial and oppressed social community, attempted nothing less than the assassination of key governmental figures of the day. The Gunpowder Plot can be aligned, for example, with the attempt by the IRA to blow up Margaret Thatcher's cabinet in Brighton in 1984. In its impact socially, it might even be compared (as James Shapiro has compared it) to 9/11.[12]

The situating of Bacon's text is important, for it clearly shapes a text that begins with a careful consideration of the King's speech and character; and relates this or sees it as important to a consideration of learning and its progress. In the dedication at the start of *The Advancement of Learning*, Bacon praises explicitly the speech of the King, finding in the manner of speaking itself the very ground of sovereign authority. He compares James to Augustus Caesar: 'for your gift of speech, I call to mind what Cornelius

Tacitus saith of Augustus Caesar: *Augusto profluens, et quae principem deceret, eloquentia fuit*' (Augustus was a fluent speaker, and where his sovereignty is revealed, there we will also find eloquence). He goes on explicitly to 'classify' modes of speech, into two categories: servile and sovereign:

> If we note it well, speech that is uttered with labour and difficulty, or speech that savoureth of the affectation of art and precepts, or speech that is framed after the imitation of some pattern of eloquence, though never so excellent; all this hath somewhat servile, and holding of the subject. But your Majesty's manner of speech is indeed prince-like, flowing as from a fountain, and yet streaming and branching itself into nature's order, full of facility and felicity, imitating none, and inimitable by any.[13]

This is in some ways the very foundation of that identification of a form of speech with sovereign authority which lies at the core of our question, the 'English question'. Yet it is also true to say that a manner of speaking is not yet equated with poetry or with the particular rhetorical eloquence that interests Vico or Blair, and which they see as being tied to the practicality of knowledge or a 'practical reasoning' whose point and purpose is the establishment of that civility or cultured civilisation that is at the very foundation of the possibility of our being social and sociable in the first place.

Bacon makes a distinction between two kinds of knowledge: the pure knowledge of nature, and the 'proud knowledge' of good and evil. That distinction between abstract and moral knowledge foreshadows the kind of 'conservative' distinctions that we have seen articulated by Daniel Bell. Bacon also argues against the patronage of knowledge, for writings and books (he argues) 'ought to have no patrons but truth and reason'. This relative austerity is further developed as he takes a stance against what he calls the three major 'distempers of learning': fantasy, contention and delicacy. Fantastical learning, he argues, leads to vain imaginings; contentious learning leads to vain altercations; and delicate learning leads to vain affectations. These three distempers might be characterised for us as irrational and anti-empirical superstition, politically interested or engaged criticism, and self-conscious aestheticism.[14] These are all to be eschewed in that they get in the way of the proper *advancement of learning*, of that 'modernisation', progress and *avant-garde* advancement that I have tied above to the function of the University. As Bacon has it in a consideration of ancient learning: 'Antiquity deserveth that reverence, that men should make a stand thereupon and discover what is the best way; but when the discovery is well taken, then to make progression' (32–3).

For Bacon, poetry has a particular function. Poetry may 'at pleasure join that which nature hath severed, and sever that which nature hath joined; and so make unlawful matches and divorces of things'. Poetry, in short, is governed by metaphor: the 'unlawful' but verbal joining and disjunction of things. For Bacon, this is important for the simple reason that it will essentially start to drive a speaker away from experience or an empirical voicing towards an imagining that leads to vanity, for it takes the material things of nature, reduces them to their linguistic signs, and 'fantastically' joins them together in ways that remain foreign to any actual or lived experience.

We can look at what happens to this view of poetry as it gains ground later. Consider, for example, Johnson's 'Life of Cowley', where Johnson takes the so-called 'metaphysical poets' – those poets who certainly make 'unlawful matches' of things – and denies them the title of poets but concedes to them the lesser title of 'Wits'. Johnson defines wit thus:

> . . . wit, abstracted from its effects upon the hearer, may be more rigorously and philosophically considered as a kind of *discordia concors*; a combination of dissimilar images, or discovery of occult resemblances in things apparently unlike . . . The most heterogeneous ideas are yoked together.[15]

Importantly, Johnson also sees that, in this falling from poetry to wit, the poets are essentially divorced from actual experience:

> . . . it will be readily inferred that they were not successful in representing or moving the affections . . . they had no regard to that uniformity of sentiment which enables us to conceive and to excite the pains and the pleasure of other minds: they never inquired what, on any occasion, they should have said or done, but wrote *rather as beholders than partakers of human nature* . . . (12; emphasis added)

Johnson is here laying bare that prioritisation of form over content that has its roots in Bacon's concern for and description of the 'sovereign voice', as we might call it. The resulting problem, for Johnson as for Bacon, is that we establish a cultural authority that has no ground in experience whatsoever, but rather in a vacuous style, a formal style explicitly unconcerned with content.

As Bacon considers how poetry operates, he compares it to the working of history. The argument here is that poetry essentially exaggerates or magnifies events; but that it does so in order to speak to a particular demand. As he puts it: 'because the events of true history have not that magnitude which satisfieth the mind of man, poesy feigneth acts and events greater and more heroic' (80). First, then, we might say that this essentially ties poetry to mathematics: poetry is a kind of multiplier of significance.

However, we might further add that, for Bacon, the human mind *requires* such magnificence for its own satisfaction. That is to say: the human cannot fully become itself unless and until it is given to itself by poetry.

In the debates of our contemporary moment, or more simply just in modern times, we are much more used to seeing this argued via Hegel's 'Introduction' to the *Aesthetics* where, specifically, the imaginative power addressed in Bacon is translated into the essential issue of *freedom*. Hegel begins by asserting that artistic beauty is of a higher order than that given by nature quite simply because of a certain contingency. While the sun, say, appears to be 'an absolutely necessary factor in the universe', nonetheless, in its being it is entirely 'indifferent . . . not free or self-conscious'. By contrast, the artistic representation of the sun is 'characterized by intellectual being and by freedom'. The 'addition', as it were, that constitutes art is a demonstration and even an enactment of human freedom.[16] What Hegel has done here is to take the predicament in which poetic metaphor has distanced poetry from experience (as in Bacon, as in the metaphysicals) and to revalorise it by demonstrating that such a divorcing of mind from material necessity can become precisely the ground of the possibility of human freedom itself. Poetry, thus, paradoxically re-establishes that connection between eloquence (in Eliot's terms, 'That was a way of putting it') and material history in its establishment of the possibility of freedom, of our potential for freedom.

This whole tradition – Bacon, Vico, Romantic Scotland, Hegel – is at odds with what has in fact triumphed in our understanding of the organisation and function of knowledge, and of its bearer, the intellectual. Vico specifically was arguing against Descartes and the triumph of a particular 'method'. As I indicated in the opening section above, the question at stake here is not really a two cultures debate but rather a mind–body dualism debate, the terms of which we have inherited from Descartes. These terms, I contend, in radically mis-shaping the argument, have limited our possibilities. Most specifically, they have reduced the question of freedom to an essentially bureaucratic notion of the form and processes of freedom (a 'method' of freedom, as it were) as opposed to a freedom that has any meaningful content. The freedom in question is abstract, divorced from practical realities. It is the freedom of the victim of rape in Milton's *Comus*: a freedom that is asserted and whose enactment requires an essential divorcing of the mind from the body. When Comus has the Lady imprisoned, she says:

> Fool do not boast,
> Thou canst not touch the freedom of my minde

With all thy charms, although this corporal rinde
Thou hast immanacl'd . . . [17]

To accept this is to be complicit with a situation in which, at best, freedom is spiritual and at worst, freedom is purely the freedom of fantasy.[18] Meanwhile, the material world goes on its merry and oppressive ways. We have seen exactly the same 'celebration' of a freedom that is purely fantastic, divorced from experience in certain strains in 'Leftist Theory', as described by Richard Rorty in his *Achieving Our Country* where he points out that 'Insofar as a Left becomes spectatorial and retrospective, it ceases to be a Left'.[19] One of Rorty's arguments in this book is that certain emancipatory theories – those associated broadly with left-wing critical theory in Europe and the US since the late 1960s (Marxism, feminism, ethnicity studies, postcolonial studies, gay and lesbian studies and so on) – have allowed us to make good social advances in genuine freedom:

> This cultural Left has had extraordinary success. In addition to being centers of genuinely original scholarship, the new academic programs have done what they were, semi-consciously, designed to do: they have decreased the amount of sadism in our society. Especially among college graduates, the casual infliction of humiliation is much less socially acceptable than it was during the first two-thirds of the [twentieth] century. (81)

This is a good thing, argues Rorty. 'We' can no longer be casually prejudiced against women, blacks, gays and other groups, thanks largely to the work of a cultural leftist theory. However, this Left has done its work in the essentially sequestered area of the academy, that ghetto of which I wrote above; and it has remained thus a Left that is 'spectatorial', onlooking, and oddly – paradoxically – not interested in historical experience. As Rorty puts it, 'there is a dark side' to this success story, because 'during the same period in which socially accepted sadism has steadily diminished, economic inequality and economic insecurity have steadily increased' (83). In the terms that I myself have been using, the freedoms that have been established have been purely 'formal' and are thus essentially fantasies of freedom: they are the freedom of the Lady in 'Comus', a freedom that remains sequestered within the academy, a freedom of the mind while the body in the historical and material world is damaged and denied the content of freedom.

The argument that I am advancing, by contrast then, is, as it were, one that adopts the route offered by Vico over Descartes, by Italy over France, by freedom over administered bureaucracy and form. To some, it will look like Forster's 'liberal' position, that can accept muddle, or Keatsian–Shakespearean negative capability, or Derridean undecidability: these, in fact, are all fundamentally remarkably similar. My claim is that we are now in a specific predicament with regard to the English question and with regard to freedom, academic and otherwise. The predicament can be described simply. A Cartesian structure, based upon sceptical doubt, negates its own doubt through an application of formal and mathematical or syllogistic logic, and thereby replaces the doubt with absolute certainty; consequent upon this is the possibility for us to make truth-claims. The truth of these claims is given and legitimised in purely abstract and formal terms, and not by experience. The claims do not require the historically present spoken or speaking voice for their validation; indeed, Cartesian thought would suspect any claim that grounded itself in the experience of the rhetorical speaking voice or in any more generalised somatic or physical experience at all. Experience might tell me, for example, that I am starving; Cartesian logic can demonstrate that this is an impossibility because the advanced economies can show in the figures in their government papers that aid has been distributed to me. Experience might tell me that the state of affairs in Baghdad is appalling; governments can absolve themselves of blame and can point to the triumph of democracy because, formally, there has been an election. The teaching that is done in a particular institution might be in fact and in the experience of all concerned mediocre, but the audit-trail paperwork shows the steady and rhythmic pulse of 'excellence' in all things.[20]

In these and similar examples, we can say that it is 'administered form' that gives certainty and legitimacy. In our time, we have learned to call this 'transparency', which we too often mistake for 'truth' or for 'justice'. Actual truth and practical justice require the messiness of content and uncertainty; in our unwillingness to live with such uncertainty, we have preferred to have the merest *forms* of truth and of justice, a 'legalism' without legitimacy, as it were.[21] What happens, we might ask, when we attend to the experience in these cases – or, as we might put it, to material history?

We can relate this directly to the question of teaching, and to the centrality of language and of poetry within that. Jacques Rancière, in *Le Maître ignorant*, describes the 'intellectual adventure' of Joseph Jacotot in 1818. The French speaker Jacotot was a teacher, who found himself in the Netherlands, facing a class of students who had no French, while he had no Dutch. In a move that sounds desperate, he turned to a bilingual edition of Fénelon's *Télémaque*, and managed to convey, through an interpreter, the instruction that the students should learn French by studying the bilingual edition of the text. Amazingly, they did so, to the point where they were able to write, in French, a commentary on the text.

Why is that 'amazing', asks Rancière? After all, it is essentially the way in which we learn all the basic fundamentals of what we call our maternal tongue. No one 'explains' that to us; rather, we more or less pick it up through a process of being saturated in it, surrounded by it, trying it out and working pragmatically towards proficiency: essentially, we work it out through experience. Rancière then is able to generalise from this. He points out that the logic of 'explication' that governs most teaching – I, the teacher, give you a book to study; but I then supplement that with my own explanation of the content of the book – is essentially problematic, for it sets up the possibility of an infinite regress: my explicatory text or speech surely requires in turn, quite logically, its own explanation and so on.

What arrests the regress is, fundamentally, two interlinked things: first, my explanation is verbal and made in the speaking voice, which trumps the authority of the written text because it is experiential, here-and-now; and second, I assert my position as teacher to decide, simply and arbitrarily, when the explanation has been 'understood'. To legitimise this understanding, I 'examine' the student, if need be in a *viva voce* exam. I am that Oxford academic asserting my essential authority before the hapless Romantic Scot, with my faulty edition of Strabo but my greater claim to authority. Thus, the structure of pedagogy that is grounded in the logic of 'explanation' is one that leads inexorably to a hierarchy that can be grounded – but not legitimised – in one thing at best: the power of my voice as the voice of the authoritative teacher. That power, of course, is not intrinsic to the voice either; for rather, what has happened is simply that I as teacher am able to assert a knowledge (my own understanding) that you, the student, do not have (or that I say you do not have) – and it is this latter fact that invests the voice with authority.

The difference, then, is that between a situation in which I, as teacher, subjugate you as student and a different situation in which I, as teacher, talk with you. As Rancière puts it:

> The would-be adult, or child is first of all a being of speech. The child who repeats the words that she hears and the Flemish student 'lost' in his *Télémaque* do not process just by chance. The whole of their effort, all of their exploration is directed towards this: addressed to them has been the speech of a man that they want to recognise and to which they would respond, not as pupils or as wise men, but just as men; as you would reply to somebody who talks to you and not to someone who is examining you: under the sign of equality.[22]

Or, as Wordsworth would put it in the Preface to the Lyrical Ballads, poetry should be 'a man talking to men'. What is important for our purposes here is that Rancière is proposing a state of affairs in which poetry – in this case *Télémaque* – is placed at the centre of an event that is essentially a pedagogical event; but the result of the event is the establishment of a kind of agora, an open and more democratic space in which civility happens; and the result of that civility is the establishment of the possibility of freedom as opposed to subjugation. The civility in question here is characterised precisely by a kind of equality 'before the text' so to speak, and the very definite eschewing of a pre-established authority that is given to me as teacher because I can claim closer intimacy with the 'essence' of a language, the formal vacuity of a Queen's English.[23] Instead, we can replace this with something that might properly be called dialogue.

2 A front story

Thus far, I have tried to show through the history of various (but certainly not all) ideas of the University that there is a link between the institution and the fact of a public domain. Leavis's question, remember, was 'does the University exist to replicate society of which it is a part, or does it exist to counter that society?' In what follows here, I want to re-pose this question, but with a different inflection: can we now say that *society* exists in order to counter the force that is the University? In other words, given that the University is shaped, in some ways, by its relation to the fact of a public domain (a nation or just a civic polity), is it the case that what we call 'the social' – by which we mean something like 'the norms of the everyday' – now exists partly as a way of *refusing* the kinds of knowledge that we produce?

Our contemporary society is one whose norms increasingly call into question the values of knowledge, the value of culture or of the arts more generally. This may be one of the reasons why John Carey can pose the question 'what good are the arts', and also find a willing audience for what is essentially an anti-intellectual stance.[24] Crudely put, our contemporary society is one that validates and prioritises the immediate, the un-mediated (reality TV; instant gratification of desire; immediate answers to problems via the web). It takes the extraordinary, and renders it ordinary, everyday. We might say that it is organised around the intensity of the present, or of that which is present: it prioritises being and *identity* – the collapsing of all that was not known (and therefore foreign) into the immediately recognisable and comforting.

In all of this, there is one certain constant: the reduction of knowledge to information. Yet, as A. N. Whitehead put it, as long ago as 1932, 'So far as the mere imparting of information is concerned, no university has had any justification for existence since the popularisation of printing in the fifteenth century'.[25] Rather, says Whitehead, the justification for a University to exist lies in imagination: 'The university imparts information, but it imparts it imaginatively . . . . This atmosphere of excitement, arising from imaginative consideration, transforms knowledge. A fact is no longer a bare fact: it is invested with all its possibilities. It is no longer a burden on the memory: it is energising as *the poet of our dreams*, and as the architect of our purposes' (139; emphasis added).

The University, we might say, exists in some privileged relation to knowledge and knowledge formation; the social, however, sees all such knowledge as being relative or 'situated' in relation to particular points of view. In order to avoid the alleged 'prejudice' or bias in such knowledge, the social claims a freedom in preferring and prioritising instead the simple 'information' on which the knowledge is based.[26] It claims, further, that such information is 'neutral' precisely *because* it is not based on any experience. Again, Whitehead would be a useful counter-weight here, arguing as he did that 'The task of a university is to weld together imagination and experience' (140). In prioritising information over knowledge, and in believing that in so doing it avoids ideological prejudice, the social claims and asserts freedom. The freedom in question is now the merest consumerism: the 'student' can choose between competing points of view; crucially, such choice *cannot* be based on knowledge. This reduction of knowledge to information – transparency – gives the merest illusion of freedom. Some universities and some Vice-Chancellors or Presidents call this the basis of a 'student-led' degree programme. Logically, such a thing is self-contradictory: it must be based on ignorance and is therefore blind stumbling based on pure superficiality, not the articulation of a substantive freedom.

Against this, the arts and culture – and perhaps above all English – occupy the terrain of mediation, of deferral and an unreality, a reality that has been or is about-to-be: a terrain characterised by the ongoing and incessant search for knowledge. We might say that English is organised around the unavailability of the present, or of presence itself; it prioritises the possibilities of becoming and thus of *difference* – the realisation that the present is not all there is, and that alterity calls me forth into answering Rilke's great demand as he stands before the sculpture of Apollo when he realises that, before art, there is no hiding place for the human: 'you must change your life'.[27]

Or, rather, we might say that English *ought* to occupy this terrain. However, it too has often become complicit with precisely the collapsing of knowledge into information that ends up evacuating the discipline of any force. In the current state of affairs, a politics of neo-Cartesian identity (the question of the speaking subject, the I and its self-identifications) pervades virtually all aspects of English study. For Leavis, the point was to identify oneself as 'English'; for us, now, the point is to identify ourselves usually in some kind of adjacency to this Englishness: 'foreign', gendered, sexualised, 'raced', ethnicised, classed and so on.

Although we may no longer simply celebrate the discovery of 'Englishness' in the felt and lived tradition, nonetheless, our discipline is still answering the questions posed by Leavis at the time of the ending of the Second War: who am I? We have been looking into texts for the confirmation and affirmation of identity; and when that identity is not straightforwardly 'English', whatever that is, we pretend that we are celebrating difference. In fact, of course, the oppressed and victimised stereotypical 'other-than-white-anglo-saxon-male-straight' is every bit as much obsessed with identity as Leavis was; when those of us who are not black, or gay, for examples, find ourselves in the presence of a text that celebrates and confirms black or gay or any other identity, we acknowledge it with all due piety – another word for patronising it (essentially similar to the way in which Leavis would patronise 'colonials' attempting the Cambridge Tripos). English is, as it were, now a supposed multicultural English; yet it is simply that we have changed the description of what it might mean to be English – being English remains the quarry and goal. Better, and much more fundamentally, *being* is the goal: being, and not *becoming*, is what has become important. It matters little what we are, so long as we are some identifiable thing; however, freedom requires not self-identification, but instead the possibility of change – 'you must change your life'. While, for Leavis, those who qualified as 'English' were a rather narrow group of the elite (and also usually white male and so on), for us, now, we have a greater motley: 'English', like 'American', can now be hyphenated or qualified in all sorts of ways. Being and identity remain the goal; and the purpose of reading has often become the pursuit, establishment and consolidation of an assured identity.

Here is a better question, and one for our times: what is education about if not an increase in freedom, in becoming, in possibility or potentiality? In 1859, Mill posed the question for us, essentially, when he pointed out in his discussion of 'Civil, or Social Liberty' that 'the nature and limits of the power which can be legitimately exercised by society over the individual . . . is likely soon to make itself recognised as the vital question of the future'. It is thus precisely because the English question (the 'Eng lit' question) is the question of the possibility of a future: it is about potentiality. Mill felt that 'the only freedom which deserves the name is that of pursuing our own good, in our own way, so long as we do not attempt to deprive others of theirs, or impede their efforts to attain it'. Actually, this can be read 'weakly' (as it usually is within liberal philosophy: do what you will as long as it doesn't affect adversely or hurt others); or we can adopt a strong reading, one which imposes on us a duty to ensure the wider freedom of others along with that of ourselves.

It is this latter reading that I take here; and I make the claim that English, as a discipline singularly and above all others in the public domain (a public sphere whose very existence – after Vico – is centred on poetry), is the site for the increase in freedom. But I have also equated that freedom with the notion of potential and potentiality. It is therefore *not* the freedom to 'be one's identity', but rather to find the possibilities of change and difference: 'you must change your life'. Identity does not make free, as it were: it is slavery to be 'emancipated' only into one's own prior identity, an identity given and inherited and essential. A literary criticism that is concerned to legitimise identity is, by definition, therefore, not a criticism worthy of the name, for its practice is anathema to the point of criticism.

In the light of this, what, then, is the place of the University, and what might become the place of English within it? In recent times, the University has become fully instrumentalised: in an odd sense, we have rediscovered the medieval university and have indeed almost fully reinstated it. That medieval university was one driven by the demands of vocation: to medicine, law, theology above all. We retain the vocational aspects of those disciplines, of course; but we tend to think of them today as 'professions', leaving the word 'vocational' for the kinds of activity that require localised skills, and not generalisable theory.

And recent developments in English – 'theory' – were entirely complicit with what we might call the triumph of the so-called transferable skills agenda (as if English were no good in and of itself, but merely as a set of skills that could be applied to other, more worthy, activities – thus, again, evacuating English of content and reducing it to a formal and instrumental exercise). As Nicholas M. Strohl has recently put it, 'What began as a progressive social movement to include *more* cultures in the academic setting has regressed into a conservative movement to *exclude* critical debate about culture within higher education'; the result is the replacement of intellectual and academic autonomy (which we used to call 'academic freedom') with the demands of marketability, trainability, accountability to a governing ideology – which, in its bureaucratic functioning, has no legitimacy and no real content.

At the centre of this instrumentalisation of English and of the University has been a massive culture of mistrust, essentially put in place by the conservatives who systematically attacked the public sector – and the public sphere – in the 1980s and since. We must all surely agree that the establishment of the Quality Assurance Agency was the worst thing to happen to higher education in recent times – and perhaps ever. QAA is, for those of us who have suffered through its tawdry posturing, a cancer that gnaws at the core of knowledge, value and freedom in education; its carcinogenic growth is now perhaps the greatest pervasive danger to the function of a University as a surviving institution. It has presided over the valorisation and celebration of mediocrity, paradoxically at the very moment when it is allegedly assuring the public of the quality of education and Universities.

How has it done this? The secret is simple: in its bureaucratisation of our work, it has encouraged – and often required – those involved in Universities to evacuate their activities of any meaningful content. QAA would not presume to question the content of my seminar; but they will require an audit trail that 'proves' that I have somehow forced students to achieve certain 'learning outcomes' that are essentially guaranteed by the 'aims, objectives and teaching methods' of my module. They can check this – and thus assure everybody about the quality of my work – not from any actual experience of it, but rather from a paperwork audit-trail. Even the content of the paper-work is less important than the mere fact of its existence, for the content is designed in turn to be so generalised and homogenising that it, too, is void of any meaningful content. QAA empties teaching and learning of content, but assures the public that the forms are being observed. It literally reduces knowledge and the work of the University to a mere 'formality'.[28]

Those who have been complicit with QAA might profitably read Julien Benda's *La trahison des clercs* (1927), and hang their heads in shame. For that agency has been the primary vehicle through which a proper discussion of what the university and its disciplines may be about in actual terms has been prevented. The scandal of audit is that the more that QAA inspect, the less there is to inspect – to the point where we now, seriously, face the demise of the university as such – the evacuation of any serious content from the public face of the University. The old question that Leavis asked, essentially about the relation of university to society, can no longer be asked after QAA. For Leavis, there was some relation – to be determined, but available – of representation between university and society; but QAA has replaced the very idea of representation with that of management – and, more sinister still, has installed, behind 'management', a culture of control of thinking and a narrowing of critical thought. The idea of a university as a site for the contestation of questions regarding freedom and democracy is now replaced by the non-idea of the university as a managed site for the efficient processing of information, the production of students characterised by the mysteries of 'graduatedness', and the endless proliferation of self-justifying statistics for a world that neither reads them nor cares about them.

There is, of course, the further and obvious question: how is QAA legitimised? Essentially, QAA in its present form has its roots in that ideological culture of distrust of the public sector that was initiated by the successive governments of Margaret Thatcher, especially during the 1980s. For no reason other than the fact that they were not private profit-making businesses, Universities were alleged to be sites of wastefulness, and their staff alleged to be workshy dilettantes. Coincidentally, the attacks on some industries – such as the mining industry – went hand-in-hand with a rhetoric of 'the right of managers to manage'. And how they have – failed. One might have expected me to write 'and how they have triumphed'; but the paradox, of course, is that we do not really have management in the public sector at all – rather, we have *managerialism*, which is, of course, the very anathema of managing. It is this culture that has placed the Business School at the centre of many institutions, of course. When Whitehead defended the idea of having a Business School in a University in the 1930s, it was for the simple reason that he thought that business would learn from the imagination that he saw as the central characteristic functioning power of the University, and that business decision-making would improve as a result; but of course what has happened since Whitehead's time is that the imaginative disciplines – especially those in arts and humanities and especially those dealing in poetry – have been told to become more like businessmen, to make their work more 'commercial' or to think of themselves as 'student-led'. It is not that businessmen lack imagination; it is that the University has centred its idea less on imagination and more on business – to the cost of both.

Managing requires that individuals take decisions, accept the responsibility for them, and ensure that they are the best possible decisions. Managerialism is that state of affairs in which no-one will take responsibility for decisions, preferring to have in place an objective *formal* 'transparent' system that will make the decisions for all concerned. The purpose of a Vice-Chancellor, in this state of affairs, is simply to ensure that the machinery keeps running. Further, in removing herself or himself from responsibility, the managerialist makes a claim for 'democratic accountability' by a process of delegation of duties (to Deans, heads of department and so on) in a system that essentially is designed to delegate blame. Increasingly, the logic of that position starts to pervade the entire system as a whole: at every level, people are required simply and primarily to keep the system – the business – running, but not to consider what the system is actually doing or to imagine what its function might be. The culture of the delegation of blame, in turn, generates a sense of pervasive victimisation with its ever-present threat of litigation; and in turn, this leads to yet more evacuation of any meaningful content (and certainly, the removal as far as is possible of 'experience') from the University's activities. This is why the system can be described as carcinogenic: it behaves like a self-perpetuating disease that, once installed, is difficult to arrest.

We talk endlessly of the 'idea of the university', as if there still were such an idea, such a unifying and presiding set of intentions. Samuel Weber has recently invited us to think not in terms of a 'what is or should be the university' kind of question, but rather to ask the question of what is the university's relation to a future (in his case, whether there might persist a university at all). For Weber, this is a question dominated by space and habitation: the campus used to be seen as the space of a transition between family and society. In the days of contemporary technology, where information is held in servers and not in libraries, that space has lost its force. Further, in the age of globalisation, for Weber, the university can continue to exist, as he points out, only if it manages to present itself as governed by a market logic that effectively leads to a state of affairs in which it has a direct relation to financial profit. These things work, of course (as I would wish to point out) if we elide the difference between information and knowledge, and see the University as a site of informing rather than as a site for knowing.

On one hand, the 'delocalisation' of the University in this state of affairs returns us to that medieval condition of the peregrine scholar – if servers are more important than libraries, there is no building to be worried about, and scholars can simply move around. However, this situation is one in which a public sphere is reduced to the mere idea of a public sphere. Dialogue, in this state of affairs, is at best 'virtual': I sit at home, divorced from any substantive society, and email my assignments to a tutor who could be anywhere; and she or he returns grades and comments, again virtually. The relation of the student to knowledge in this state of affairs is jeopardised. If knowledge is something that happens, and whose happening effects a modification in the self (you must change your life), then knowledge requires the active experiencing of alterity – in its most basic form, dialogue on the model of Rancière's 'maître ignorant' – and not the mere abstract relation to the idea of otherness that we can get through the images and representations of otherness offered by contemporary technology. In short, we may be losing the requirement of the actual University plant, but we are in danger of throwing out the necessity of our own peregrine relation to knowledge, to becoming, with that loss of plant; and we replace it with the other aspect of Weber's analysis: the relation to commerce or finance.

After this, what has happened to poetry? I don't mean this in any simple nostalgic or mystical sense; rather, I refer back to the proposition that poetry is necessarily imbricated in the social, that eloquence requires that all knowledge be a matter of public debate, and that, for better or worse, the relation of university to society – if it is to mean anything – must be based in the production of freedom. Our globalised economy understands freedom in the purely limited sense of 'freedom of choice' and therefore consumption; but freedom as understood here is, rather, the production of change and of difference, the non-identification of a subject with her or his goods, the non-identification of I with my characteristic qualities – it is the realisation that I, insofar as I live at all, can be and must be different: you must change your life. That difference we usually call 'the future'.

We might say of the kind of revolution that is required in University education what Marx said of the nineteenth century: 'The social revolution of the 19th century cannot draw its poetry from the past, but only from the future'.[29] The chapters that follow in Part II of this book look at some of the various ways in which we might start to write that poetry.

PART II

The Comfort of Strangers

CHAPTER 2

The Fate of Culture

Die Welt ist alles

I begin, then, with a beginning that is not my own, but one that I appropriate from a text written over eighty years ago, by one who has been dead for over fifty years. There will be some readers who will recognise Wittgenstein's opening gambit in his *Tractatus Logico-Philosophicus*, and others who will not have done so immediately, but who will infer (now that I have mentioned it directly) that this text, from 1921, is what I am citing from above. Yet others will gain little from this new knowledge, if they are unacquainted with Wittgenstein and the *Tractatus*. Are these facts regarding the readerships for this piece significant? Would it be more significant if I had opened a poem with such a kind of allusion or direct citation? For example, is it a significant or important fact that some readers 'hear' Chaucer when, in 1922 or even today, they start to read Eliot's 'The Waste Land' while others do not?

My opening tactic divides the readership into at least two groups at once.[1] In so doing, it operates in a mode akin to the parable. In 1977, Frank Kermode explored this in a rather different context. In *The Genesis of Secrecy*, his Charles Eliot Norton lectures at Harvard, he explained the operation of biblical parable, taking his source from Jesus as reported by Mark:

> When Jesus was asked to explain the purpose of his parables, he described them as stories *told to them without* – to outsiders – with the express purpose of concealing a mystery that was to be understood only by insiders. So Mark tells us: speaking to the Twelve, Jesus said, 'To you has been given the secret of the kingdom of God, but to those outside everything is in parables; so that they may indeed see but not perceive, and may indeed hear but not understand; lest they should turn again, and be forgiven'. (4:11–12)[2]

In the context of biblical narrative being analysed by Kermode here, the point is that there are different levels of cognition for the audience: although they all 'see' or 'hear' the same text, they do not all 'perceive' or 'understand' it. Some are excluded from its interior sense, while others have a kind of 'access' to it. The same, I suggest, operates in the reading of poetry, as in my allusion to Eliot; and it can also happen (as I hope it has) in the reading of criticism, such as at the start of this present chapter.

Some readers, we might venture at this point, can appropriate texts more than others; all will appropriate them variously. Some readers can give blood to the ghosts of the dead that they hear, identifying them as, say, Chaucer or Marvell or Kyd or Middleton in Eliot; some audiences can hear the spirits of Handel or of Telemann when they are at a concert played by the Michael Nyman Band; some spectators can see Seurat in Hodgkin's paintings, and so on. In all these cases, there will be those who remain 'outside' of such an appropriation, though they will still have a view on the works of art, perhaps enjoying Nyman's ability to weave certain rock-rhythms into pieces played on instruments not normally associated with rock; or admiring the particular play of colour in Howard Hodgkin's small canvasses, say.

Is the difference between these audiences – (and let us perhaps identify them, for shorthand purposes, as those 'inside' and 'outside' of the University; those 'inside' and 'outside' the institutions of criticism, aesthetic evaluations: that is to say, *those inside and outside of 'culture' itself*) – is this difference important or noteworthy? If it is not, then how might we propose to deal with the resultant incommensurability of views – even the consequent impossibility of serious or meaningful communication – when the divergent audiences emerge from the same concert-hall or library or art-gallery and try to talk with each other in the public domain? If the difference between audiences is important, on the other hand, should we strive to reduce the distance between them, to establish a new or third audience, one that would be able to *share* a reading in common, or to find a commonality around a text or other work of art?

Another way of putting this question would be to ask whether it would make a positive difference to an individual reader in their engagement with a text if she or he learns to recognise Wittgenstein at the start of the present piece, or to hear the echo of Chaucer at the start of Eliot? That is: if they do not know the Chaucer, ought we to introduce the reader to the text that ghosts the one that she or he is reading presently? Yet more pointedly: should we teach literature and its history? The alternative might seem, at first glance, to be that we should teach an active forgetting of what we might already know, so that some readers acquainted with Chaucer will ignore or forget that knowledge while reading Eliot, say, in the interests of being able to communicate with 'those outside', those who do not share the perception that is aware of Chaucer behind Eliot, a perception that, in aligning *The Waste Land* with a text of pilgrimage, helps shape and govern the range and purchase of its meaning and value, or its status *as a signifying practice* (the reasons for my stressing this phrase will become clearer later). This willed ignorance is (for me at least) an unattractive option.[3]

The question of whether we should teach literature and its history is not a trivial one. There are many – and many in positions of power – who would respond to it in a firm negative; and that fact is surely important for those academics involved in the disciplines of the humanities in today's University. Successive governments over the last three decades in Europe and the US (though I shall focus primarily here on Britain) have certainly been suspicious of the teaching of literature and its associated business of criticism in the University; and it is a simple fact that many of the governmental directives and 'initiatives' aimed at a supposed improvement in efficiency in higher education and the claimed widening of access to it in Britain over thirty years have been concerned to stifle the humanities out of existence on the grounds that they appear to offer no immediate and substantial financial return either to the general economy or to the individual engaged in their study. They are not giving the kind of instrumental knowledge that, we are told, the society and its individuals need.

That is to say, there are some 'outside' of the institution of literary study (the government) who cannot understand what it is that we do, for the language in which we speak of what we do is one that is simply unrecognisable to them. Where we might speak of 'quality of living', they prefer to speak of 'measurable outcomes'. Their language, as Lyotard presciently pointed out in 1979, is that of 'performativity', and, largely because we are involved in an entirely different language-game from this, there is little chance that we will be able successfully to encapsulate or describe adequately what we do in terms of the measurements of input and output that governments regard as the only legitimate language-game in town.[4]

It is as wise to make my position clear at the outset and get what some might read simply as 'polemic' over with (for there is a substantive argument regarding democracy behind the ostensible polemic here). Thus: the world of business does not want a highly educated workforce with 'transferable skills', but does want a pliant – even a compliant – workforce that will do whatever is required whenever it is required of them (in other words, it does not know what it wants until it has a problem to be solved or a specific task to be completed; and then it wants someone capable of solving the problem or carrying out the task, promptly, efficiently, cheaply); the world of business has made it abundantly clear that it does not wish to contribute in any way to the funding of education but wants simply to benefit from it (even if some industries involved in arms and drugs manufacture, for the obvious instances, will fund some scientific and pharmaceutical research); the British government, at least, is not interested in the establishment of a number of outstanding Universities in the UK;[5] the government, and the public that it forms through its presentation of itself and of its values, mistrusts the intellectual, especially the 'non-scientific' or critical intellectual, preferring (at best) the investigative reporter or the mediatic interviewer (in Britain, Jeremy Paxman, John Humphreys and their ilk: interviewers who start to become the story and thus enter the frame of mediatic celebrity).

Those extremely influential British governments that we have seen under Tony Blair have laid bare the underlying realities of governmental interest in education: there is no interest in the *contents* of education; instead their interest extends only as far as the *politics* of education. That is to say, all that governments require is a set of statistics that can be entered into a manifesto for re-election. If it were not education, then it might well be hospitals, or police forces – and, indeed, it is these things too. What these 'public services' have in common is the fact that they are concerned with issues relating to the quality of our social and public spheres, a quality that can impinge directly on the lives of many individuals (though not all individuals);[6] what they have further in common is their intrinsic resistance to the languages of performativity. Yet these are all now homogenised by a bureaucratised administration and managerialist governmental system that speaks only to and for its own internal discourses, where government officials speak to journalists and provide 'news' that is of interest primarily to other politicians and journalists – that is, it is news about which non-politicians can do nothing; and then they wonder why the electorate does not bother to turn out for them, as even participation in general election ballots slump to the point where more people vote in the 'deselection' of candidates from the prize in the TV show called *Big Brother* than bother to turn out for governmental elections. At this point, one might return to the initial question: is it important that the audience for *Big Brother* has a full awareness of the literary source behind its title and what it means? Would such an awareness change their view of the TV programme? If the phrase 'big brother' had some semantic content returned to it, might it affect how its viewers relate their activity of 'voting' in the programme to how they might vote in elections or otherwise participate in the public sphere?

Are these large and pressing issues linked? Is the effective disenfranchisement of a people linked in any way to the predicament of the humanities? In this chapter, I will argue that there is a fundamental link between them; and that an attack on humanistic cultural study leads inevitably to the demise of democratic (or indeed any) participation in the social or public sphere. Further, I shall argue that the institutionalisation of a relatively new University discipline, that of Cultural Studies has been, despite itself, complicit with precisely this barbarism, even as it has set out most firmly to oppose it and to try to empower and enfranchise those who have been traditionally or historically excluded from the centres of power or of self-expression in our society.

My contention here will be, reversing Williams, that culture is not ordinary. Culture, further, is not a state of affairs or a stable condition, nor is it a specific and identifiable archive of books, musical compositions, paintings and other artefacts; rather, culture is something that happens, an event (one that typically renders the ordinary extraordinary); it is episodic rather than constant. Further, I shall take the view that culture is *edifying*, that it is an event marked by the growth and development of the individual lucky enough to undergo it. In line with the etymology of 'edification', culture makes 'dwelling' possible: it delays or holds focused our attention to a specific event, and intensifies it.[7] In so delaying us, the event that is culture, arising within history, nonetheless arrests history for its duration as an event, for our enduring of the event; it makes a space or a place for it, allows it to *take place*, and to take place in a space that is necessarily shared, the focal point for the possible establishment of a community. I shall contend also that this cultural event, in its bringing together of history and the arrest of history, is akin to the commitment that we have to the dead and to their memorialisation. Finally, my argument at this stage will show that, without such an understanding of culture, democracy is impossible (but also that even with this understanding, democracy is not guaranteed, but only possible).

In the first part of what follows, I diagnose the predicament that has led to the establishment of our 'new paradigm' of Cultural Studies; I try to show where I believe it is complicit with the conservative forces that it would contest. Secondly, I outline in more detail what it might mean to think of culture as an event, and how it relates to the memorialisation of the dead. Finally, I explore the political dimension of this view, in an effort to show how intrinsically radical it might be to evaluate positively, especially in the pedagogical context, the old icons of what used to be called 'high culture'.

I Cultural Studies and the End of the University

In the very earliest University institutions, including those that pre-date my 'brief history' in Part I of this book (Bologna, Paris, Salerno for examples), the disciplines were organised as a particular combination and collocation of the subjects of the quadrivium and of the trivium. The quadrivium comprised the study of arithmetic, geometry, astronomy and music; the trivium that of grammar, rhetoric, and logic. It is not too diffi-cult to see in this a combination, broadly understood, of the mechanics of language with the mechanics of number. Another way of formulating this would be to describe the two together as a combination of structures (quadrivium) and speeches (trivium), a combination of the abstract (quadrivium) with the particular (trivium); in short, and in that Saussurean terminology worn almost to death by now: *langue* and *parole*.

This mode of thinking is one which views the University as a place in which we find out not only the conditions governing the possibility of thought, but also the specific content of that thought itself. The structure is one that mutates readily into that governing most actual medieval insti-tutions, where study was organised around the four faculties of the liberal arts, canon law, medicine, and theology. What is it, however, that makes it appropriate that these diverse bodies of knowledge are bodies that can be properly housed in the same building, the same dwelling-place, even, *à la rigueur*, in the same individual who studied them? What is it that makes a *uni*verse of such knowledge? There are four disciplines here (arising from the seven of the trivium and quadrivium), and they are distinctive; yet it is soon realised that there is, at least tacitly, a governing idea that allows for their unification. Usually, that idea is located in the non-discipline called philosophy. In this view, philosophy is not yet a separate body of study: rather, philosophy is simply the lived world and its presiding ideas as they are served and understood by the disciplines of the University itself (*Die Welt ist alles, was der Fall ist*). It is a kind of metadiscipline, not yet articu-lating itself yet existing as the unstated ground on which the other disciplines stand (it 'under-stands' them, literally) and which makes their self-realisation possible.

The modern University, though it has come a long way from this, nonetheless retains some elements of its structure. In his posthumously published *The University in Ruins*, Bill Readings offered a splendid analysis of the University in Europe and North America since the time of the forma-tion of the modern University of Berlin, under the rectorship of Humboldt, in 1810.[8] Readings pointed out that this modern institution has, as its mission, the question of culture itself. It is the task of the University to describe the shape and condition of the national cultural identity of the citi-zens of the nation-state in which it is operating; it is also the task of this University to offer models of the kind of citizen required by its nation-state. Thus, for instance, Berlin gives the citizens of the nascent German nation-state an idea of the nation state that they should strive to live up to, and, at the same time, it produces individual citizens (its students) who are capable of becoming the 'good Germans' required by that idea. There is a circularity to this, of course; but the answer to 'what comes first: the nation or its appropriate citizen?' is provided by the very institution that is required to pose it, the University itself. The University, as it were, intervenes in the historical process to get the process of history itself started. In such a kind of institution, named by Readings as 'the university of culture', it is clear that the humanistic disciplines must play a central role, concerned as they are with issues of value, ideology, morality and other such metaphysical ideas. It is important to note, in passing here, that this university of culture is thus the place in which the idea of the nation state and the idea of citizenship are made into a material and historical reality.

However, one central point of the analysis advanced by Readings is that the university of culture is no more, that it has outlived its usefulness and purpose; and, consequently, the University might best be seen as an institution in transition. The central problem for the university of culture is that the nation-state has ceased to matter in the ways in which it mattered two hundred years ago. 'Americanization' (Readings' synonym for globalization, a synonym 'that recognizes that globalization is not a neutral process in which Washington and Dakar participate equally'[9]) has effectively put paid to the nation-state; and, as far as the University is concerned, it has thus undermined the possibility that the institution can be a 'cultural' entity in the ways that it was during the period of the nation-states and of national governments. As a character in Wenders' *The Kings of the Road* has it, 'the Yanks have colonised our unconscious'; or as Lyotard had it in *The Postmodern Condition*, 'Eclecticism is the degree zero of contemporary culture: one listens to reggae, watches a western, eats McDonald's food for lunch and local cuisine for dinner, wears Paris perfume in Tokyo and "retro" clothes in Hong Kong; knowledge is a matter for TV games'.[10] If it is the case that the point of the University was the acclamation of a culture, and of a culture that was specifically and intrinsically tied to a national identity, then it follows that when the national identity disappears, culture as such becomes – at least in the substantive sense of culture as an instantiation of edification – redundant. It is then easily replaced by a notion of culture as 'habits of life' or 'the everyday' or simply, 'what happens round here' in very vague and generalised senses.

There are, according to Readings, three options open to us for dealing with this predicament. The first, which he termed the conservative option, would be simply to try to ignore what is going on in the era of Americanization, and to continue to teach as before. The second, which he termed the multicultural option, would be to adapt to the new situation, to open up to the interest of an eclectic range of other cultures, other identities. The third – and this Readings saw as the most likely outcome – is to abandon the notion of the University as an institution with a mission linked to the project of national identity at all; this would also imply that we give up the role of the intellectual (the thinker whose thought might have purchase on matters of public import and interest as well as on her or his disciplinary field), and also that we acknowledge that we 'have done the state some service; but enough of that' – Othello-like, we abandon the idea of being in service to the state.[11]

It is perhaps paradoxical that it is precisely at the moment of this crisis, the moment when 'culture' is effectively redundant, that we see the almost exponential growth of Cultural Studies, especially during the 1990s. Yet Readings offers a logical and persuasive rationale for this. It is only when culture, as a governing idea (like philosophy, like the *langue* of the ancient trivium/quadrivium), ceases to matter for the University that it can most readily and easily become a discipline within it. That is to say, Cultural Studies becomes a discipline precisely *because* culture as a metadisciplinary idea for the institution (and indeed for society) has ceased to matter. In short, if there has been a 'culture war', then culture has lost it, and we have lost culture.

How did we lose something so 'ordinary'? It was Williams, famously, who gave a currency to the idea that 'culture is ordinary'. His case was one that was concerned to circumvent the apparent consensus that culture equated with 'high culture' and that, as such, it was an entity that was particularly appropriated by a bourgeois or ruling class, with the consequent effect that the working class was effectively excluded from culture. In making the case for the ordinariness of culture, for its 'everyday-ness', Williams effected a semantic shift in the term, such that it began to mean not just the arts, but rather a whole 'way of life', a system of values and priorities – values that were not in the first instance perceived as economic – that shaped and conditioned our being and the possibilities of our horizons of perception. In this way, the mode of life of the class that appeared to be excluded from culture would be legitimised; and the category of 'culture' would be widened to accommodate all those activities of a people that could not be immediately classed as 'instrumentally efficient' activities.

From this, it is not a massive step to the position of the institutionalised forms of Cultural Studies that have risen to such dominance in the University. In the argument advanced in his *Literary into Cultural Studies*, Easthope understood culture to embrace virtually anything and everything, provided only that anything and everything can be understood in terms of its being a *signifying practice*. Culture, therefore, is not painting only; it would now include visual advertising, say, provided that the advertising in question is seen to signify something beyond its immediate function of selling. Culture is not just Mahler; it is also, say, Britpop and boy/girl-bands, provided these latter phenomena are construed as signs pertaining to a wider arena of values in contemporary youth. Culture is not just *Ulysses*; rather, it embraces all forms of narrative, including televisual and cinematic narrative provided that these latter are available to be read as symptoms of the values of a mass society and of the power relations (especially those of 'race', gender, sexuality, class) that shape and control it.

In Cultural Studies, then, things are translated into their value as signs, becoming the signs of things.[12] Cultural Studies becomes possible precisely because it allows 'things' to carry on their merry way, undisturbed, while it goes about its relatively harmless (and, effectively powerless) business of analysing the 'signs' of those things. It forges a wedge between the realm of significations and the realm of material being; and limits its purchase to the realm of the sign. In this respect, practitioners of Cultural Studies are precisely akin to those politicians satirised above: they speak to and for themselves, while the world to which they refer carries on without them, working to a different set of priorities, values, and understanding. Cultural Studies, then, effectively divorces culture from material reality, establishing a separate sphere for its study and for its being: that separate sphere is what we call a 'discipline' in the University. As Readings has it:

> Culture finally becomes an object of study in direct proportion to the aban-donment of the attempt to provide a determining explanation of culture. Cultural forms of signifying practice proceed from culture, and culture is the ensemble of signifying practices. In this sense, there is a direct ratio between the intensity of apocalyptic claims for the institutional potential of Cultural Studies and their absence of explanatory power. What allows Cultural Studies to occupy the entire field of the humanities without resist-ance is their very *academicization of culture*, their taking culture as the object of the University's desire for knowledge, rather than as the object that the University produces.[13]

Now, then, there is paradoxically no culture as such to be analysed, precisely as the analysis of this absent object grows exponentially. As Readings pointed out, all that there is left to do for Cultural Studies in this predicament is to 'oppose *exclusions* from culture . . . Cultural Studies finds nothing in the nature of its object culture that orients its intervention, other than the refusal of exclusion'.[14] Once this is established, the only validated position from which one can legitimately speak 'within' the culture is that which is located 'outside': that is to say, one can *only* speak now with authority if one speaks from a margin of some kind. The crude and slightly reductionist way of putting this would be to say 'to everyone their own victimhood'.[15]

In this state of affairs, another contradiction arises. If everyone is a victim, then victimisation ceases to have any substantive and *specific* semantic content. As Readings put it, 'the effect of multiculturalism is necessarily to homogenize differences as equivalently deviant from a norm';[16] or, in other words, who will *judge* 'my' victimhood (as working-class Scot, say, facing a colonialist imperialist English 'centre') to be *more* or *less* significant than 'yours' (as Irish lesbian, say, in a similar context). The faculty of judgement itself is what is paralysed in Cultural Studies, because there exists no culture as such, and therefore no cultural norms as such, from which to measure our several critical distances.

Indeed, it is the paralysis of judgement that lies behind this predicament. In the late 1970s and early 1980s, to be 'authoritative' in one's judgement regarding the value of a text (the 'Keats vs. Dylan' debates) was construed as being 'authoritarian', especially if the authority found herself or himself in a teaching situation. The authority of the teacher, based in her or his greater experience of the subject (literature, say), was spectacularly undermined by a Thatcher government that insistently attacked the quality of teaching (at all levels) and of the individuals carrying it out; perhaps worse, it was even disavowed by those, especially on the left, who were engaged in the teaching itself. In both instances, there is a false notion of democracy at work: Thatcher's government wanted a democracy that it could control without the possibility of facing a 'critical' electorate; the left believed in a premature democracy that wanted to value and legitimate everyone's judgement, even if it was ill- or under-informed. This latter view has its roots in Williams's assertion, in another context, that 'culture is ordinary'. When we have lost culture, and we have also lost the will to judge, something has gone wrong; when the academic left finds itself complicit with a Thatcherite barbarism then, too, some wrong turning has been made somewhere.

2 Culture as Waking

There is an intimate link between what we typically call 'culture' and what we might think of as the memorialisation – the 'waking' – of the dead. Hartman thinks of culture as that which 'keeps hope in *embodiment* alive';[17] by this he means that culture is what is able to give a reality to the ghosts of the past, to those who have gone before, the dead. Culture activates or realises the dead in our memory, in the edifying Arnoldian figure of 'the best that has been thought and said', allowing the living to say and think, or to quote and inhabit, to appropriate or 'embody', this 'best'. It 'wakes' the dead, remembering, celebrating, embodying them, and thus 'possessing' death, accommodating it and turning it to wakefulness, watchfulness (the words are the same etymologically).

What is at stake in the memorialisation or waking of the dead? In remembering the dead, we are effectively calling attention to the absolute singularity of the individual recalled, her or his Benjaminian 'aura'; paradoxically, we are simultaneously aligning the dead with ourselves, aligning that absolute singularity with the present living self in an act that brings the two together, even identifying the dead and identifying ourselves with the dead person (and thus ostensibly denying singularity, replacing it with community), such that the living are, in a certain sense, 'possessed' of and by the dead. Death, as Derrida recently argued, is the one thing that we cannot get anyone else to do on our behalf: it is the locus of a calling to responsibility, and 'only a mortal can be responsible'. Though it is the one thing that cannot be done on our behalf, the living still can live on behalf of the dead, can 'survive' them or live on on behalf of them.

In the literary sense, we remember the dead or waken them by reading them. It should be noted, in passing, that the central figures in my analysis so far, although regarded as very much 'contemporary', are dead (they are also white and male): Wittgenstein, Readings, Easthope, Williams, now Arnold. Should we forget them? Is it all right to know their work while they are alive, but to ignore it the day after they die? Obviously not. We remember them by quoting them; and so we speak in words that are not our own. I began this present chapter in words not my own; but there is no other place from which to speak. We are spoken by the dead – and that is what we call culture. As Eliot put it in another context:

> Someone said: 'The dead writers are remote from us because we *know* so much more than they did'. Precisely, and they are that which we know.[18]

'Culture' is what happens when death makes its presence felt through the very intensity of our sensory being.

Culture is therefore not a commodity. Even Arnold was aware of this when he proposed a view of culture that was not at all static but rather dynamic. For him, culture, as 'a study of perfection', the pursuit of a 'best self', was 'not a having and a resting, but a growing and a becoming'.[19] Culture considered as commodity – even in the form of the library, archive, museum, conservatory and so on – is, effectively, a means enabling the characterisation of culture as nothing more than 'entertainment'; and in its capitalist form it is controlled by the 'leisure-merchants' of the culture 'industry'.[20] Culture as event, however, as the memorialisation of the dead who can possess us and whom we can also possess through knowledge of them and of their voices, is antipathetic to such entertainment, to commod-ification as such. The mode of 'possession' in this case is non-capitalist, non-economic; the dead have gone beyond the system of exchange and of exchange-value that makes commodification possible in the first place; and to 'possess' the dead is also to be possessed by them and of them. It is only in the latter form, as I shall argue in the final section here, the form of culture as event, that there arises the possibility of democracy.

What does it mean to think of culture as event? By event, here, I mean something rather specific, of course. An event is what happens when the outcome of an action cannot be pre-programmed in advance, when the outcome is *not* contained in the input. Events are things that are anathema to our oppressors at QAA: radical irruptions of the unexpected into the norm; and, as such, they are episodic. (Indeed we might argue that the primary function of QAA is to put a stop to any such episodes.) I identify this moment with culture precisely because it requires a growth of the indi-vidual who undergoes the event in question in order to accommodate it, in due course, at some future moment. In Kantian terms, this is a shift between the operations of the analytic *a priori* and the synthetic *a priori*. An *a priori* knowledge given to us by the power of our analytic methodologies, for instance, simply operates to confirm the power of the methodology; it cannot offer us any genuinely 'new' knowledge of the world. For this, Kant argued, what is required is a *synthetic a priori*, an operation that exceeds that of the analytic insofar as it not only confirms our analytic methods of gleaning knowledge but also allows for the simultaneous structural modi-fication of those methods in order to allow consciousness to appropriate a new knowledge, a new given, data that would not be amenable to compre-hension under an existing analytic methodology.[21] In short, the event is that which requires synthetic knowledge, for it requires that our modes of comprehension grow and develop to accommodate new data: in this case, specifically, we are required to develop consciousness to the point where we can know and appropriate, be possessed of, the dead.

The culture-event, then, we might describe as the encounter with death. Levinas saw death as a limit-point of 'responsibility': death, he argued, is 'le sans-réponse'.[22] It is the point that cannot be accommodated into any 'economy of signs', and thus marks a kind of end of economy as such.[23] Further, it is a moment of an absolute transition; and, in this regard, it becomes a liminal and exemplary instance of non-capitalist change itself. Maurice Blanchot (for whom literature can be aligned with 'the right to death'[24]) offers a useful way of thinking how this works. He considers the case of the writer as one who is analogous to the man building a stove. The building of a stove brings something new, absolutely new, into being; it eliminates that which was there before (it 'denies' the 'mere' existence of the raw materials). The stove *transforms* the world; more importantly perhaps, the activity of making it (by analogy, the activities of writing and reading) *transforms* the maker (where before he was cold, now he can be warm), and does so in ways that are practical in an empirical sense as well as edifying in a metaphysical sense.

Writing, reading: these can both be seen as precisely this kind of 'limit' encounter in the aesthetic sphere. The culture-event, then, can be seen precisely as the encounter with death; but one that is edifying, one that requires the growth or development – the *Bildung* – of the individual who undergoes it and who is produced by it, possessed of it. To be possessed of and by culture in this way is to grow as human potential.

3 On political culture, briefly

Democracy requires community. It requires that there be a people able to communicate with and to influence each other. It requires that I be able to cite the arguments of others if they are better than my own; it requires that I 'possess' and that I am 'possessed of' others, not in the sense of owning them as commodities but rather in the sense of embodying them, such that my body is the general body, my sphere is the public sphere. This, in its most basic form, is what we might call 'political representativeness'. Democracy requires love and hospitality, therefore, as the basic relations governing the people as such.

It is culture – in the form of the culture-event described above – that, in a privileged fashion, can offer this as a central effect of its happening. This is why we ought to study culture; this is why we cannot have a democracy without a knowledge of the dead (the ultimate 'other', of course); and this is why we might consider abandoning Cultural Studies, as we try to wake culture once again. As critics, this is our duty; as teachers, we owe the young a knowledge or experiencing of the dead, not just of the living, not just of themselves, not just of their status as victims: we owe them instead the weapons to fight back – together, in hospitality and love, however 'soft' and unbusinesslike it may sound – against victimhood, the weapons that will arm democracy itself, by giving them an autonomy and, yet more importantly, a freedom, through the encounter with the dead.

CHAPTER 3

On Reading

Towards the end of *The Reader*, Bernhard Schlink's 1997 novel and meditation on the 'responsibility' or answerability of the post-war generation of Germans towards the past, Michael Berg receives a letter from Hanna Schmitz, the elder and formerly illiterate woman to whom he used to read and who is now in prison for crimes that she committed during the Nazi regime. His reaction reveals a classic attitude to the value associated with reading and writing:

> I read the note and was filled with joy and jubilation. 'She can write, she can write!' In these years I had read everything I could lay my hands on to do with illiteracy. I knew about the helplessness in everyday activities, finding one's way or finding an address or choosing a meal in a restaurant, about how illiterates anxiously stick to prescribed patterns and familiar routines, about how much energy it takes to conceal one's inability to read and write, energy lost to actual living. Illiteracy is dependence. By finding the courage to learn to read and write, Hanna had advanced from dependence to independence, a step towards liberation.[1]

What *The Reader* has shown by this point, of course, is that, as I started to hint in the previous chapter, reading can also be a matter of life and death. In the camp where Hanna was a guard, she had 'special prisoners', girls whom she would protect so that they could read to her; and, during her trial, in a move that effectively condemns her, Hanna admits to writing a controversial document rather than acknowledging her illiteracy (115–16; 128).

The classic attitude, as reiterated here, is that reading is emancipatory, that it sets us free by establishing not only our capacities for negotiating a contemporary world of business, getting through documents, finding offices or streets, entertaining guests in restaurants and so on; but also, in that it can be a matter of life and death, reading establishes our capacity for autonomy and freedom, 'liberation' from dependence.[2] There are two understandings of 'freedom' here: the first sees freedom as that which is exercised (and exhausted) in the enactment of *choice* (as in the menu, say); the second sees freedom as the search for and enactment of *autonomy*, becoming a subject who is not entirely predetermined by her or his 'situatedness'.[3] This latter suggests that reading is connected to, indeed is a condition of, the very possibility of subjectivity. I want to modify this slightly to suggest that – or indeed to show how – we might better think of reading, in this second and stronger sense, as determinant of the possibility of our becoming *citizens*. In this way, and through the exemplifications I will advance in this chapter, my Viconian argument that reading is intrinsic to civics and even to civilisation will be further strengthened. The idea here is that, in reading, we can become more fully ourselves, can more fully realise our humanity: we can find the conditions of our *becoming*, and not just the conditions of our economic being. This is an idea with a long history; and, for many, it is what will validate and indeed give value to the activity of reading itself. In a troublingly haunted phrase relevant to *The Reader*, we might say that *reading makes free*.

Reading, to yield such benefits, comes at a heavy price: it is difficult. Not only is it difficult to make one's first step towards deciphering the hieroglyphic mark on the page (if you doubt this and have forgotten how you learned to read, try looking at a text that uses a different alphabet from the one with which you are familiar); more than this, criticism in the last thirty years, as if in obedience to an economy in which the benefits of reading must be paid for, has consistently stressed how odd and how perplexing it can be to try to read aright.

In 1984, David Trotter, in *The Making of the Reader*, suggested that one issue that shaped modern anglophone poetic writing was the attention that a writer would have to an audience. The making of a reader was also the making of a readership, or of a community that might be able to avail of the poetry that Trotter discussed. Yet the value of putting the question of the reader in this way is that it recalls to us that the awareness of an audience is not, of course, an entirely 'modern' phenomenon. It is found not only in the 'Oyez' of medieval romances, but also, most famously, in Milton's invocation of Urania in Book VII of *Paradise Lost*:

> Still govern thou my song,
> Urania, and fit audience find, though few.
> But drive far off the barbarous dissonance
> Of Bacchus and his revellers . . . [4]

Milton here is profoundly aware of his reader; and he is already making a critical distinction between those who can read and the rest – between, as Kermode would have had it in his book on parables, *The Genesis of Secrecy*, to which I have already had recourse above, those 'inside' and those 'outside'. Milton was not one for 'widening participation' in any easy sense, by assuming that the simple instrumental skill to read was somehow adequate to what might be called an unbarbaric or a civic reading.[5]

The sheer difficulty of reading became a recurrent refrain, even a theme, in late twentieth-century criticism, especially though not exclusively in that associated, however tangentially, with deconstruction. For Bloom, for instance, in 1975, all reading was, of necessity, misreading: 'Reading . . . is a belated and all-but-impossible act, and if strong is always a misreading'. For de Man, at the end of the seventies, if reading was good, it was so partly because it was of necessity strewn with error, and thus reading 'has to bring in this unstable commixture of literalism and suspicion'. For Hillis Miller, as late as 1987, 'Reading itself is extraordinarily hard work. It does not occur all that often'.[6] More recently, and from entirely different theoretical persuasions, we can find similar attitudes in, for example, Eric Bolton's account of his own developing reading habits, in which he found that 'pleasure was more complex than fun; satisfaction craved more than having one's prejudices stroked, and there was some relationship between effort made and pleasure gained'.[7]

The emergence of this kind of view, from differing critical angles, in university literature departments throughout the last decades of the twentieth century is a response to a particular issue or problem: how does the study of literature – and by extension, the very existence of the arts or humanities faculty – justify itself in *economic* terms? If reading is *work*, and especially if it is *hard work*, then in that very *askesis* it can legitimise itself: the axiom is that pleasure costs effort – and is therefore not 'pure' pleasure, but is rather productive in some way, a contribution to an economy that is normally served by the exploitation of one's body or physical capacities in a work that generates a sickness unto eventual death.

The growth and development of 'reader-response' criticism, in the wake of Barthes' announcement of the birth of the reader in 1968, and as developed in the early work of Iser or Fish in the late sixties and early seventies, prefigures a Thatcherite economics of reading. In this mode, the reader, counter-intuitively, not only becomes more important than the author (as the 'buyer' would dominate the 'market'), but also becomes an individualistic hero of sorts, 'struggling' with meaning or against hegemony, concerned with the 'violences' of the text, 'engaged' fully within the articulation of the text, 'interpellated' by it, and thus always, of necessity, 'committed'. Eagleton's satiric remark, for once, was not entirely wrong when he described this as the RLM or 'Readers Liberation Movement'.

Yet the roots of this attitude pre-date Barthes. If we turn to 1943, we find I. A. Richards, in the midst of war, indicating that:

How a page was read has often been a matter of life and death. Misread orders
on the battlefield have sent thousands to unnecessary destruction. Their
readings of a page of Scripture have led as many to the stake. . . . All [I]
could do . . . would be to help us to understand some of the difficulties.[8]

First here, note the relation of reading to matters of public life and death,
and its relevance to contemporary affairs in the war. Reading is part of the
struggle, part of the war effort. Yet more interestingly, however, Richards
sees the kind of emancipation proposed by this difficult and dangerous
reading as one that involves quite radically the edification and expansion of
the self. A key to our understanding of what is at stake here is given in
Richards's view that it does not follow from the fact that texts have many
meanings that any reading is as good as any other. Rather:

> These things have many meanings because they touch us at points at which
> each one of us is himself many-minded. Understanding them is very much
> more than picking a reasonable interpretation, clarifying that, and stick-
> ing to it. Understanding them is seeing how the varied possible meanings
> hang together, which of them depends on what else, how and why the
> meanings which matter most to us form a part of our world – seeing
> thereby more clearly what our world is and what we are who are building
> it to live in. (13)

The freedom at stake here is not that of the choosy consumer; it is that
of the citizen. It is clear, thus, that, at least since Milton, there has been
'reading' and reading; and the two modes (consumerist; civic) are not the
same. Indeed, they may even be opposites. My first contention in this
present chapter is that there are at least two senses in which we might think
of reading; that one of these – the dominant one at the present time – insofar
as it is political and instrumental, is precisely barbaric (in Milton's sense);
that only the other can be emancipatory (in Schlink's sense). I shall argue
that, in its more positive and civilising sense, its cultural sense, reading
delays us, that it forces a lingering dwelling in a place and in a time, in a
nation and in a history, say (and the characteristic marker of both of these
is the specific language); and, insofar as it forces this dwelling, it is antipathetic to matters of *economy* and thus, by extension, resistant to political
assimilation. Finally, in exploring reading as a matter of life and death, I
shall explore more fully than heretofore in this book the intimacy that exists
between reading and dying, between the ways in which a reading is always
of necessity an act of a structural commemoration that requires a discourse
with and among the dead. It is thus 'angelic' or 'hermeneutic', concerned
with messages from other places and times; and thus always an act of translation that requires the mastery of more than one tongue. It is best done by

those who, like Milton, could become ministers of foreign tongues. The only literature is comparative literature; the only reading, by analogy, is comparative reading.

I The two literacies

In chapter 4 of Austen's *Emma*, Emma asks Harriet Smith about Mr Martin and, trying to get to the core of his character, she asks:

> 'Mr Martin, I suppose, is not a man of information beyond the line of his own business. He does not read?'
> 'Oh, yes! – that is, no – I do not know – but I believe he has read a good deal – but not what you would think any thing of. He reads the Agricultural Reports . . .

When Emma then reads, in chapter 7, Mr Martin's letter proposing marriage to Harriet, she is surprised:

> The style of the letter was much above her expectation. There were not merely no grammatical errors, but as a composition it would not have disgraced a gentleman; the language, though plain, was strong and unaffected, and the sentiments it conveyed very much to the credit of the writer. It was short, but expressed good sense, warm attachment, liberality, propriety, even delicacy of feeling. She paused over it . . . [9]

Between these two passages, we get a view of Mr Martin that is constructed precisely in terms of his literacy. At one level, his reading (Agricultural Reports) is instrumental rather than edifying; yet, in his writing, he is able to deploy a correct grammar that contributes to the success of his self-expression and style. Indeed, this is such a 'very good letter' in relation to what she expects from a man of such reading that Emma initially wonders whether it is plagiarised from the writings of his sisters. The aesthetic delight of reading the letter gives her pause; and in that pause, she is able to reflect, to think, to change her mind about the author, about the value of the writing; and, in our pause, we too are able to reflect not only on Mr Martin but also on Emma herself as well as Harriet.

Judgements about persons here are being made on the grounds of aesthetics, on a foundation of the style of one's writing and the substance of one's reading. The ethical relation (not only between characters in the text, but also between ourselves as readers) is dependent upon the aesthetic. This has become, during the last two centuries, a fraught issue relating to the massification of culture and the widening spread of a certain literacy. It was clearly a matter of concern in the nineteenth century, and government took an interest in it.

That interest is striking for its similarity to present-day predicaments and governmental responses to them. In 1862, Robert Lowe, then Vice-President of the Education Board in Palmerston's administration, accepted the Newcastle Commission's findings on the costs of education, and promulgated what became referred to in simple shorthand as the 'Revised Code'. The Code essentially established a system explicitly based on 'payment by results': schools could claim payments from Government depending on the attendance of their pupils, and with a significant supplement if the children passed some tests in reading, writing and arithmetic. There would be an annual assessment by Her Majesty's Inspectorate (staffed, at the time, by Matthew Arnold among others); and, inevitably, as Arnold pointed out, teachers started quite reasonably to teach to the test in order to secure the funding for their schools. Arnold's complaint against this was that government policy, under the guise of raising literacy standards, effectively *reduced* education to a series of instrumental and potentially thoughtless tasks. Instead, of course, what he wanted was what he called 'a fresh and free play of the best thoughts upon [one's] stock notions and habits'.[10] Arnold took the side of a Frenchman (Renan) against an Englishman, the northern radical John Bright, this latter believing in the efficacy of a policy of quantitative and measurable 'target-setting', against Renan's preference for a notion of high quality in education, a notion in which quality does not translate easily into quantity.[11]

It would be an error simply to lambaste Lowe and his contemporaries, for they – no doubt like more recent British and other governments – were trying to deal with an irresolvable problem: they wanted a good education system, but one that was cheap. The consequence, when a government has not the will to do what is necessary to pay for a mass education, is an education that concentrates on certain 'basic' or 'fundamental' aspects of an education for the mass or 'the many' ('the few' taking better care of themselves, and making their own increasingly private arrangements); and the further consequence is that pupils are taught precisely to those basic levels and in a fashion that sees education – here reading – simply as an instrumental means of the gaining of money. The net result is the production not of citizens but of consumers. It is in relation to this that we should revisit Hoggart.

One aspect of the fundamental argument of Richard Hoggart's influential 1957 study of *The Uses of Literacy* is that there is, within working-class life, the potential for a certain resistance to the blandishments of a mediatic culture driven by unreflective consumerism; but that there is also, equally clearly, a threat to that possibility of resistance effected by the sophisticated deployment of the new and widening literacy on which the mass and populist culture depends. The 'culture merchants' and 'leisure merchants' depend precisely upon the very literacy that was supposed to be emancipating the previously illiterate classes.[12] The anxiety expressed by Hoggart was not new, nor was it being expressed for the last time. Indeed, there is a lengthy history of lament for the demise of what Hoggart has, more recently, identified as 'critical literacy'. Plato, indeed, was ostensibly troubled by the schooling of his day, having Socrates argue, in *Republic* Book X for one random example, that a mimetic learning by heart ('to the test') and recitation was rather dangerous, a threat to the self of the student; and that much preferable would be the diegetic skills associated with narrative (and also, by extension, with the critically discursive document). More pertinently for present purposes, a thinker such as Steiner follows Hoggart in 1963 by calling for a 'humane literacy', and writing that 'He who has read Kafka's *Metamorphosis* and can look into his mirror unflinchingly may technically be able to read print, but is illiterate in the only sense that matters'.[13]

Hoggart and Steiner, from utterly divergent class backgrounds, are, in their convergence on the issue of reading in the age of mass culture, essentially echoing the Miltonic anxiety about the fitness of a readership. For Steiner, the fit reader must, in a sense, have read all of literature. He feels a certain pathos as he walks along the library shelves now, in his later life, and realises that there are certain things that he simply will never read; in this, he echoes Calvino, in *Se una notte d'inverno un viaggiatore*.[14] For Steiner, for Calvino, and in the end for Hoggart too, *what* we read is important: 'creative reading' (Steiner) or 'critical reading' (Hoggart) both derive from an engagement that is directed towards the text that is edifying precisely to the extent that it does not address our direct and contemporary concerns, precisely to the extent that it offers us a different or foreign world. That is difficult; but it is no more difficult than learning to decipher those hieroglyphic marks on the page in the first place. Further, this kind of priority in reading precludes easy consumerism; in its stead, it offers the difficulties of freedom, democracy, emancipation: all those ideals of a classic defence of reading. Such reading must take as its object something called *literature*; and this literature can be characterised as that which opens its reader to otherness, difference, or simply *foreignness*.

One way forward here might be to consider Steiner's distinction between 'critics' and 'readers'. For Steiner, the critic is she or he who is able to establish a proper distance between the text and herself or himself. Reading critically is a matter of 'placing', of establishing the space of the critic in relation to the text. By contrast, the reader is she or he who is, in one sense, always intimate with the text.[15]

What I want to take from this is the *placing of the reader*: critical reading gives one a *place*, a place that is different from the place of the text; and, in the establishment of that very difference, one can see one's 'habit' and 'habitations'. Yet, distanced in this way, one is also *distanced from the habitation*: self-conscious, self-critical. Literature 'calls' to its reader, calls for its reading; critical reading is what happens when the answer to that call searches precisely for the adequacy of response; and that search in turn 'calls' to literature, calls for its writing. This is a matter of place, of placement and habitation: a matter of dwelling.

2 Dwelling among the remains

To write presupposes reading; to read presupposes writing. It follows from this that Barthes cannot be correct when he argued, in what is his most famous and most trivially cited 1968 essay, that 'the birth of the reader must be at the cost of the death of the Author'.[16] That position suggests a purely *economic* relation between the forces of reading and writing; but the relation is, I have argued, properly a *dialectical* one. Some eight years later, Barthes argued his case differently, suggesting that reading is itself productive of writing, that 'it will never be possible to liberate reading if, in the same impulse, we do not liberate writing'.[17] Long predating Barthes, Proust, whose final days coincided with the infant Barthes learning to walk, was profoundly aware of the potentially dialectical relation (we might now say deconstructible relation) between these activities. In *A la recherche du temps perdu*, Proust offers us two matching scenes, one of an imagined writing, the other of an imagined reading. They are separated by some two hundred pages; but they are intimately related to each other, for both concern the communication and relation – or lack of it – between the Narrator and Gilberte. A consideration of these scenes will allow me to argue for a specific preliminary understanding of what it might mean now 'to read', an understanding that will link the activity of reading explicitly to the concept of *habitation*, to dwelling in a dialectic or an undecidability. Dwelling, in this sense, is precisely the inhabiting of *indeterminacy*, non-determined-ness, Beckettian end-less-ness.

During one January, having still not received a New Year letter from Gilberte with whom he imagines himself in love, the Narrator realises that it is not Gilberte but rather he himself who, by prolonging their separation, is effectively making it impossible for them to have any future serious erotic or even romantic relation. He tries to imagine himself telling her that it is all over between them; but realises that she would not hear or understand exactly what he means. The reason for this is simple but important for the text of *A la recherche* as a whole. Indeed, one might even suggest that, at root, it is what the text is about: the difficulty – if not impossibility – of telling the truth straightforwardly in words. Communication can never be straightforward:

> Mes paroles ne seraient parvenus à Gilberte que deviées, comme si elles avaient à traverser le rideau mouvant d'une cataracte avant d'arriver à mon amie, méconnaissables, rendant un son ridicule, n'ayant plus aucune espèce de sens. La vérité qu'on met dans les mots ne se fraye pas son chemin directement, n'est pas douée d'une évidence irrésistible. Il faut qu'assez de temps passe pour qu'une vérité de même ordre ait pu se former en eux.[18]

> [My words would only have reached Gilberte by deflection, as if they had to cross the moving curtain of a falls before reaching my friend, and so, unrecognisable, sounding ridiculous, having no kind of sense any more. The truth that you put into words doesn't trace its path directly, and isn't endowed with an irresistible clarity. Enough time needs to pass for a truth of the same order to have formed itself in them].

Proust does not suggest simply that he will be misunderstood. Rather, lurking in here is an entire theory of communication. Proust has it that there is a discrepancy between words as they are uttered or written and the order of truth to which those words and their speaker or writer strive to be adequate: in short, that communication has a temporal dimension and a *delay* that must be there if the truth is to be articulated or felt. You may put the truth into your words, but that truth does not reveal itself in an unmedi- ated – immediate – fashion in the hearing or reading of those words. It takes time for the truthful sentiment that you have 'put into' words to come and *inhabit* them. Reading is intrinsically and structurally *belated*: its condition of 'being late' is of its essence.

This is to say two things: first, if we want to understand the truth of a text – if we are to read it aright – we must come to it always belatedly (the commonplace reading of Proust, of course); secondly, truth is a matter of *habitation* – it 'lives in' or dwells with words ('dwell' in the sense of 'delay', 'linger'). There is a temporal *décalage* here, that we have already seen drama- tised in earlier pages of the text where the matter is thematised for us as the very substance of the novel. The Narrator imagines himself as a reader, reading a letter that he has received from Gilberte much earlier:

> Et quant vînt l'heure du courier, je me dis ce soir-là comme tous les autres: 'Je vais recevoir une lettre de Gilberte, elle va me dire enfin qu'elle n'a jamais

cessé de m'aimer, et m'expliquera la raison mystérieuse pour laquelle elle a été forcée de me le cacher jusqu'ici'. (I: 401)

[And when the moment came for the arrival of the mail, I'd say to myself on that evening as on all the others: 'I'm going to receive a letter from Gilberte, she'll tell me at last that she has never ceased loving me, and will explain the mysterious reason why she has been forced to hide it from me until now'].

He imagines receiving this letter every evening, figures himself reading it, knowing its every phrase by heart. Then, suddenly, he realises that if he ever were to receive a letter from Gilberte, it could not possibly be the one that he has imagined reading, for it is he, not Gilberte, who has composed it. So, from then on, he has to try to conjure the words that she will say, or that he wants her to say, precisely by *not* reading them, *not* imagining them.

The psychology of this is precisely the phenomenology of reader-response criticism; it is also that of a Marxian reading as described by Jameson when he claims that texts come to us 'as the always-already-read'.[19] In such criticism, the reader necessarily *prefigures* what it is that she or he is about to read; and thus, as is shown by my first citation from Proust here, necessarily gets it wrong or, as is shown by the second, reads only herself, not the text and not the author. The prefiguration obviously involves a disjunctive temporality: we read before we read, before we have the materials to read. Reading here presupposes that a writing will take place, not that it has already taken place; yet it must imagine that future, must project itself towards futurity.

This said, we have already been told very early on in Proust that truth, if it comes at all, comes from reading (in a passage commented on at length by de Man). The servant Françoise says that the 'adventures' read by the Narrator as a child are not real; but his retort is that all reality depends upon the intermediation of a text:

Tous les sentiments que nous font éprouver la joie ou l'infortune d'un personage réel ne se produisent en nous que par l'intermédiare d'une image de cette joie ou de cette infortune . . . (I: 84)

[All the feelings that the joy or misfortune of a real person make us experience are only produced in us through the mediation of an image of that joy or that misfortune . . .].

To read, thus, is to mediate the real. Moreover, truth in reading is a matter of inhabiting or of dwelling; all reading is a matter of passing time, of dawdling in a location. It gives a 'local habitation and a name'.

Very early on in the novel, we have a simple scene of preparation for the reading of Georges Sand. In this scene, the mother who is about to read excises the love scenes, deeming them unsuitable for the audience, the young boy who is not yet a reader himself. In this she is an unfaithful reader, 'une lectrice infidèle'; yet she is also a reader to be admired for the respect and simplicity of her interpretation: 'une lectrice admirable par le respect et la simplicité de l'interprétation' (I:, 41–2). The first thing to note, however, about this reading is that it too is done 'out of time', out of its proper moment: the book is a birthday present that has been opened two days prior to the birthday. The text read here is, in every sense, 'premature'. The unfaithful reading is an act of translation by the reader (the mother) for the audience. In this sense, it is an act of 'comparative reading' in the sense that I offered above, right at the start of this chapter, in my opening allusion to Schlink's *The Reader*. It is also a reading carried out in a time that is out of time: it is somehow taking place in the two days that have not yet elapsed.

I use Proust here to show that reading is a matter of entering a realm of epistemological uncertainty, an exercise in negative capability. Reading is that which allows us – even requires us – to *inhabit* undecidability, a realm of shadows and hauntings; and to inhabit this sphere as a place marked by belatedness, by 'being late'. Others endorse such a view: in his *History of Reading*, Alberto Manguel uses the example of Kafka whose stories 'nourished by Kafka's reading experience, offer and take away, at the same time, the illusion of understanding'.[20]

This, however, is a trap. The activity of reading – of the non-instrumental and anti-consumerist reading that I celebrate here – is the paradoxical one that tries to deal with the uncertainty provoked by one text through the engagement with another in the hope of finding certainty; but reading precisely exponentially expands the uncertainty, for every further text serves simply to add exponentially to the uncertainty, to double it, to resolve nothing. This is what Steiner means when he claims that 'the mark of good criticism is that it opens more books than it closes'.[21] As Borges knew, to read one word with an adequate form of attention is to enter a labyrinthine library in which we must of necessity dwell, and from which there is no immediate exit. The foreignness that such reading invites us – requires us – to inhabit is thus both a spatial and a temporal foreignness: it alerts us to what we might call the 'question of the present', a presence conditioned precisely by its relation to that which is absent, a presence that, literally, *makes itself absent*. Such an inhabiting of undecidability, of course, is but another word for thinking, for a thinking that is a humble not-knowing. Further, to dwell in such consciousness is to seek an identity that must always elude us, thereby making us constantly differ from ourselves, constantly grow: and the word for this is culture.

In a sense, what this amounts to is a call for us to 'dwell among the ruins', to dwell in the remains, to inhabit culture as a mode of undecidability, endless-ness. Reading exposes that which is present to its potential absence; reading is precisely this dwelling in uncertainty, in this wasting expansiveness of time. It is antipathetic to 'basic' literacy of the kind required to process the 'Agricultural Report' or any document designed to bring us home to ourselves, to reassure us of our present being, to deny us the possibility or potential for becoming other than we are, or in another time than the present.

3 Reading as dying

Eliot famously argued that 'No poet, no artist of any art, has his complete meaning alone. His significance, his appreciation is the appreciation of his relation to the dead poets and artists. You cannot value him alone; you must set him, for contrast and comparison, among the dead'.[22] Before Eliot, it is Hamlet who poses the question, and poses it as the great question of modernity.

In the midst of that most famous soliloquy, he describes death precisely as an 'undiscovered country, from whose bourn / No traveller returns'. Not only is death the paradigmatic instance of an absolute foreignness, it is also precisely the site of uncertainty and undecidability. Blanchot, who in theoretical terms has most insistently tied literature to death, is instructive here, in remarks that sum up an entire tradition of philosophical perplexity over the fact of death. He writes:

> . . . when we die, we leave behind not only the world but also death. That is the paradox of the last hour . . . to die is to shatter the world; it is the loss of the person, the annihilation of the being; and so it is also the loss of death, the loss of what in it and for me made it death. As long as I live, I am a mortal man, but when I die, by ceasing to be a man I also cease to be mortal. I am no longer capable of dying, and my impending death horrifies me because I see it as it is: no longer death but the impossibility of dying.[23]

Reading, such as I have described it here – that is, a reading that is *dyseconomic*, a reading that provokes *becoming* (and difference) and denies being (or identity) – is that which confronts precisely this paradox. Dying, here, *like reading*, is the necessity of an impossibility. The impossibility in question is the 'endlessness' of the literary, its 'pointlessness', its endless becoming, its endless dying in a death that marks the impossibility of its dying. This is the real sense of Eliot's remark: it is not just that the living, the present writer, is to be placed among the dead; it is also that the dead are, precisely, not-dead. Literature 'happens' and reading becomes possible if and only if we acknowledge this paradoxical position: the famous 'dead white males' are not dead (for dying is impossible), the contemporary 'counter-traditions', from feminism to postcolonialism, say, are not 'living'. Both are to be read precisely because, as literature, they call us into that point of uncertainty, hovering between two conditions, a 'present' whose shape is given as being between life and death, between the possibility and the impossibility of dying. It is here, in this undecidability, that we find it possible to read.

CHAPTER **4**

The Question concerning Literature

I Polemical

The question concerning literature is complex, in that it involves at least three separable strands of inquiry. In the first place, we have a question of definition, of course ('What is literature?');[1] secondly, ghosting the question of definition is a concern regarding the place or places in which we read and study ('What is the nature of literary *studies* and, by extension, what is the nature and function of the *university,* here considered as the place in which we study literature and the place that often decides the question of the literary, in our time?'); and, further, what might literature have to do with the linguistic – and, through the linguistic, finally, the *national* – identities of human citizens or subjects (that is, what is the status of 'English' literature or literary study with respect to English people or to the category of Englishness as an ethnic marker; and, by extension, what is the nature of a subject's or citizen's *participation* in the national via the linguistics and literacy that govern the literary)?[2] One reason for rehearsing the question concerning literature in our time is that, despite recent controversies within literary departments or national cultures, debate has circled and, indeed, circumvented what is at stake in posing the question.

In 1983, at the height of the 'theory wars', it all seemed so simple; and it was presented in a cunningly simple fashion by, for a highly typical instance, Terry Eagleton. In his very influential textbook primer, *Literary Theory*, Eagleton poses the question 'what is literature?' with his characteristic rhetorical flourish, knowing all the while that to present the question concerning literature in this simple fashion is to ensure that no satisfactory answer will be available; and, consequently, he will therefore be able to divert attention from the question to some other matters. To look for a definition of 'literature' that will be necessary and sufficient to all cases in such a way as to allow perfect, clear and distinct typological or taxonomical classification for all instances of writing is a search doomed to failure – which may be why Eagleton asks it in the first place. The very notion of having a 'clear and distinct idea' of the *essence* or *being* of something that is continually evolving or *becoming* is ill-judged and misplaced; to draw inferences, as Eagleton does, regarding politics and power from the fact that certain individuals subscribe to the notion that 'literature' is a usable and workable term, is an exercise in the purest rhetoric, and one that will not stand scrutiny in any serious critical fashion.

Eagleton has little difficulty in dismissing those who argue that literature can be defined through its supposed distinction from 'factual' writing. Empirical evidence itself, he remarks, deals with this, when we reflect on the fact that 'Seventeenth-century English literature includes Shakespeare, Webster, Marvell and Milton; but it also stretches to the essays of Francis Bacon, the sermons of John Donne . . . [and] might even at a pinch be taken to encompass Hobbes's *Leviathan* or Clarendon's *History of the Rebellion*'.[3] (What Eagleton means, of course, is that these writings have been often taught in university 'English' curricula; and not that they 'are' or 'are not' intrinsically 'literature' – that is what he is allegedly trying to define in the first place.) He has much more difficulty when he tries to dismiss the notion of there being some peculiar uses of language that mark out characteristically distinct moments in writing or reading. What he has to accept is that the Russian Formalists – who broadly subscribe to this view – did not themselves try to define literature as such, but rather confined themselves to noting the instances or happenings of 'literariness'. Eagleton then insists that:

> Anyone who believes that 'literature' can be defined by such special uses of language has to face the fact that there is more metaphor in Manchester than there is in Marvell. There is no 'literary' device – metonymy, synecdoche, litotes, chiasmus and so on – which is not quite intensively used in daily discourse. (5–6)

Yet the Formalists did *not* define 'literature' in this way; rather, they acknowledged precisely the kinds of anxiety displayed by Eagleton, and restricted themselves to the attempt to define 'literariness', or moments when the aesthetic function in writing asserted a specific kind of autonomy. The sloppy misrepresentation of their argument allows Eagleton to knock down a straw-person, and to imply that anyone who subscribes to a *value-system* that would see more literary worth in 'Marvell' than in 'Manchester' is fundamentally mistaken, or that she is doing so on shaky philosophical grounds. (Let us leave aside the clear implication or invitation to consider a value-system that would see more worth in Manchester than in Marvell; it is this particular kind of rhetorical jolt that Eagleton seeks, not committing himself to any such position, but implying an allegiance to those who might scorn or feel threatened by Marvell or by their ignorance of Marvell). The point at issue, however, has not (yet) to do with value, but rather with the difficulty of proposing some stable definition for something that develops historically and culturally.

As Eagleton knows, to ask 'What is literature?' is a bit like asking 'What is a sofa?' When Cowper, in the early 1780s, was invited by Lady Austen to 'write on this sofa', he immediately made the phrase itself into the base for his great poem, 'The Task'. Playing on the double sense of 'on', he wrote *on* the sofa, *about* the sofa; and, at the start of the poem, he gave his brief cultural history of the development of the sofa and what we might call its standing in England. Cowper displays a number of items on which people have sat, from the three-legged joint stool on which King Alfred sat, through to the more stable four-legged version, then, with the arrival of cane from Indian trade, the lattice-chair, on through to the simple chair, then the arm-chair, contrived by 'an alderman of Cripplegate', until eventually we reach, after many variants, the sofa itself. He writes:

> So slow
> The growth of what is excellent; so hard
> To attain perfection in this nether world.
> Thus first necessity invented stools,
> Convenience next suggested elbow chairs,
> And luxury the accomplish'd Sofa last.[4]

These lines, full of innuendo (the 'nether' world, the necessity of our passing 'stools' in our progress), and following on from the obvious political implications regarding England's trading position in the world (the cane from India), describe the slow evolution of a single item from its variant models or sources. To define a sofa by the fact that one might sit or lie comfortably on it is, clearly, not an adequate definition; since there are so many other items satisfying this description. Each different form of seat has a different historical and cultural position, clearly; but are we to infer from this simple fact that it is now impossible to accept the existence of the sofa as such? After all, Cowper is in the process of demonstrating the worth of writing about it (just as the critic might demonstrate the worth of writing about something called literature). Are we to say, in acknowledgement of the fact that sofas are not naturally occurring phenomena, and that we have appropriated a word for them, that they are 'merely' an arbitrary construct and therefore not to be treated differently from other kinds of furniture?

The fact that we 'merely' linguistically describe certain items as 'sofas' does not, of itself, invalidate the claim that there may be a distinguishable something called a sofa, and that its *being* a sofa is somehow independent of my – or *my community*'s – strategic or tactical desire to call it such. Nor does it follow that my acceptance that there *is* something called a sofa – or, by analogy, literature – implies some fundamental essentialist or monotheological or unhistorical or damningly elitist view of the world on my part. Rather, all that is implied in accepting that there *is* a category called 'literature' is that I agree to participate in meaningful discussion of the topic. To push the argument by analogy further, I can accept that there is a useful category of those called 'men', which will allow me to talk meaningfully of gender. I can even accept that the notion of maleness or of masculinity might be constructed. Yet the fact that transsexuals exist and that gender is located on a spectrum, rather than on one side or other of some absolute barrier, will not disallow my conversation or prove it to be inherently sexist, vacuous or, worse, elitist. On the contrary, without such a category, talk of transsexuals, even talk of gender – or, by analogy, talk of 'boundary cases', even of texts, in the category of literature – would itself be meaningless and thus lacking in any interest.

Further, although we may have culturally 'invented' literature or constructed it as a concept, it does not follow from this that *anything* can become literature. To be sure, many things – especially written artifacts or events involving language – can be treated *as if* they were literature; but such a view is functionalist, reductivist, and fails to acknowledge the facts of cultural or aesthetic difference. Although some universities may use TV programmes as raw material in a literature course, TV programmes are not literature; nor are films or advertisements or comic-strips or the semiotics of body-piercing and so on, however interesting these things may or may not be. It follows, polemically but also logically, that although one may legitimately study such phenomena, they have no place as legitimate, fundamental objects of study in a university literature programme.

I shall get up from my sofa and put this argument polemically at this outset. There are some who will argue that one of the consequences of the introduction of 'theory' into English literature programmes has been to propose a more inclusive approach to legitimate culture. There are some who argue that the introduction of 'theory' into English literature programmes has served a positive political purpose, in that it has led to the necessity of our describing curricula that are more 'representative' of social groups who did not previously figure in an older curriculum; and, further, that the *inclusion* of that which had previously been excluded has served the purpose of *legitimizing*, culturally and socially, those who had allegedy been excluded or unrepresented in 'English'.[5] Such an argument, ethically and politically attractive, is worth examining. Catherine Belsey is among those who have claimed that, with theory, 'the discipline of studying English literature comes to embrace a form of cultural history and cultural analysis that takes us beyond the handful of "great works" that used to be selected for study in order to preserve good taste'.[6] Well, she must have pretty big hands. My own undergraduate programme (at the University of Glasgow, 1973–78, typical of the kind that Belsey would regard as unhelpful) required that I had some detailed knowledge of, at a conservative estimate, the works (usually multiple, rarely if ever anthologised) of at least ten, and usually around twenty, writers from each of six centuries; and that I would be able to write ably about these texts up to four years after I had studied them in classroom situations. Compare this with a contemporary 'modular' system, driven in the UK by 'quality assessment/control', which forbids an examiner legitimately requiring knowledge of what has been taught anything later than about a month after it has been studied; explicitly requires that no knowledge 'outside' of that which has been taught be examined; and requires that students of literature should only be asked to read minimal quantities, usually anthologised and 'selected' beyond recognition. The simple, if polemical, question is this: 'Have we genuinely expanded the possibilities for the realisation of a rational social democracy by extending the literacy of students; or, on the other hand, have we been forced, however unwillingly, to capitulate to a set of 'market-forces' that have driven quality steadily ever downwards, that have allowed us to preserve the forms of education while emptying those forms increasingly of content, and that have served the purpose of pushing a hoped-for participatory democracy further and further into the receding distance?' The question, of course, is rhetorical in that it does not require much reflection before offering a reply.

In the same piece from which I have already quoted her, Belsey is rightly pleased that 'To be worth reading, texts written by women, members of the working class or colonial and post-colonial authors no longer have to be measured by standards of taste established a generation ago in white, patrician and patriarchal senior common rooms'. My own contention, however, would be that we are *not* reading these texts, *nor* even the older, allegedly 'exclusivist' curriculum; we teach *neither* of these, but rather a banalised form of 'cultural semiotics' that blandly homogenises *all* writing, such that we are fundamentally unable now to distinguish *texts*, not to mention texts *by* women, say. The reason for this is, I allege, simple: we have lost the category of the literary; and, in the particular ways in which we have tried to achieve something politically through the university, we have thrown the baby of political change out with the bathwater of 'traditional' studies of 'literature'.

It will be clear from the foregoing that, in this chapter, I shall be mounting a defence of literature as the 'proper' object of study for a university English department and its students. This position, I believe, is not reactionary or conservative; and I stress at the outset that I do not endorse in any way the by now familiar rantings of the conservatives – the Blooms (both Allen and Harold), Hirsch, D'Souza, Bennett, for random examples – in the so-called 'culture wars' that have deflected many within the American academy from its proper work. That said, I argue in what follows that it is time that we reconsider the 'question concerning literature' in terms of the complexity that lurks within that question. I shall explore slightly more fully, therefore, the questions of definition and the rhetorical gestures of 'theory' in the debate; following which, we should be able more fully to explore the place of literature in the university and the place of the university in our communities; and finally, I shall outline what we might call 'the persistence of the literary' as our proper object of study; and in this, we will see that 'the question concerning literature' is, in fact, the question – and, perhaps troublingly, the questioning of – democracy.

2 Rhetorical

In her recent book, *Cultivating Humanity*, Martha Nussbaum follows the general tendency according to which anything can become a legitimate object of inquiry in a literature programme. The ethical (and also political) argument behind this has to do with giving voice to the previously unheard or delegitimised within our societies. Having argued for the positive ethico-political values of including Richard Wright's *Native Son*, or Ralph Ellison's *Invisible Man* (a development, she argues, of Sophocles' *Philoctetes*) in our contemporary literary curricula on the grounds that they encourage what she calls 'the compassionate imagination', she then writes that:

> These works are all written in a conventional literary language, a fact that explains their relatively easy acceptance into the realm of 'literature' despite the radical character of their subject matter. It can also be argued, however, that literary art most fully fulfills its Whitmanesque mission of acknowledging the excluded when it allows the excluded to talk as they really talk, to use a daily language that is nonliterary and that may shock our sensibilities.[7]

The example she gives of such a text is James Kelman's *How Late It Was, How Late*, 'a novel of working-class life in Glasgow, Scotland', which 'uses throughout the working-class Scots dialect that [its Glaswegian protagonist] would actually speak, and includes all the words that such a character would be likely to use in thought and speech' (98). Nussbaum's argument, which she thinks aligns her with Kelman, is that Kelman is giving a voice to those who had typically been excluded, rendered invisible, by the dominant literary forms; and that this is a positive thing in itself, on the grounds that a democracy must inherently be able to encompass cultural difference and a multiplicity of diversities.

The notion of democracy that lurks behind this is one based, as I believe Nussbaum herself would accept, upon the rather imperfect models offered by the ancient world, upon which we can only improve. The ancient model is that of the *agora*, the public sphere or arena in which deliberation takes place and in which there is an exchange of voices or views. Through debate in this public sphere, it becomes possible to align oneself with one specific voice or speaker rather than with another: to make what is now a choice within and for the *polis* in which one identifies oneself with what is spoken by another, or in which one finds one's own voice adequately represented in the speech of another. Thus, *voicing* can be seen to be cognate with *voting* (as it is in Latin); and what we now call 'representative democracy' occurs. Central to this is the notional primacy of discussion, and specifically of oral debate, to any proper democracy. For democracy to work in an ethical fashion, it is incumbent on all participants that they strive to hear the voices of those who, for whatever reasons, do not figure in the *polis*, the excluded or 'those outside'.[8] It is by giving voice to those dispossessed of the usual forms of legitimised speech that we can enact an ethical version of representative or 'deliberative' democracy. Nussbaum's arguments for the inclusion of many new works into the curriculum of literature departments rest precisely on this ethical ground: an inclusive democracy must correct the tendency to monolingualism or to authoritarianism or even just to the coercions of social normativity, by attending to the voices of those who have been silenced in the past.

There are problems with this notion of democracy, one fundamentally indebted to the Marxian idea that 'these people are not represented. It is vital to represent them'. This much-cited *dictée* from Marx's *Eighteenth Brumaire* might usefully be placed alongside a lengthier passage from that same work in which Marx argues that

> the democrat, because he represents the petty bourgeoisie . . . imagines himself elevated above class antagonism generally. The democrats concede that a privileged class confronts them, but they, along with all the rest of the nation, form the *people*. What they represent is the *people's rights*; what interests them is the *people's interests*. Accordingly, when a struggle is impending, they do not need to examine the interests and positions of the different classes. They do not need to weigh their own resources too criti-

cally. They have merely to give the signal and the *people*, with all its inexhaustible resources, will fall upon the *oppressors*.[9]

Some might find this a more or less adequate description of the kind of 'democracy' understood by leftist literary theory in the last three decades of the twentieth century. What is at issue in it is primarily the concept of cultural 'representation'. To 'represent' those who have not been represented, it is first necessary to 'invent' them, in the sense that it is first of all necessary to consider them *abstractly*, as a homogenised class with shared qualities or properties.

An anecdotal example of this might suffice to show the point. In a public debate in Cambridge in March 1998, Wlad Godzich and Margaret Anne Doody defended this kind of ostensibly admirably 'democratic' line of argument. A counter-argument was proposed, in which a participant in the debate alluded to the case of his relatively uneducated mother, a woman who had left school at the age of thirteen, with no qualifications, limited literacy, and absolutely no 'cultural capital' in that she had no knowledge whatsoever of what counted in her society as legitimate culture. All she knew was that it was not for her; and that, as a consequence, she was the poorer in every sense. The woman was described as an avid reader, but of low-grade romance-stories and of court-room detective stories. Her son suggested that critics such as Godzich and Doody were failing in their ethical and social responsibilities: they had the opportunity to give this woman cultural capital that would enrich her life and her social standing, but, by pretending to 'legitimise' culturally the low-grade books that she more or less partially read (for the most part books that they themselves would not read, they themselves preferring 'high culture'), they were effectively simply saying to her that where she stood was in itself already 'legitimate', requiring no further education (and all the while keeping the riches or cultural capital – literature – away from her). In response, Doody said to me (for it was, of course, my mother) that it was so typical of a male critic that he should stigmatise *woman* for her low levels of literacy and that he should so negatively dismiss the kinds of reading done by *women*. This manoeuvre won the predictable applause, despite the fact that Doody had simply effaced all presence thereby of this particular and singular woman. Why, I inquired, should an audience of would-be radical literary critics and teachers applaud Margaret Anne Doody's incapacity, as a supposed feminist, to fail to see the specifics of a particular case; why applaud the failure to see a specific woman, submerging her historical being under the wraps of an abstraction? The abstraction can be easily discussed, of course, so long as we keep it void of content; as soon as we give it some actual content, specific cases requiring specific judgements replace the vacuities of a homogenized abstraction. It is this failure to see specificity that is the direct result of the kind of 'representative democracy' – fundamentally a bourgeois concept, as Marx points out – that makes me wonder why a critic such as Doody bothers to teach at all. My point was – *is* – that it is the responsibility of the critic to make some judgements, even in the absence of universalisable criteria; and that the failure to make a judgement that says, for example, that *Middlemarch* is more edifying than, say, the novels of Georgette Heyer or of Danielle Steele, is an total abnegation of responsibility, and one that has potentially dire social, ethical, and political consequences. To validate equally *everything* that is read in 'cultural' terms – that is, in terms of its capacity for enabling a participatory democracy and for establishing the autonomy of human citizens or subjects – is to validate nothing, and to render fragile the link that obtains between literature, or literacy, and freedom.

In relation to this, let me introduce here what appears to me to be a potentially devastating intervention. In his examination of 'The Expressive Force of Language: on the function of rhetoric in gaining knowledge', Gadamer indicates at the outset that there has been a shift in the operations of rhetoric whose consequence cannot be stressed enough:

> In modern civilization the topic of rhetoric is no longer what it was at its ancient origin, nor is it the same as the 'rhetoric' that has attended our cultural tradition for so many centuries. For us, the change has to do with converting the art of talking into the art of writing and the art of reading. . . . This at once makes clear a problem hidden behind this whole range of topics: the dissociation of writing and reading, which has brought about a fundamental modification of understanding. How to bridge the distance between the meaning fixed by the writer and that understood by the reader is the basic question of hermeneutics. For modernity, this is also its pre-eminent problem.[10]

In this, Gadamer draws attention to the simple fact that it is inappropriate to 'translate' a form of polity based on the primacy of the immediacies of spoken dialogue and debate into the extremely heavily mediated forms of communication that are central to a literate culture without significant modification. As he argues, talking always takes place within the immediate relations between a speaker and a definite addressee; and both speaker and addressee are identifiable – defined – through the polity that arises from the conversation. Writing, too, requires an addressee, but in this case, the addressee is necessarily indefinite, and the temporal immediacies of speaking – which allow for the classical construction of democracy as that based on a spatial consciousness (democracy as applied in the *agora*, establishing a *polis*) – give way to the *problem* of establishing a democracy that is guided and characterised by time or by *mediation*. As Gadamer says, 'It cannot be sufficiently emphasized that today what is at issue is not speakers but writers. Here, in literary aesthetics . . . lie many as yet unsurmounted problems' (124). The problems, as I shall argue here, are not simply problems relating to stylistics or aesthetics, but also relating to precisely the forms of democracy that we might relate to the question concerning literature.

3 Democratic

I have remarked above that the posing of the question of literature in the form of the simplicity of 'What is literature?' was a rhetorical gesture. For a theorist such as Eagleton, the rhetoric drew attention to questions of power supposedly inscribed in any act of definition, with the clear implication that such an assertion of power was unwarranted, suspect, and (usually, and by implication only) anti-emancipatory. The reason for this is that any act of definition must, *by* definition, *exclude* from its ambit those elements – in this case, writings – that do not satisfy the terms of the definition; such categorical, but *linguistic,* exclusion is then rhetorically treated as if it were *social* exclusion, the exclusion of certain people from access to political power or social standing. Behind the analysis here (which is either extremely weak intellectually, or extremely cunning – or both) there lies a serious issue – the question of the relation of literature to politics, especially under the sign of autonomy. How might literature relate to the production of autonomous human individuals, subjects, citizens?

Alongside this, one might usefully consider the history of literary studies in the academy or university. It is by now something of a routine at this point to rehearse the by now dispiritingly familiar story of 'the rise of English studies' as a story punctuated by the names of Arnold, Eliot, Leavis, Williams, and culminating in our present predicaments. Rather, as we have seen from the introductory section above, I take a slightly wider scope for the question, allowing us to see the stakes of the rise of national literary studies in various locations. For present purposes, we should properly explore the implications of noting that what we now call 'English' in university departments is a mutation from something that used to be known, perhaps more technically, as 'rhetoric'.

Let me recapitulate some of the central nodal points from my introductory section, here showing their purchase on the question of what we can call the persistence of the literary. When Hugh Blair was appointed to the

Chair of Rhetoric and Belles Lettres in the University of Edinburgh in 1760 (it becoming the Regius Chair in 1762, and Blair the first holder of that royally-endowed and influential, if still politically sensitive, position), he proposed an annual series of lectures on the topic of rhetoric, exemplifying the tropes and figures of rhetoric through analyses of a significant number of passages from some works that we have come to treat – either positively or negatively – as among the 'canonical' texts of English literature. One of Blair's great themes, let us recall, is the superiority of spoken over written forms of communication. For Blair, speech is sensible, immediate: it gives the present act of communication its full presence as the *content* of a specific material experience. Writing, by contrast, may be powerful; but in its lack of immediacy, its necessary capacity for abstraction, it gives but the *form* of experience without the specific content that would be there in the immediacy of a speech or dialogue situation.

We can now add to this. As Gadamer would have it, there is, then, a dissociation of the act of reading from that of writing, such that the rhetorical encounter is necessarily muted or mediated; the consequence – with which the whole trajectory of reader-response literary criticism has always tried to deal – is that the 'experience' of the reader is always somehow merely formal, vicarious, distanced from the self of the reader. In such a state of affairs, it is clear that there is a particular sense in which the 'experience' of the reader is 'inauthentic', in that there is a dissociation of the reading-subject from itself such that, unable to be 'present-to-itself', it cannot genuinely be present to the site of the textual dialogue either; consequently, it is not fully participating in the great democratic project of dialogue or conversation itself.

Blair, in following this line suspicious of writing is, as we all know after Derrida, simply one thinker among many in this regard. More important for present purposes is that, for Blair, as previously for Vico in Naples, speech had an intimate relation to the social: eloquence or rhetoric were to be placed at the heart of a university education. It is through the proper inhabiting of a language (and, in the European post-medieval universities, this is increasingly a vernacular language) that we will be able to assert our autonomy, to distinguish sense from sensibility, and to prioritise reason in our construction of the social itself, at the cornerstone of which is the intellectual life. If our societies – and our linguistic communities or nations – are to persist at all, they must be based on reasonable and reasoned grounds; and if we are to have reasoned grounds, we must master rhetoric.

The culmination of this kind of thinking is to be found in Humboldt's report on the founding of the University of Berlin in 1810. There, as Bill

Readings pointed out, we find an articulation of the 'university of culture'. The University such as this is an institution that, in Readings' words,

> draws its legitimacy from culture, which names the synthesis of teaching and research, process and product, history and reason, philology and criticism, historical scholarship and aesthetic experience, the institution and the individual. Thus the revelation of the idea of culture and the development of the individual are one. Object and process unite organically, and the place they unite is the University, which thus gives the people an idea of the nation-state to live up to and the nation-state a people capable of living up to that idea.[11]

In Humboldt, the function of the University is to address and even to constitute a national culture, thereby making the nation *available* to, or *inhabitable* by, its people; such people become specific citizens, able now to live the nation-state empirically or to embody it in their actual practices. It is these practices that we can now call culture – and, in the case of Berlin, the culture in question is specifically that which emerges, at this early moment of the nineteenth century, as 'German' culture, forged through the literature of Schiller and Goethe, and the philosophy – in particular the aesthetics – of Kant, Hegel and Schopenhauer.

In all of these thinkers, as in Newman too in Ireland, the centrality of grammar and rhetoric to a university education is unquestionable. It is axiomatic that one can *participate* culturally and socially as a citizen only to the extent that one can participate adequately in meaningful dialogue. However, as Gadamer points out, that dialogue is not voiced as such in modernity, but rather it is the case that information is primarily a matter of written documentation. It is here, quite simply, that the link of literacy to democracy is forged: to participate within a modern democracy, one must be literate; and, further, one must have so mastered rhetoric that one is able to speak in different voices, in different registers, in order to assert one's autonomy. For every participant in such a polity, *prosopopoieia* is fundamental. That is to say, in certain circumstances, I, as a working-class speaker of a Glaswegian dialect, must learn how to speak precisely in the person of a Glaswegian; yet, if I am to participate in other social relations, I must also master other forms of speech or rhetoric. Thus the speaker herself becomes not just dialogical (able to engage in dialogues with others unknown to her or different from her); but also multivocal, plural in her voicings, and thus able to *think* or to speak to herself. This is the real consequence of following the Wittgensteinian line regarding the impossibility of a private language: one must always be speaking in and through borrowed voices if one is to 'hear/understand' oneself at all. If I speak 'authentically', that is, always in the pure presence of my own 'proper' voice, then, quite simply, I do not speak (or think) at all. A linguistic difference – and a *persona* or act of personification – is necessary if I am to be able to represent things to myself or to think.

It is not the case, therefore, that Kelman, say, 'gives a voice' to those who have been unheard. Does Nussbaum really think that upper-class snobs have no awareness of the voices of Glasgow? Is it really the case that middle-class students will herald a new revelation when they 'hear' or read Kelman? 'Oh, so this is how the Glaswegian working-class male speaks.' It may come as a surprise to those who agree with Nussbaum, but there is no such thing as *the* Glaswegian working-class male; there are only singular people, speaking in singular fashions, sometimes denied access to the centres of culture, and sometimes delegitimised by others, and especially by those who feel able to categorise them as an abstract, if homogeneous, type. If we are to read Kelman in a university literature syllabus (as we should), it is assuredly *not* primarily because he 'represents' some class that has typically been excluded from cultural forms of representation; it is rather because his work is *literature*.[12]

In conclusion, then, we must reconsider the claims for the supposed intrinsic link between literature and democracy. At the core of this, as Badiou has recently argued in his *Petit manuel d'inesthétique*, is the troubling link between art and philosophy. Badiou proposes that the link between art and philosophy has traditionally been thought in one of three ways. In the first way, which he calls *didactic*, it is proposed that art is incapable of truth, yet that it offers the semblance of truth; accordingly, philosophy's task, here, is either to correct art, or to banish it, or to treat it in a purely instrumentalist fashion. The second way, called by Badiou the *romantic*, claims that it is *only* art that is capable of the truths that philosophy can merely hint at or suggest or imply; thus art, here, is a kind of *incarnation* or realisation of a truth that can be felt, lived, or experienced *only* through the medium of art. The third way, the *classical*, accepts that art does not propose the truth, but doesn't feel any concern at this fact; for it says, following Aristotle, that the purpose of art is therapeutic; and thus, its domain is not that of truth but rather of *vraisemblance*, and of probability. In this classical schema, art is not to be described as a kind of thinking or 'thought' at all; rather, it has its being fully in its enactment or in its public service in rendering pleasure. These three schemes, argues Badiou, have dominated throughout the twentieth century; but the consequence of such domination has been the effacing of a third term that should properly hover between art and philosophy: education.

In the face of this impasse, Badiou asserts that we might re-think the relations of art – and from now on I shall limit this to literary art, *literature* – and philosophy (or criticism). In doing this, we should note first of all that literature is itself what Badiou calls 'une procédure de vérité':

> L'art est une pensée dont les oeuvres sont le réel (et non l'effet). Et cette pensée, ou les vérités qu'elle active, sont irréductibles aux autres vérités, qu'elles soient scientifiques, politiques ou amoureuses. Ce qui veut dire aussi que l'art, comme pensée singulière, est irréductible à la philosophie.
>
> [Art is a thought for which the works [of art] constitute its [the thought's] reality (not its effect). And this thought, or the truths that it activates, are irreducible to other truths, be they scientific, political, or amorous. Which means to say, further, that art, as a singular thought, is irreducible to philosophy].[13]

In this, to be literature, a specific literary text will demonstrate both 'immanence' and 'singularity'; by which we can claim that the literature is 'rigorously coextensive with the truths that it propagates' (immanence) and that 'these truths are given nowhere else' except in the specific literary text (singularity) (21). In this state of affairs, Badiou would ask what becomes of the third term in our set of relations, that is, the educational function of art. For him, art is educative simply because it produces truths, and:

> Ce pour quoi l'art éduque n'est rien d'autre que son existence. Il ne s'agit que de *rencontrer* cette existence, ce qui veut dire: penser une pensée.
>
> That for which art educates is nothing other than its own existence. It is only a question of *encountering* this existence, which means to say: to think a thought. (21)

The distinguishing characteristic of literature, thus, is that through an encounter, it forces the thinking of a thought. Yet, as I remarked earlier, following Wittgenstein, such 'thinking' cannot take place within the realms of a private language. It thus requires the reader of literature to be always other than herself, to be *essentially* 'hypocritical', in the sense of that term given by its etymology. The 'hypocrite lecteur' is, as it were, an *actor*, one who can inhabit various voices and who can, thereby, 'speak' to herself and, simultaneously, 'hear/understand' herself *without this being an immediate – unmediated – encounter*; that is, this reader is one who occupies not the *space* of the *agora* but rather the *time* of becoming. That is to say, literature is literature precisely to the extent that it produces a reader who, of necessity, is 'inauthentic'. Such a reader will not be distinguished by finding some adequate representation, in the text, either of herself (i.e., allowing the text to speak 'for her', or 'identifying' with its characters or ethos) or of an other (that troubling 'Glaswegian', say, whose dialect is not usually transcribed in the history of the texts we have thus far encountered, but whose being I can now 'locate', 'identify', or homogenise).

Literature, in this way of thinking, is that which renders somewhat problematic the easy or straightforward relation that would suggest that an increase in autonomy and democracy is proportionate with an increase in literacy. To put this simply: it is folly to hope that we will establish autonomous democracy by representing classes, 'races', genders, sexualities and so on in our curricula, as if we were trying, like Borges, to imagine a map that describes perfectly and totally the world it supposedly only represents: such a map would have to *be* the reality it supposedly represents, in some kind of Cratylean fantasy. The error of some recent theory has been to believe that one can easily translate from the representation to the real; that to imagine the world differently is to make it so.

Now, what happens to democracy in this? Badiou suggests that there should be a 'co-responsibility' of art and philosophy:

> une coresponsabilité de l'art, qui produit des vérités, et de la philosophie, qui, sous condition qu'il y en ait, a pour devoir, et tâche très difficile, de les montrer. Les montrer veut essentiellement dire: les distinguer de l'opinion. En sorte que la question d'aujourd'hui est celle-ci, et nulle autre: y a-t-il autre chose que de l'opinion, c'est-à-dire, . . y a-t-il autre chose que nos 'démocraties'?

> [a co-responsibility of art, which produces truths, and of philosophy which, on the condition that there is any [art], has for its calling, and a difficult task this is, to demonstrate these truths. To demonstrate them essentially means: to distinguish them from opinion. Such that the question today is this, and none other: is there anything other than opinion, or in other words . . . is there any thing other than our 'democracies'?] (29)

Given its propensity for establishing an 'authentic democracy', those versions of contemporary theory that dispose of the exclusivist category of 'literature' manage to circumvent the complexity of the relations between literature or literacy and politics. In particular, they depend upon a simplistic version of 'identity-politics' in which the task is to legitimise an authentic identity for the reader. Yet, as we have seen here, such 'authenticity' is itself that which exerts a *limitation* on the possibilities of democracy; for a democracy such as that desired by our Left – a genuinely historical or participatory democracy – requires that specific form of inauthenticity that I called above *hypocrisy*. The version of authenticity espoused by inadequately considered Leftist criticism is one in which authenticity is guaranteed by the supposedly adequate representation, in a text, of certain voices (homogensied as those of specific classes, or 'races' or genders and so on). The version of 'democracy' espoused, likewise, is that rather bourgeois one which is nothing other than the triumph of 'opinion', in the multiple voicings of what Marx satirised as 'the people'; and, further, it is a notion of democracy that, while it may possibly have been adequate to non-literate cultures, is simply inappropriate for the highly developed cultures within which we have literature at all.

As we must.

CHAPTER 5

For a Literature that is Without and Beyond Compare

Preceding chapters here have tried to address a general question of the importance of literary experience as being a 'worldly' or material and historical activity. Following from this, I turned to a general question of literacy (through which I have tried to reclaim the importance of reading as such); and then on to a more specific question of literariness (through which I have tried to reassert the necessity of the critic's requirements to make value-judgements that are grounded in experiential specificities). Central to these issues is the idea of 'comparativeness', of the critic being able to make comparisons between and among discrete and specific particulars. An experiential comparativeness, as it were, is becoming central to our question; it follows from this that if we are asking a question about 'English', we must also be situating that English question in a broader context where English can be compared with that which is not-English. In short, the English question is also turning into a 'comparative literature' question. Insofar as it is touching on the necessity of experience as well, we are now in a position where we can claim that the experience of 'English' requires the experience of that which is 'not-English' or, simply, foreignness. In this chapter, I relate this to two questions that are, I claim, central to our concern: love (which requires the experience of alterity) and freedom (which I claim, by analogy, equally requires the experience not of selfhood but rather, again, of a kind of othernness within).

|

It has become something of a commonplace in our times that any critical intervention that proposes itself as foundational should begin from the assertion that our subject is in crisis in some way. Criticism is inaugurated with and by the requirement to make a decision; but this is done in the name of the making or production of a critical state of affairs: *krinein* in all its etymological force. This is perhaps all the more true when the intervention in question pertains to matters of 'theory' or, in general, where matters of conceptual or definitional interest are at stake. Thus, when one is minded to consider, for example, the present state of the discipline of Comparative Literature, the nearly immediate tendency is to start from the assumption that if the question has any import at all it must be because the discipline is 'in crisis'. Comparative Literature, we assume from the outset, is 'critical'; or, at the very least, our object of inquiry is thought of as contentious.

That attitude shapes some recent responses to the question concerning comparative literary study. It stands at the cornerstone of George Steiner's Inaugural Lecture for the Wiedenfeld Chair in Comparative Literature in Oxford in 1994 ('What is Comparative Literature?'), where he ponders the issue in fairly formalist or aestheticist terms. Equally, it shapes Gayatri Spivak's Wellek Library Lectures, published in 2003 as *Death of a Discipline*, though there it also addresses political issues more directly, yet still with some circumspection. It centres Haun Saussy's 2004–2005 report to the ACLA (American Comparative Literature Association), where we see a further exploration of the rather 'parochial' nature of the institution of Comparative Literature coming under pressing scrutiny. In the present ferment of interest, this sense of crisis or of paradigmatic shift within the discipline is also being shaped by the arguments around Franco Moretti's recent work in the *New Left Review* following from his 'Conjectures on World Literature' (2000).

For decades now, further, we have been living in the shadow of eschatology: ever since the famed 'end of ideology' debates inaugurated within the sociology of Daniel Bell in the 1950s and then revived in chiliastic fashion by Francis Fukuyama in the 1990s, we have been presenting or imagining ourselves as being at the end of things, witnessing the death of this or that, finding ourselves to be 'post-just-about-everything', effectively ghosting ourselves and our own present tense as 'posthumous people'.[1] Beckett might have enjoyed all this, but for the observable fact that, as in the case of our great modernist precursor T. S. Eliot, we find that our ends are tantalisingly close to our beginnings: all those hypothesised endings – whether feared or welcomed – of Comparative Literature are themselves proposed in the form or in the name of establishing new beginnings for it.

A note of humility in these matters might also be apposite in the present times. Talk of 'crisis' in our discipline might properly be measured against what crisis might mean in Baghdad under occupation, or Louisiana under water, or Orhan Pamuk under the threat of imprisonment for his description of an event in Turkey's fraught history as essentially an act of genocide.[2] Put in the framework of these kinds of crisis, is it genuinely the case that our discipline is in any real sense 'critical'? What might Comparative

Literature have to do or to offer to that realm of decision-making that we know as comparative politics; or what might a revived *Weltliteratur* offer to world politics or to world affairs? Moretti comes fairly close to the correct modality of humility, I think, when he accepts an essentially limited purchase for our work: 'Forms are the abstract of social relationships', he writes, and therefore 'formal analysis is in its own *modest* way an analysis of power' (emphasis added).[3] In the present chapter, I will offer some considerations of how the questions of Comparative Literature impinge directly on the English question by looking at what I see as the driving priorities of comparativeness in relation to the question of freedom; I will also aim to set those priorities against other issues by asking about the place of Comparative Literature in a more general state of literary politics – an 'ecology' of literature, as it were.

The talk of crisis in the discipline compels us to think of ourselves as being at the start of something new or at least something refreshed. Crisis, like the schizophrenic's present tense, is explosive precisely because it is always a turning-point, a revolutionary instant in which we move from an old to a renewed condition. It is as if we are compelled to 'make it new' or to originate some new foundation for our concerns, some novel ground for our practices. As 'critics' in this particular mode or mood, we are 'moderns' through and through ('modern' here refers not so much to Eliot as to Swift and his satirical characterisation of the 'modern' author in *A Tale of a Tub*). This modern asserts an authority that is derived entirely from his being in the present moment, a being 'here, now': 'I here think fit to lay hold on that great and honourable privilege of being the last writer. I claim an absolute authority in right, as the freshest modern, which gives me a despotic power over all authors before me.'[4] The essential triviality of such a position is itself revealed by Michel Serres in his *Eclaircissements* interviews with Bruno Latour. Serres indicates our propensity for viewing intellectual and other forms of progress as, fundamentally, the gradual correction or elimination of errors. Such a stance leads us towards a 'here, now' where, as he satirically puts it, we have finally entered the realm of truth: 'Ouf! Nous sommes enfin entrés dans le vrai'.[5]

Two things drive this mood, and both are related to a global market. In the first place, and quite crudely, talk of crisis sells books: crisis, confounded in that word with the material substance of what happens in Baghdad, or Palestine, or burning cars and buses in the dix-huitième arrondissement in Paris (for random examples), is serious, worldly, of import. Secondly, and I hope less crudely, 'modernisation' (and all its correlates) is what drives the global by the bureaucratic homogenising of history across the world. Sadly, institutional forms of literary criticism have a tendency to be complicit with precisely these forms of marketisation and homogenisation of our work: who would not want to be Swift's modern author, in a banal sense? Who would eschew the possibility of inaugurating and being a founding originator of the next big thing – even something called, for example 'distant reading' (Moretti) or 'planetarity' (Spivak)? In the old sense of 'author' given by Foucault, who would not want to authorise a new school of literary criticism, a new inflection of comparative literature? Influence, authority and prestige are conferred by – and accommodated to – the market-place in which, for example, the honour of giving the Wellek Library lectures can be measured and quantified.[6]

More telling, though, is the drive towards homogenisation hinted at here. In my previous chapters, I have been at pains to show that there is a tendency within the University towards homogenisation in many convergent ways. First, in the interests of efficiency, degree programmes have to be 'modularised' into units that can be exchanged. They must therefore be constructed in ways that, quite literally, chop literature up into marketable pieces: marketable in the sense that, whatever size the pieces may be, their size must all either be the same or must be factorable as multiples of each other. Secondly, in the interests of a supposed equality of treatment of all students taking different modules, the volume of work required for each modular unit must also be measured and found to be exactly the same (or, again, factorable as a multiple): the purpose being that there then exists a homogeneity between the degree result in medicine and in art history (for two random examples). The 'value' of the first-class honours in each of these is based upon exactly the same amount or weight of work. Thirdly, these modules must be inserted into a temporal structure that allows for exchange of students between institutions; it follows from this that the modular structure must be universalised and then the term structure must likewise follow homogenising suit universally as well.

Key to all of this is the idea of exchange-value; or, more precisely, key to this is the idea that value is measured precisely by exchangeability. In the exchange, the specificity of the exchangeable items is less important than the merest *fact* of their exchangeability. The end result is an evacuation of all intellectual space of any meaningful content, at least in terms of social and cultural value. Thus – and this explicitly is the drive being led by the Quality Assurance Agency, for example – we would or we *should* be able to say that a First Class Honours in medicine is the same as a First Class Honours in art history, say, in the sense that both are based upon similar weights of work, similar volumes of study, similar intellectual demands upon the student. It should follow from that, logically, that my friend the art historian can be called upon to diagnose and then treat my illness.

Thankfully, of course, we do not actually *believe* that all degrees are the same: and, as I shall argue in my final chapter to this present book, we actually do as teachers smuggle in all sorts of degree-specifics. Yet, formally, the drive towards homogenisation is there, and it is there institutionally and socially in the interests of allowing us to claim or to assert a (bogus) 'democracy' in matters pertaining to the relation between the intellectual and the masses, between the University and society.

In literature, it is also there in the ostensible counter-movement of theory, which also homogenises. I wrote above of Doody's homogenisation of 'woman-as-such', or of Nussbaum's homogenisation of the 'working-class Glaswegian male'. Yet, I would claim, it is also there in virtually all theory that is grounded in a politics of identity and a politics of being, rather than in a culture of becoming and a culture of alterity. Identity politics in cultural criticism does two contradictory things. On one hand, it asserts an identity – and with it various rights for autonomy and self-governance – for an individual who, usually for political reasons, has either been denied a legitimate identity in the past or whose identity is given but in a position of victim.

For example, the assertion of an identity as working-man, say, makes one whose existence had no 'official' appearance within literature or culture, say, visible once more; it claims a right to be seen not as victim and object of another class's history, but rather as an autonomous subject and agent within history. This is potentially emancipatory and, many would argue, it is absolutely necessary for the question of freeing this individual. On the other hand, and simultaneously, it asserts an identity between this specific individual and others who can also be aligned with the 'working-class' position. To do this, however, the identity in question needs to be homogenised, such that the second individual (who may be a woman, say), loses her specificity in the interests of the more general position. The wider and greater the identity (and the more powerful in effecting emancipation), the more it has to become abstract, generalised, non-specific: homogeneous to the point where the specificity of (in this case) a particular woman is eradicated. This, clearly, is less emancipatory; and, indeed, it starts to reproduce precisely the very structure of oppression that caused the working-class male to assert and re-assert his identity in the first place. To deal with this, of course, we now have, as it were, multiplied our victimhoods and identities; but insofar as these new identities are also caught up in a logic of identity-politics, they will be forever condemned to repeat the very gesture against which they protest so rightly and so vigorously. That is to say: they assert their own freedom, but always at the cost of another's. The issue of freedom has, in turn, essentially been 'marketised' here: we now have many 'freedom(s)' among which to choose, as if the very fact of the choice was a realisation of freedom as such. The predicament appears to be greater than ever; and yet, as I shall argue here, all is not lost. It will be possible to find a position that is 'without and beyond compare' in its effecting of a freedom, and a freedom that has its roots in literary criticism and in the University's work.

I shall therefore aim to avoid this marketisation, at least in the structure of the present argument. I start to find this new grounding – more modestly even than Moretti, I hope – from the position that Comparative Literature is not 'in crisis' at all. If whatever I advance here could have been predicted from the logic and structure of an incidental – such as a market-driven demand for novelty – then the argument becomes less useful, less marked by something that we might call an 'event' of thinking.[7] It is important to note, however, that while I may try to resist a position where this book will have a market-ideology as its presiding impetus, I shall also, nonetheless, attend to the importance of certain political issues pertaining to the current condition of our work. It is simply that politics will not act as the central determinant of the argument (if I am successful). As a corollary, I shall also be trying to avoid the natural tendency in which talk of 'crisis' polarises opposing sides into a polemic, and therefore to move beyond the necessary polemicism of preceding chapters. In the spirit of *comparativism*, I hope it is better to allow for a comparison of positions that need not be seen as opposed or polarised at all. This is a position that, I believe, Moretti tries himself to respect when he points to the modesty of his own reading ('Many people have read more and better than I have');[8] but it is also a position that tries, quite genuinely, to accept that the mastery of the field, of the kind that I, for one, assumed was natural to thinkers of an earlier generation such as Auerbach, Curtius, Etiemble, Steiner and others, is rather impossible to achieve. It is still desirable, but difficult.[9]

2

In 1994, Steiner indicates that the first and essential issue specific to Comparative Literature is and has to be that of language: 'Comparative Literature . . . is immersed in, delights in, the prodigal diversity of natural languages. Comparative literature listens and reads after Babel'.[10] This position respects the traditional axiomatic view of the operation of Comparative Literature: to be a comparativist, it used to be the case that one had to be able to claim competence in at least three languages and in the literatures of those languages. The obvious logistical issue that follows from this is that not all comparativists share the same linguistic competences. Therefore, for the reader or audience of any article in the institution of Comparative Literature (including its journals, centrally), there is a strong chance, indeed a likelihood, that an act of translation will be required. I may understand the French and Italian, say, but as for those passages in Portuguese or Arabic, I am at a loss; and my own reader, proficient in German, say, may struggle with my Italian; and so on. This is obviously a matter of logistics, but I want to suggest here that it is also philosophically and structurally fundamental and intrinsic to the discipline.

Steiner is correct, but trivial, when he opens his Inaugural by stating that 'Every act of the reception of significant form, in language, in art, in music, is comparative. Cognition is re-cognition . . . '[11] His lecture, however, is more significant when it focuses on the primacy of translation as an issue for Comparative Literature. The statement might have more purchase were it re-phrased to suggest that a philosophy of translation is required for any and every act of comparative reading – and, indeed, for any act of reading. Reading, I shall claim here, is best carried out by those who are, as Milton was, 'ministers of foreign tongues'.[12]

We have a consequent issue which might be regarded as happenstance but which is, in fact, of great theoretical importance: the language that grounds most of this translation is English. Increasingly, English is the root language – our Latin, as it were, almost no longer a vernacular – into which everything is 'resolved'; and it is the ground – spoken or unspoken – on which all Comparative Literature stands. This remains an issue of substantive importance for two reasons. First, there is the implicit assumption in the institution of Comparative Literature that, in the end, all linguistic difference can be rendered a matter of commensurability: French and German literatures can be 'compared', and therefore can share a common (if unspoken) ground. Although unspoken, this ground nonetheless is the foundational language – the old Saussurean *langue*, if you will – of Comparative Literature; thus, language differences are resolved, finally, into superficial differences which mask an essential homogeneity. Secondly, and as a corollary of this first position, it is assumed that the tacit translation of all difference into an unspoken English is the end of translation. In fact, of course, it is but the start of our difficulties, for it assumes that English is itself internally homogeneous, and not subject to an internal or intrinsic logic of translation. The merest glimpse at the history of English demonstrates that it is not one language; and the merest understanding of its historicity demonstrates that the English spoken at any single moment in the world is multiple and various, not single and unified. 'Tacit English', as we might call it – that ground on which the functioning of Comparative

Literature stands – does not answer the problem of translation, but merely displaces and extends it.

Let us then revisit Steiner, with this problem now to the fore. We might say not just that all acts of reading involve translation, but rather something yet more far-reaching. A distinguishing characteristic of Comparative Literary study is that, by its attention to non-native languages, it serves the purpose of altering or 'othering' and alienating the relation that a 'native' speaker has to her or his first tongue. That is to say, Comparative Literature fundamentally undermines the very structure of 'nativity' as such, with the corollary that it calls into question the link of language to nation. That my 'first' language is English gives no substance to any claim for the primacy or priority of my 'national' links to England, or indeed to any Anglophone nation-state.

Two final glosses on this are important. The first is that, although English is routinely recognised as a world language, it is of course nothing of the kind: at best, it is a series of languages spoken and written in diverse ways in diverse parts of the globe. It may globalise our work *in principle*, but in fact globalisation of our domain remains essentially a matter for the economic and publishing markets. In this regard, it may well be the case that, ostensibly counter-intuitively, we can say that the world's *divisiveness* is occasioned precisely by the triumph of English, and especially of American–English.[13] Secondly, we can learn from Agamben. As his work on the figure of the refugee in *Homo Sacer* makes clear, one of the reasons why the figure of the refugee disturbs us so much is not due to contingent matters pertaining to specific political situations. Rather, refugees disturb the operations and, indeed, the very concept of the nation-state; and they do this 'because by breaking the continuity between man and citizen, *nativity* and *nationality* . . . they put the originary fiction of modern sovereignty in crisis. Bringing to light the difference between birth and nation, the refugee causes the secret presupposition of the political domain – bare life – to appear for an instant within that domain'.[14]

If we put these two glosses together, we reach the hypothesis which suggests that Comparative Literature is, properly speaking, the literature of refuge, the literary practice most intimately tied to the refugee. This would explain that historical reading of the discipline (shared by Spivak) which sees its roots in the wastes of Europe after the Nazi period; but it explains that reading in theoretical terms, and in such a way as to demonstrate the *intrinsic inevitability* of the condition of Comparative Literature. It makes refugees of its readers, and therefore disturbs the link of nativity and nationality. This is all the more so in the case of a literature whose tacit underpinning lies in an ostensibly global language, such as English. For

those whose first language is one of the Englishes of the world, it demonstrates the foreignness of English to itself. That is to say, it suggests that
there never was a 'first' language for any speaker, and that what appears as
such a first language was itself and is itself always a translation, always
grounded in an intrinsic translatability that would call into question its
status as originary or authentic. The realisation that English is grounded in
the variety of Englishes offers us a key to the alterity that lies within any
identity that is characterised not by some chthonic nativity, not by any
dangerous claims of blood or soil.

When Gayatri Spivak laments the 'politics of hostility' that she sees at
the source of contemporary Comparative Literary Study, she is touching on
the implicit desire for a certain commensurability among cultures. That is,
though she wants to advocate substantial differences in our theoretical
stance and procedures, she nonetheless retains the demand for a grounded
and foundational comparativism. Like many, she traces a certain history of
Comparative Literature to the flight of the intellectuals from Nazi Europe:
'Comparative Literature was a result of European intellectuals fleeing
"totalitarian" regimes', she writes; and, in the light of this, which she sees
as contributing to the inevitability of politics in the discipline, she
continues 'I am proposing an attempt to depoliticize in order to move away
from a politics of hostility, fear, and half solutions'.[15] Her moves, effectively,
attempt to replace a politics of hostility with one of friendship, *à la* Derrida.
That too will have difficulties, of course. This friendship is structurally
shaped by inequality, and requires a demand for justice and grace.

The position outlined by Spivak is not that far removed from a sparkling
analysis once made by Edward Said of the work of Auerbach's *Mimesis*.
Having noted that *Mimesis* looks the way it does partly as a result of the
library in which Auerbach found himself working in Istanbul while in
flight from the Nazis, Said is able to attend to what is essentially a rather
fantastic set of speculations in the work. One example will stand for many.
Looking at Woolf, what Auerbach finds to say is that in Woolf's apparent
interest in the random, we 'cannot but see to what an extent – below the
surface conflicts – the differences between men's ways of life and forms of
thought have already lessened'.[16] The burden of the thought (and the
language of the rest of the passage is clearly marked by this, too) is that,
even in a regime such as Nazism, dependent upon extreme discriminations
among people, there is a fundamental and underlying unity that can be
revealed in literature. It is as if Auerbach wants to use literature as a way of
apotropaically warding off the threat of Nazism and even difference as such.
Yet, however much literature may offer such solace, the reality differs. The
key aspect important for the present argument is that Comparative

Literature has itself been driven by this demand for an essential 'lessening' of the differences among people's ways of thinking and of living. It may be admirable, but it remains fantastical.

To put this into the language of Franco Moretti, it is as if we have been seeing Comparative Literature as essentially governed by the metaphor of the tree; and, as Moretti shows us, such a situation leads inexorably to a prioritisation of the question of the nation: 'Trees and branches are what nation-states cling to'. While this metaphor proposes an underlying unity (one tree, many branches), by contrast, as he points out, waves – as a governing metaphor – 'observes uniformity engulfing an initial diversity'. Waves, therefore, 'are what markets do'.[17]

It follows from my foregoing observations that, in fact, trees and waves, in Moretti's terms, do indeed have something in common above and beyond being metaphors that work as metaphors, despite his more modestly stated claims. Both attempt to regulate the relations between uniformity and diversity. Both accept the principle that such a regulation is available.[18]

What, however, if the task of Comparative Literature is the task of producing difference as such? What if we entertain the possibility of real diversity, as it were? What if there is a diversity that cannot be regulated under the sign of any uniform?

3

This difference – or even let us call it divisiveness – is and might properly be the end and aim of Comparative Literature. Starting from an analysis carried out in the mode of comparison, with a tacit assumption of commensurability among or between the elements being compared, it might be more appropriate and productive to stress the other aspect of comparison: contrast. There is, however, another way of looking at this and another way of formalising it. In this final section, I want to think of what it would mean to describe Comparative Literature as being 'without and beyond compare': that is, to characterise it in a language appropriate neither to conflict nor to the blandishments of that fallacious and potentially fantasy-governed demand of 'commensurability' of which I write above. The language in question here would be a development of the language of friendship: we might call it rather the language of love.

The model I have in mind derives from a combination of Lyotard and Badiou. It is from Lyotard that I am taking this particular notion of a differend that will be at the root of Comparative Literature; and that, in turn, derives from his earlier pronouncements, in his 'Answering the

Question: What is Postmodernism' programme-essay. There, he wrote against the kind of unification and totalisation of thought that I myself have described as being, silently, at the core of much Comparative Literature. He wrote:

> We have paid a high enough price for the nostalgia of the whole and the one, for the reconciliation of the concept and the sensible, of the transparent and the communicable experience. Under the general demand for slackening and for appeasement, we can hear the mutterings of the desire for a return of terror, for the realization of the fantasy to seize reality. The answer is: Let us wage a war on totality; let us be witnesses to the unpresentable; let us activate the differences and save the honour of the name.[19]

The multiplication of difference in the name of a counter-terror – or, more positively, in the name of love – is what I am after here.

Badiou's thinking on the issue of love closely resembles that of Lyotard on the differend. Badiou describes the situation of love as one of relatedness between positions. There are two positions, he argues; and, for the sake of argument, we might characterise them as 'man' and 'woman' (with no determinate biological or any other overtones). These two positions are absolutely disjunctive with regard to each other; the characterisation as man/woman simply serves to illustrate the disjunctiveness in question. This is like Lyotard's two argumentative positions in a differend. Further, the disjunction between the two positions cannot be the object of an experience or of any direct knowledge; for such knowledge or experience would imply the existence of a third position that can assume or 'contain' the two disjunctive positions (the Lyotardian bar of a higher authority, as it were, to which both positions can subject themselves willingly). This is impossible for Badiou, because, axiomatically, there is no such third position.

Now, this is rather like the position I have described for Comparative Literature: there are (let us say) two literatures, in two languages; they are disjunctive with regard to each other (this is the question of the difficulty of translation: no matter how hard we try, 'amore' is not 'amour', neither of these is 'Liebe'; and they cannot all be 'contained' in the Anglophone 'love'). There is no third position (no single English) that will totalise and adequately contain the two divergent positions.

For Badiou, it follows that we cannot 'know' that there are two such positions in the first place; for any such knowledge depends on the existence of a third position that transcends the two – and there is none. Thus, a *knowledge* of love gives way to an *experience* of sorts; and that experience is, for Badiou, 'a singular event. This event is what initiates the amorous procedures; and we can call it an encounter'.[20]

The result of this now is that we can no longer even say that there are two positions, for to say that would imply, in arithmetical terms, a third position from which we could count back to two; and there is no third position. Thus, we now have a state of affairs in which there is a 'position-one' and a 'position-one', and these can never add up to a two or a couple. There is, as it were, a position and another position; a literature and a literature – the two can never be reconciled. This, however, is extremely positive news, for it means, in brief, that two separate literatures can now, for the first time, encounter each other without one 'containing' the other. By analogy, my 'identity', asserted in a criticism based in identity-politics, can now – and for the first time – accept that there are other identities that are simply not there to be assimilated by 'mine'. Moreover, both resist containment under the general sign of a totalising 'English'.

By analogy, my own 'identity' asserted in a criticism that is based in identity-politics, can – and for the first time – accept that there are other identities to be asserted in relation to any given text, that these identities are fundamentally other than mine, that they are not there to be assimilated by mine or located in opposition to mine – finally, that they are perhaps not even there to be understood by mine, much less judged from my own position. In short, what happens then is that there is a realisation that 'my' identity is, of necessity, always in the public domain; but the public domain is not itself fixed and stable. In the very mutability of the public domain, I am made to realise that more important than my 'being' is my 'becoming'; and that I can find out what I may want to become precisely by the encounter with alterity that actually constitutes the very possibility of my being and of my being sociable in the first place.

On one hand, we are in a predicament here; but, following Badiou, we might say that love is that mood that treats precisely of this kind of predicament. We are not in crisis; rather, we are – or can be – in love.

To read Comparative Literature in this way is to open ourselves to the possibility of reading for the first time; such reading does not place an understanding at the centre of our work, but replaces that with the experience of an 'encounter'. This event of an encounter, like love, is what is without and beyond compare.

PART III

Foreign Friends

CHAPTER 6

Newman: The University and Universalism

'Non judicavi me scire aliquid inter vos,
nisi Jesum Christum, et hunc crucifixum.
(Newman, citing St Paul)[1]

I Irish Souls

On the 12th of November 1851, John Henry Newman, a Doctor of Divinity but not yet a Cardinal, was formally appointed as Rector of the Catholic University of Ireland, the institution that would open formally almost exactly three years later, on 3 November 1854. In Dublin, almost immediately, he began what he called his 'campaign in Ireland' with a series of 'Discourses' – lectures 'On the Scope and Nature of University Education' – that would eventually become the first part of the completed text of *The Idea of the University*. Published initially in fortnightly instalments during 1852, more or less exactly contemporaneously with their oral delivery, the Discourses caused some small stir in their immediate audience and more widely abroad. Central to these texts is Newman's view that, in a fundamental sense, the phrase 'Catholic University' is a tautology. What is often taken in Newman's writings post-1851 simply as the ecumenism that one might expect from a convert is, in fact, more precisely his *militant* alignment of Catholicism with a totalising Universalism.[2]

For Newman, 'globalisation' – had he ever had the opportunity to comment on the term – would have described the process by which the world would come to accept and to practise Catholicism; and, importantly for our purposes, the University as an institution would play a part in this process. In some respects, Catholicism is to Newman what the neo-liberal market-economy is to the contemporary globalist: something that ostensibly diminishes the importance of local laws and allegiances in the interest of some immanent and transcendent condition. However, the strict opposition that is implied in this – between Catholic and Protestant, or between 'universalising-global' and 'localist' (with all that this latter implies: historically located, geographically located, geo-politically located, individual-ising and so on) – is not in fact quite so clear-cut as the rhetoric of the opposition might imply. Newman, on occasions, resembles a pragmatist thinker such as Rorty, who once explained his 'postmodern bourgeois liberal' stance by arguing that the socio-political arrangements of the 'western democracies' were 'right' in the sense that those arrangements allowed us to live in the way that we were choosing to live: they were right because, in effect, they were suitable and adequate to our concerns. Rorty then argued for a kind of 'frank ethnocentrism', in which 'We await . . . the time when the Cashinahua, the Chinese and (if it should prove that there are any) the Martians will take part in the same social democratic commu-nity'.[3] In some ways, Newman too expects that, insofar as humans will fulfil themselves, then they will emerge as Catholics on a global stage.[4]

A more direct comparison of Newman's thinking might even be made with that of George Soros, who is unapologetically a 'globalist', but who sees that there are at least two orders of globalisation always in question: the economic and the political.[5] Soros is at pains to distinguish between what he calls the *economic* triumph of global capitalism on one hand, and the failures of global *political* emancipation on the other. (To phrase this in our terms, we might even go so far as to say that the formalities of the global academy have triumphed over the actual content of setting people free through some pedagogical institutional process.)

In what for many outside of the business-audience that he is addressing would be an obvious truism, Soros writes that 'Capitalism and democracy do not necessarily go hand in hand'.[6] Indeed, he points out that one of the major threats to freedom and democracy in our time is precisely the over-intimate relation between business and government, the relation that (in other times and places) has been a major characteristic of fascism. The key to the position adopted by Soros is one that would not be entirely anathema to Newman, in fact. Newman was also well aware of these two distinct realms, noting that the business realm in his time is effectively dominated by Protestants and Protestantism; but in his case, the question of govern-ment is primarily an issue concerning the 'government of the self' and, as such, is for him primarily a theological and not 'merely' a political one, though no less 'universal' for that.

Soros states unequivocally that 'business is conducted for private gain', and so it follows that 'If we care about universal principles such as freedom, democracy, and the rule of law, we cannot leave them to the care of market forces; we must establish some other institutions to safeguard them'.[7] While Rorty effectively follows a kind of logic of the 'market forces' of competing discourses, subscribing to those that 'work' or that triumph over the others (the question always being 'work for whom?' and the answer seemingly being 'for Americans'), Newman would have taken a position closer to that of Soros, in which there exists the world of business on the one hand (economics), and, on the other, a world that underpins and shadows that business realm but that is regulated differently from it, a world of 'universal principles' (politics; or, for Newman, a world governed by theology). In short, while the world of business in Newman's day is a world controlled and regulated by educated Protestants, for educated Protestants, to the detriment of Catholics who are systematically denied the opportunities of education, Newman also sees that that world is properly underpinned by a more universalising set of forces, the force of Catholicism, that currently lies latent.

The purpose of the University will be, among other things, to set these conditions right so that the latent Catholic realm gradually is revealed and gradually comes to be seen as a universal – global – condition for our social, political, cultural and, above all for Newman, *spiritual* well-being, survival, 'resurrection'. Soros criticises what he calls 'market fundamentalists', those who ask that the logic of the so-called 'free' market determines all social and political being; Newman, far from being such a market fundamentalist, sits close to the opposite end of Soros's spectrum, as a kind of political funda-mentalist, holding the view that a politics of emancipation (determined essentially in terms of theological salvation) underpins all else, including the business markets that are currently controlled by Protestants. (It is worth noting, in passing, that many of these religious-fundamentalist argu-ments have now been displaced onto secondary-level education, where so-called 'faith-schools' are increasingly being legitimised and favoured by many political parties in search of what we should call 'faith-votes'.)

Yet Newman is not what Eagleton once identified as 'prematurely utopian' regarding this. In his Field Day pamphlet, *Nationalism: Irony and Commitment*, Eagleton advanced a simple deconstruction of the opposition of Catholic to Protestant:

> . . . the claim of the Roman Catholic church to universality is in any case only necessary once that status has been challenged by Protestantism, and so is no sooner raised than refuted, denying itself in the very act of assertion . . . Catholicism itself already contains a certain Protestantism – *ecclesia semper reformanda* – without which constant deviating from itself it would not be truly itself; and Protestantism cannot exist as such without its historical antagonist. All that remains now is to explain this on the Falls and Shankill roads . . . [8]

Such a simplistic view is what Eagleton describes as typical of a premature utopianism that 'grabs instantly for a future, projecting itself by an act of will or imagination beyond the compromised political structures of the present'.[9] Newman does not simply assume that by arguing *theoretically* for this universal or global validity of Catholicism that it will inevitably come about, much less that it somehow has come about just by proving its *logical* inevitability. Rather, Newman sees the real and material conditions of Catholics in the two islands that most concern him in his Discourses;[10] he is well aware that there is a job of work to be done if the equation of Catholicism with Universalism is to be established as a self-evident truth; and the site for this work is precisely the institution of the University.

Newman was at pains to establish the singularity, or, better, specificity of the Catholic as well. In lines that show he was alert to political history he wrote that 'Insulted, robbed, oppressed, and thrust aside, Catholics in these islands have not been in a condition for centuries to attempt the sort of education, which is necessary for the man of the world, the statesman, the great proprietor, or the opulent gentleman'.[11] While Protestants have enjoyed the benefits of such education, Catholics have not; and, for Newman, the convert of some six years' standing, the time has come to change this iniquitous and unjust state of affairs. So much, so uncontroversial, we might think: Catholics have been deprived; it is time to redistribute power more equitably. Yet Newman's position is profoundly controversial, in fact.

It is controversial not just because the nineteenth century – perhaps especially so in Ireland – is not yet ready to acquiesce comfortably in notions of egalitarian democracy that are ostensibly axiomatic to the formation of the most contemporary 'developed' societies. More than this, it is controversial because it explicitly attacks the 'Protestant' Universities (Berlin, and, closer to home, those in England; but most particularly Oxford, Newman's own former institution) on the grounds that, fundamentally, they are not really 'universities' at all; rather, they are like self-sustaining factories for the production of 'gentlemen' who will always be in social and political power. There is nothing wrong with being a gentleman, argues Newman, except that if that is the limit of one's aspirations then one is failing in a duty to educate; for education implies the fulfilment or achievement of the self – and such an achievement of the self is properly measured, for Newman, not before the market (the bourgeois and mercantile realm dominated by the rule of the gentleman) but before God. Thus, when the Church founds a university in Ireland, as it now intends to do, the project is not concerned with wisdom for its own sake, but rather concerns itself with the spiritual welfare of the student. The proper task of the university, in this view, is the salvation – indeed the *resurrection*

– of souls; and as such it has a properly metaphysical dimension. Being a 'gentleman', with all the material benefits that this implies, is but incidental to this larger project, focused on the soul.

This gesture – in which Newman (like Marx, in fact) re-asserts the rights of the oppressed or of society's victims as being the most basic and fundamentally shared rights of all (in short: as universal rights) – is one that is replayed in more recent populist Irish culture, by Roddy Doyle in *The Commitments*, the novel that was turned into an internationally successful film by the English director Alan Parker.[12] *The Commitments* asserts the rights of the impoverished youth of Dublin to 'soul'. Trying to give his newly-formed band a model of the kind of music that they should be playing, Jimmy Rabbitte, the entrepreneurial manager, shows them a video of James Brown. As Brown falls to his knees, overwhelmed by soul, Deco, the abrasive singer in the band says 'I'm not doin' that. I'll knee-cap meself'; he gets support from the rest of the band, who comment hesitantly (and intrinsically racist in this) on the fact that Brown is, well, brownish, even black, and that they are 'a bit white' for that kind of thing.

The implication is that soul is the property of the American black, to which Jimmy replies: 'Don't you lads see? That's exactly it. The Irish are the blacks of Europe; the Dubliners are the blacks of Ireland; the Northside Dubliners are the blacks of Dublin. So say it once and say it loud, "I'm black and I'm proud"'. Those that are systematically excluded thus become included in a comic (and essentially irrational) act of identification with victimhood, a gesture that effectively universalises humanity as victims, but essentially as helpless victims, for if we are all victims then where are the victors against whom we might struggle? The thinking here is either desperate, or paranoid, or both. A much more serious parallel gesture would be that which I have already discussed in relation to Auerbach's extraordinarily poignant analysis of Woolf. In that analysis, Auerbach claimed that the style of the writing showed that 'below the surface conflicts [of the contemporary world] . . . the differences between men's ways of life and forms of thought have already lessened'.[13] This, in the face of Nazism.

This more recent gesture in *The Commitments*, though, is more complex. At one level, it is simply a supposed exemplification of the cliché that music – especially a music that derives from the soul – is a universal and quasi-Levinasian language of suffering ('they had nothing; but they were willing to sacrifice it all', as the publicity material for the film stated). At the same time, more complexly, the Irish is identified here not with the Asian (as in the metaphor of the Celtic tiger) but with the American black such that the Irish person can become, effectively, a black person.[14]

Following Nicholas Canny, Seamus Deane critiques the early modern

English view of Ireland in which the Irish were going to be 'compelled to be free' by the good governance (after a victorious war) by the English: 'To become free and prosperous the Irish were evidently going to have to become English'.[15] If that is the early modern (and even modern) view, the more recent view (one that we have already seen exemplified in Rorty) is that to become free and prosperous the Irish will evidently have to become in some fundamental and universalised way 'American'; the impoverished, deprived – and, centrally for our purposes, 'uneducated' or 'uncultured' – youth of Ireland will evidently have to take the position of the American black (this latter being *not* a position endorsed by Rortean philosophy, a philosophy that is based essentially on the optimism associated with the expectation of success or achievement, and not shaped by the more pessimistic facts of suffering).[16]

Here, then, is a version of globalisation in which difference, while certainly being maintained, is also paradoxically being erased at the same moment: difference is maintained (the Irish are different from the Americans) as a marketing ploy or commercial and economic gesture (in the thinking of both the fictional Jimmy Rabbitte and the real Alan Parker); yet difference is simultaneously erased in a political gesture claiming equality of worth (the Irish, like James Brown, have soul, identified in the film with 'authentic being'). It is interesting to note here that the 'Dublin Soul' that is validated in this film is constantly being contrasted with Elvis Presley. Rabbitte Snr is a great admirer of Elvis (his picture hanging above that of the Pope in the Rabbitte household); but the thing about Elvis is that he whitens the black music that he takes over, making it more acceptable to the white American and European audience. The white has access directly to black suffering or to the blues, even if in a watered-down form: but the white can now claim to understand black suffering, even to 'feel' it, and therefore also can claim the rights to deal with it on behalf of the sufferer, with whom the white can now patronisingly identify. The key element in all this is that authenticity, thus, is aligned with – even identified by and grounded in – victimhood or suffering, but a suffering that is authentic precisely to the extent that it is *fundamental* and thus potentially universal or global.

We should note that there is an important distinction to be made between globalisation, represented in the figure of James Brown as authentic universal suffering on the one hand, and, on the other, 'Americanisation', represented in the figure of Elvis. As Bill Readings indicates, Americanisation is virtually a synonym for globalisation, but a synonym that draws attention to the fact that 'globalization is not a neutral process in which Washington and Dakar participate equally'.[17] In a particular sense, globalisation is not happening at all as yet; but what is happening is this Americanisation, as the triumph of those already in power. Soros also takes the view that globalisation is being obstructed (and for him this is a bad thing), and it is being obstructed by market-fundamentalism. In my terms here, 'America' is just another name for such market fundamentalism, in which the world is seen simply as a potential market for American interests, a market in which every High Street eventually has its McDonald's, next door to its Starbucks, where American popular music, punctuated only by the ringing of mobile phones playing tunes from populist Hollywood movies, is the aural backdrop.

In what follows in the rest of the present chapter, my view of the question of globalisation will no doubt be regarded as 'theoretical', on the grounds that (for the most part) I do not directly address questions concerning economics or global capital. As I am not a specialist in these matters, let me give my position here insofar as I am able to describe it in directly economic terms.[18] Globalisation is, in some senses, not a new phenomenon. The world of the European Renaissance, say, saw similar movements of goods and services in untrammelled fashion; in fact, globalisation was then not even an issue. In an age of fledgling mercantile empire-building, it is not at all controversial for writers to present the world as an entity that can be somehow experienced all at once, here, now. This is what lies behind that gloriously ambivalent moment in Milton when Adam and Eve, freed from Paradise, step out into their ambiguous freedom where 'The World was all before them'; it also lies behind that so typical metaphor adopted by another thinker whose writing (perhaps like that of Newman) is shaped by apostasy – Donne – when he can celebrate the unification of the world in the shape of a female body under his own guiding and shaping hands, where 'both th'Indias of spice and mine' are to be found at once, the world contracting into the here, now of a woman's body, a body whose 'availability' is exactly the metaphor for mercantile – bourgeois – globalised power.[19]

Globalisation becomes an issue when politics and economics diverge; that is to say, it is an issue if and only if the world is organised around the existence of sovereign nation-states that are seen to determine their own political and economic conditions of local living, culture or identity. Thus, globalisation requires the existence of national *political* boundaries precisely in order to transgress them *economically*: a global economy can be identified only because it operates at a level beyond that of the more usual national economies that have shaped a modern world organised around the nation state. In terms of my fundamental argument regarding the University, something important is happening here. It will be recalled that I have shown how the modern University gains its functions and principles from the alignment of number, law and medicine: economics, the social, and the bodily or sexual. In globalisation, what we are seeing is the *divergence* of the economic and the socio-political; and this, in turn, may help explain the present predicament concerning the function of the University in a 'west' that identified its nation-states in relation to 'Universities of culture'.

It will be seen, therefore, that Ireland is in a rather odd position here (and one that may well be paradigmatic). In brief, it is widely accepted that Ireland has been a net beneficiary in economic terms of the globalising tendencies that have brought much inward investment. However, the crux of the matter for Ireland is that there are contradictory forces at play here. Globalisation in these terms assumes the transgression of or the ignoring of national boundaries. The free traffic in goods and services and, most especially in capital itself, has established a state of affairs in which the fiscal powers of the State are weakened: if the State taxes highly, business will move its capital elsewhere, to a State that taxes less highly. That movement across borders presupposes the already stable existence of such borders around established nations. However, Ireland's self-identity, precisely during this period of globalisation, has been given to it precisely in terms of the struggle to establish such national borders in the first place: it is an 'incomplete' nation so long as the fraught question of the North remains unresolved.[20]

Ireland's 'identity' thus is fractured around this issue, in that there is a contradiction between its re-emergence as a nation-state (its historical identity since the start of the twentieth century, say) and its new-found economic powers as an economy attracting significant numbers of foreign nationals (if such a term as 'foreign' is even permissible in a genuinely global economy), establishing its identity not in relation to a local history, but precisely in relation not even to a European but rather to an *Asian* identity or affiliation, as a quasi-mythic 'Celtic tiger' (pulling Ireland's identity eastwards, and thus contradicting the earlier typically westering movement of a Yeatsian 'revival' of the nation-state).

I will claim here merely that the position I take is philosophical, and that it addresses primarily what Bourdieu long ago identified as 'cultural capital' much more than it will address economic capital. This is important for a consideration of the question insofar as it impinges on a certain 'Ireland', not just because the Irish economy is one that has never 'simply' industrialised, moving instead from what might be identified as a 'premodern' agricultural economy to a so-called 'postmodern' knowledge- or technology- or virtual-economy, but also because the question of the identity of 'Ireland' is still, of course, a matter of disputed boundaries. Here, the nation-state that global capital would ostensibly swallow up has not yet fully established itself as a single entity, a simple nation.

2 Modern Celtic Memories

Yet globalisation is, most certainly, a question of 'where we are' or 'where we're from'. It might better be regarded as one available means of regulating the potential conflict between a local habitation (the 'where') and an identity (the 'we'); or of the proper boundaries of a place and its proper inhabitants. Depending on how we might construe these things – as Ireland, as the UK, as Britain, as the North or as Northern Ireland, as a global village and so on – we give a local habitation and a *name* to the self. As in Newman, this self must be amenable to an identifiable self-description.

This was the starting-point of that lengthy meditation so formative of modernity that is Proust's *A la recherche du temps perdu*. The Narrator, pondering that mysterious time between sleep and waking, offers a praise of *habit*; but does so in a way that relates *habit* to *habitation* or to the feeling that we have of being-at-home in the place where we are:

> L'habitude! aménageuse habile mais bien lente et qui commence par laisser souffrir notre esprit pendant des semaines dans une installation provisoire; mais que malgré tout il est bien heureux de trouver, car sans l'habitude et réduit a ses seuls moyens il serait impuissant à nous rendre un logis habitable.[21]

This text also relates this question of the 'habit of inhabiting' – the habitual as that which makes a place habitable – to the question of the past itself; and, in what is the first proper invocation of the workings of memory in the novel as a whole, it relates memory to a 'celtic' belief:

> Je trouve très raisonnable la croyance celtique que les âmes de ceux que nous avons perdus sont captives dans quelque être inférieur, dans une bête, un végétal, une chose inanimée, perdues en effet pour nous jusqu'au jour, qui pour beaucoup ne vient jamais, ou nous nous trouvons passer près de l'arbre, entrer en possession de l'objet, qui est leur prison. Alors elles tresaillent, nous appellent, et sitôt que nous les avons reconnues, l'enchantement est brisé. Delivrées par nous, elles ont vaincu la mort et reviennent vivre avec nous.[22]

Habit, in allowing us to forget, allows us also to inhabit a particular place; memory is precisely the emancipation from such located identity – but the price of such memory is the death and resurrection of the self, in an identity that is constituted as a constant changing or continual self-differing, self-transformation. This, in fact, is almost exactly like Newman's approach to a Catholic University, whose teaching will bring the dead protestants – those 'êtres inférieurs' – back to life, back among 'us', the 'catholic' we present or the we who are 'here, now' and whose here/now is thus effectively potentially of global reach: 'Trieste–Zurich–Paris', say. This memorialisation is also a part of our conception of the University as an institution: a repository or archive of what we call knowledge, but what is increasingly simply the active forgetting of knowledge and its replacement with information.

When Joyce famously signs *Ulysses* off with that by-line – 'Trieste–Zurich–Paris' – he omits – or perhaps forgets temporarily or conveniently – its starting-point, which, according to the correspondence, was either his schooldays in Ireland where he studied the Trojan wars, or Rome where he came up with the title (if little else) in September 1906. What interested Joyce at this time –1906 – was the position of the 'outsider' in Europe, most especially in the figure that Lyotard would later call 'the jews'. For Joyce, of course, the Jews were specific individuals, such as Italo Svevo (to whom Joyce taught English); but, as *Ulysses* itself makes clear, Joyce would have been sympathetic to the more generalised position of Lyotard, for whom 'the jews' is a term that comes to have a much wider range of reference.[23]

For Lyotard, 'the jews' is a name given to a structure of a necessary amnesia. There are events to which no memorial words or memory can ever be adequate; and which yet demand to be recalled and recounted. The Holocaust is the most extreme form of this; but it is not the only such event, even if it is singular and specific. Here, I want to discuss the relation of such amnesia – in which victims can be forgotten, passed over in a silence that is *at once entirely necessary and entirely unacceptable* – in a globalising institution such as Newman's University. Newman is clear that his University is a teaching institution; he explicitly separates teaching from research and argues that research is the activity proper to 'academies' but not to the University. The University is 'a place of *teaching* universal *knowledge*', concerned thus with 'the diffusion and extension of knowledge, rather than the advancement'.[24] In this respect, the University becomes rather like the archive of the best that has been thought and said: its orientation is towards the past, towards that which has already been established as knowledge. Teaching, accordingly, is akin to that Platonic view of all knowledge as outlined in *Meno*: the recovery of a memory.

As Augustine (another great convert, whose philosophy of conversion is key to an understanding of Newman and of Lyotard) knew, however, memory is an eminently deconstructible concept. He asks himself if it is possible to remember forgetting:

> I can mention forgetfulness and recognize what the word means, but how can I recognize the thing itself unless I remember it? I am not speaking of the sound of the word but of the thing which it signifies. If I had forgotten the thing itself, I should be utterly unable to recognize what the sound implied. When I remember memory, my memory is present to itself by its own power; but when I remember forgetfulness, two things are present, memory, by which I remember it, and forgetfulness, which is what I remember. Yet what is forgetfulness but absence of memory? When it is present, I cannot remember it . . . It follows that the very thing which by its presence causes us to forget must be present if we are to remember it.[25]

In a peculiar sense, forgetting itself requires memory; and the structure of memory is characterised precisely by this impossibility of forgetting. Yet it is, of course, precisely this fact that we must forget if we are to be able to think at all, for as Borges once wrote, in his great story 'Funes the Memorius', 'To think is to forget differences, generalize, make abstractions'.[26]

Such generalisation is, in linguistic terms, analogous to globalisation in economies. The problem is that in a peculiar sense, we are all Funes the Memorius. It will be recalled that Funes has a fall from his horse that paralyses him, but that leaves him cursed or blessed with an archival memory, whose effect is somewhat akin to certain types of schizophrenia. His perceptions are extraordinarily intense, for he is unable to ignore or forget the slightest detail. The consequence is that everything is, in a peculiar sense, always intensely present. He is, as it were, a convert to memory itself: a library. Yet the memory is disabling, for although it allows him the facility for learning Latin, say, more or less overnight, it deprives him of the capacity for thought or for imagining. He is, to put this into the terms we have taken from Newman as it were, a 'Protestant' in his education. He has the means of knowledge (like business acumen, acquisitive, individualistic and ever expanding), but not the substance of knowledge (like universalising principles, catholic in their universalism).

The parentage of Funes is slightly uncertain; but it is suggested that his father was an Englishman, though an Englishman with what looks like an Irish name: 'O'Connor'. In Borges, there is an evident interest in Ireland and its memorial history. We see it, for instance, in the 'Theme of the Traitor and Hero', a meditation on 'the impassioned memory of Ireland'.[27] The 'story' is not a story at all, but rather the basic structure of a plot. 'The action takes place in an oppressed and tenacious country: Poland, Ireland, the

Venetian Republic, some South American or Balkan state . . . . Or rather it has taken place. . . . Let us say (for narrative convenience) Ireland; let us say in 1824'.[28] This story, of potentially 'global' reach therefore, is nonetheless situated (for narrative convenience) in Ireland. The tenor of the text is that the facts of history, though remembered with passion, belief and commitment, are themselves not really 'facts' at all, but rather the enactment of literary plots. It is precisely when we recall a national history (such as that of Ireland) that we are most in thrall to stories, to literature; for everything that seems to be spontaneous, autonomously lived, in the narrative that is told (the narrative of an act of betrayal conflated with that of heroism) is, in fact, scripted in advance. Memory, here, is precisely an act of forgetting: the facts are what are forgotten, the story is what is remembered; and it is the story that gives the present its identity.[29]

Borges has another important Irish figure in his stories, particularly in 'The Shape of the Sword', another story of betrayal in Ireland, this time in 1922–23. This is the story of 'the Englishman from La Colorada', an Englishman who is not English but Irish. He tells the tale of how he got his facial scar to one 'Borges', a stranger, in a Spanish that is rudimentary, cluttered with Brazilian and Portuguese phrases, and interrupted at one point by French: a language that is not sited in any one place, but is tending towards the global, therefore. It is a tale of betrayal. The 'Englishman' tells 'Borges' of his history as a republican in the fight for Irish independence. His group is joined by one John Vincent Moon, who seems to be something of a Marxist; but he is a Marxist theorist, seemingly afraid of action and of fighting.[30] One evening, the Irishman sees an example of Moon's cowardice, when Moon is confronted by a British soldier. At this point, we are told, 'This frightened man mortified me, as if I were the coward, not Vincent Moon'. At this point, the Irishman offers Borges a gloss on the tale:

> Whatever one man does, it is as if all men did it. For that reason it is not unfair that one disobedience in a garden should contaminate all humanity; for that reason it is not unjust that the crucifixion of a single Jew should be sufficient to save it. Perhaps Schopenhauer was right: I am all other men, any man is all men, Shakespeare is in some manner the miserable John Vincent Moon.[31]

The reference to Schopenhauer is, in some ways, a red herring here (though one that is relevant to our argument in that Schopenhauer's task, set against that of Hegel, was to unify or globalise western philosophy with eastern). Actually, the intertext is Biblical; and is to be found in Paul's first letter to the Corinthians.

For since by man came death, by man came also the resurrection of the dead. For as in Adam all die, even so in Christ shall all be made alive.[32]

This chapter in Paul is all about death and resurrection; importantly, Paul prefaces what he has to say here by pointing out that 'ye are saved, if ye keep in memory what I preached unto you'.[33]

Paul, like Newman, like Augustine, was a convert. Yet the Biblical figure to whom Newman appeals is not Paul, but rather Peter. Against all those who will detract from his proposals for the University as somehow being impractical, he says he offers the one word reply: 'Peter'. In that name, however, is contained an entire narrative; and it is the narrative of a movement of globalisation, explicitly.

What do I know of the state of things in Ireland that I should presume to put ideas of mine, which could not be right except by accident, by the side of theirs, who speak in the country of their birth and their home? . . . Why then should I be so rash and perverse as to involve myself in trouble not properly mine? Why go out of my own place?[34]

In this, Newman is profoundly aware of his position as an outsider; yet this is so in what are for him merely technical or geo-political terms, the terms that are those of the business-world and so not the terms relating to the globalising project of the Catholic University.

His response to the predictable criticisms is that 'After all, Peter has spoken'. This Peter is not a single historical individual, but it is whoever sits in the 'Chair of the Apostles': that is, the Pope. The truth of Peter is one that lives through the ages, claims Newman; he also claims it as an empirical truth that 'All who take part with Peter are on the winning side'.[35] The passage that follows this is remarkable as a kind of history of the globalising – and militant – tendency of the Catholic Church, which figures here in a synecdoche that takes the name of Peter for the Church in its entirety. Peter has defeated, among others, 'the 'savage hordes' who 'came down from the north', 'Lawless kings . . . sagacious as the Roman, passionate as the Hun'. Importantly,

The gates of the earth were opened to the east and west, and men poured out to take possession; and he and his went with them, swept along by zeal and charity as far as they by enterprise, covetousness, or ambition.[36]

And, against that business world, Peter still prevailed. Catholicism, unlike other religions that offer mere spectacle and myth, argues Newman, 'addresses itself directly to the heart and conscience of the individual'.[37]

Moreover, the education associated with Peter in this way has already overcome 'the schools of Antioch and Alexandria, Athens and Edessa, Saracenic Seville, and Protestant Berlin'.[38] Newman claims that 'it was the See of Peter' that brought faith to 'Celt and Saxon alike', civilising them from their savagery; that it was from Rome that Patrick was sent to Ireland and Augustine to England. Eventually, from this, when Charlemagne wanted to establish proper scholarship and knowledge in France, it was to England that he 'sent for masters', with Alcuin 'the scholar both of the Saxon and the Celt . . . [as] the chief of those who went forth to supply the need of the Great Emperor';[39] and it was from this that the University of Paris was founded.

Newman then makes his great claim:

> The past never returns; the course of things, old in its texture, is ever new in its colouring and fashion. Ireland and England are not what they once were, but Rome is where it was; Peter is the same; his zeal, his charity, his mission, his gifts, are the same. He, of old time, made us one by making us joint teachers of the nations; and now, surely, he is giving us a like mission, and we shall become one again, while we zealously and lovingly fulfil it.[40]

Here, then, is the mission statement of the University: to bear witness to the authority of 'Peter'; and to see to it that this is a global mission and a mission that stands for all time, unchanging.

The real Peter, however, was challenged in AD 50 (or 50 CE) by the more militant Paul. Peter saw his task at this time as one that allowed some of the old ways to continue, such that the new 'truth of Christ' would conserve and continue, in highly modified forms, the old ways; and this way lies sectarianism, of course.[41] Peter's case in the argument in Jerusalem in that year was that the new religion of Christianity would effectively be grafted on to the already existing ways of one dominant older religion; Paul, the more radical in this, saw Christianity as an entirely new era. Peter's way explains – and to some extent legitimises – not only sectarianism but religious and fundamentalist imperialism; Paul's rather stresses the ways of grace.

Paul, in this way, becomes the real model for Newman, for Paul sees the 'Christ-event' as much more radical, exploding all ideas of the privilege of Judaism and the jewish community. This, in fact, is closer to Newman's sense that the Catholic church speaks to the heart directly and individually. Paul, like Joyce, is neither Jew nor Greek, but both. This makes him, for a thinker such as Badiou, not a prophet or philosopher, but an apostle; and, more importantly for present purposes, it brings him into a specific relation with memory, memory that – we will remember – is the foundation of Newman's University.

Badiou writes that an apostle is neither a witness to the facts as they happened nor is she or he a 'memory' or remembrancer. There are at least two important things to bear in mind when discussing memory. First, in our own time, acts of memoration have become a kind of substitute for politics; as if it is enough simply to try to remember (for example) the victims of the Holocaust or, in Lyotard's terms, 'the jews', or, in the terms proper to this present book, the victims on whom globalisation is structured (such as 'The Commitments', say). Secondly, memory is 'neutral' in that, of itself, it decides no questions and engages no actions. Badiou is unhappy with this:

> . . . 'memory' decides no questions. There is always a moment when what is important is to declare, in one's own name, that what has happened has happened, and to do so because what one envisages of the *present* possibilities demands it.[42]

This, argues Badiou, is the position of Paul. There is, for him, a present or actual demand that he declare the resurrection; the debate over it is not a matter for either witnesses or for historians. To which must also be added that, for Paul, the resurrection is not of the same order of historical fact as most happenings, being rather a 'pure event', the 'opening of an epoch'. In other words, the resurrection is an event that is actually 'the changing of the relations between the possible and the impossible'.[43]

The consequence of this, in Badiou's reading of Paul, is extremely significant. The resurrection of Christ is of no intrinsic interest in and of itself, as would be the case for what we might consider as 'normal' historical occurrences. Rather, its proper significance is that it marks the possibility of overcoming death itself. From this it would follow that we must always link *the* resurrection to *our* resurrection: that is to say, we must go 'from singularity to universality'.[44] Thus, as Badiou writes,

> Contrairement au fait, l'événement n'est mesurable que selon la multiplicité universelle dont il prescrit la possibilité. C'est en ce sens qu'il est grâce, et non histoire.[45]

Grace is that which ignores the economy of debt; and debt, of course, is the great and pervasive, if usually unspoken, question of globalisation.

For Newman, it is important to see that the University is not a mechanism for redressing some kind of economic imbalance between Catholics and Protestants, as if the Protestants who had benefited from education now owed it to the dispossessed Catholics. Much more fundamental than this, education in Newman's University is a matter precisely of this grace. It bypasses the economics of debt by the assertion of a universal singularity, in which souls are to be resurrected, brought back to Catholicism in exactly the way that he saw pertaining to his own case.

Globalisation in these terms becomes neither simply an economic issue, nor a political issue, nor even some dialectic aiming to regulate the relations obtaining between the economic and the political. What Newman helps us to see is that globalisation might be a *cultural* issue. In describing it thus, I mean to indicate that globalisation might be considered in terms of what I have called here, following Badiou, 'grace'.

3 Of Grace and Nation

Joyce's great story, 'Grace', tells of yet another convert, Tom Kernan, who finds himself at the centre of a plot organised by Martin Cunningham to come to a retreat where he can 'wash the pot'. Tom, whose tongue has been 'shortened' in the incident with which the story begins – a 'fall' akin to various other literary and biblical falls, including that of Funes the Memorius – has 'inexplicable debts', out of which Mr Power has occasionally helped him with 'many small, but opportune, loans'. The plot works, and Kernan accompanies his friends to the retreat, given by Father Purdon.

The service for the retreat is full of businessmen, moneylenders, pawnbrokers, registration agents, journalists and the like. The priest's text is one that allows him to make a metaphorical slippage between the everyday work of capital (economics) and the religious life; the metaphor to be used is that of accounting:

> He told his hearers that he was there that evening for no terrifying, no extravagant purpose; but as a man of the world speaking to his fellowmen. He came to speak to business men and he would speak to them in a businesslike way. If he might use the metaphor, he said, he was their spiritual accountant; and he wished each and every one of his hearers to open his books, the books of his spiritual life, and see if they tallied accurately with conscience.[46]

If it transpires that there be some discrepancy in these accounts, the priest recommends that the men ask that 'with God's grace, I will rectify this and this. I will set right my accounts'. However, the entire point here is that the slippage between these two realms – the economic and the religious – is *merely* metaphorical: that is to say, it has no more reality than as a linguistic trope or figure. 'Grace', by definition, is not a matter of accounting. As Badiou has it, 'la grâce est le contraire de la loi, pour autant qu'elle est ce qui vient *sans être dû*'.[47]

The priest here resembles, in at least one respect, Newman facing his own audiences in Dublin some half a century before this text was written. Newman too addressed businessmen and men of the world. His arguments for a Catholic University, fundamentally, were also arguments that set the world of business (run by Protestants, such as was Kernan before he married, in Joyce's story) up against a different order of things, a religious order. For Newman, the University was, effectively, the site of a particular kind of grace or diseconomy. In this regard, he was making something new and distinctive in the formation of the idea of a University.

The more dominant European version of the University as an institution at this time was, as we have already seen in the figures of Humboldt and others, one that was essentially tied to the establishment of the modern nation-states.[48] It is in the face of this Humboldtian idea of the University that Newman was working. The Humboldtian idea is, of course, what Newman describes specifically as a 'Protestant' kind of University. The thinking here is one that aligns the Protestant not only with the business-world, but also with the narrowly nationalistic. That is to say, for Newman, the 'university of culture' (as Readings terms it) is one that serves what are fundamentally and merely economic purposes: their task is the production of the citizen whose function is to play a role in a national economy. In this regard, this kind of University is, for Newman, precisely the contrary of a 'global' University. Newman's Catholic University is one that wishes to circumvent the economics of business, and to place before us the possibility of a different kind of social order, one based upon a *universalism* that he equates with Catholicism.

In the end, we would have to say that we have failed to fulfil Newman's idea of a University. The University, in most contemporary instances, is 'Protestant' through and through, in that its universalising idea, its capacity for a globalisation based upon the diseconomy of grace, has been entirely and thoroughly betrayed by national governments of every political hue. Those governments see the University simply as an arm of national capital, and thus use the institution precisely as a weapon in the further 'Americanisation' of the world's economy. In this state of affairs, the only possible outcome is further global inequality, both political and economic. Perhaps it is time to reconsider the possibility of an ethical globalisation, such as that called for by Mary Robinson, in terms of the establishment of a University whose scope and ambit will be, genuinely, universal.

CHAPTER 7

The Existence of Scotland

It has become clear that we have some particular questions that have emanated from our initial consideration of 'The English Question'. At one level, of course, and at least since 1707 if not from the time of James VI/I, that question has also been the question concerning the existence of Scotland. In relation to the University, the issue of the speaking voice, the location and self-identification of the autonomous subject of history, and the relation of literature to nation-state have all come under speculative and historical pressure. In this present chapter, I want to take the case of Scotland as a kind of paradigmatic example that will allow us to advance the exploration of that predicament given to us essentially after Modernism and after the Catholic Universalism (confused or confounded with the University) by Newman. I will therefore work towards a new configuration or constellation, in which the relation of English to literature to University to nation-state will find a new shape – and that new shape might be one that also offers us a way of linking English more directly once more to the issue of freedom.

I Really existing places

In their critique of the culture industry, originally written in 1944 while the authors were exiled in America from the Nazi terror, Adorno and Horkheimer complain about what we might call a specific kind of realism or reality-effect in mass culture. Their complaint is that there is a clear tendency in mass culture to advance the notion of the world as unchangeable; the corollary of that would be the impossibility of history and of historical change. The further corollary is the impossibility of criticism making any substantive change to the way in which we conceptualise the world, for what is now at stake is not the condition of the world but rather its mere (unchangeable) existence. They point out first that, in the 'transition to the administered life' that they are diagnosing, there is a 'conversion of enlightenment into positivism' and the rise of a concomitant 'myth of things as they actually are'. That combination establishes the ostensibly dismal pointlessness of critique, indeed, even its impossibility; and, for those who remain uncritical of this state of affairs, the task facing us is not how to *change* the world but rather how to *manage* it as it is. As they put it:

> The new ideology has as its objects the world as such. It makes use of the worship of facts by no more than elevating a disagreeable existence into the world of facts in representing it meticulously. This transference makes existence itself a substitute for meaning and right. . . . Not Italy is offered, but evidence that it exists.[1]

In this – a description that in some way matches a prevalent understanding of the postmodern as a mediatic age – there is what Jameson characterised as a 'waning of affect'.[2] The 'massification' of information and its dissemination in various media leads to a state of affairs in which the world is too much with us, and the superfluity of information and of what is alleged to be 'knowledge' leads to the demise of *pathos* on which the possibility of motivated human agency has traditionally been thought to rest.

Gianni Vattimo, in *The Transparent Society*, explores the hypothesis that in our technocratic age, when mass-media are capable of offering us 'real-time' history (as when we watch history unfolding 'live' on television, say), we might have reached a moment of an ostensible total transparency in history and knowledge.[3] That is to say, it looks as if we have reached the stage in which the Hegelian Absolute Spirit has fully realised itself, in that there is now no 'mediation/knowledge' to come *between* the subject and her or his history. (Another way of putting this, in my own preferred terms, would be that we have reached a stage in which we confuse information with knowledge, and ignore the latter in the immediate availability of the former). This, however, is for Vattimo a too simplistic view; in its place, he advances the argument that the massification of the media has in fact established a state of affairs in which there is no longer any belief in 'history-as-such'. The multiplication of media leads us to take the view that there is not one history unfolding at all, but rather that there are multiple histories, many of them overlapping, all of them 'situated', and all vying for position with regard to truth-claims.

'Scotland', in this view, would be both the site of a local history that takes its place amidst a crowd of other, no less viable, histories (that of 'England', that of 'France', that of 'India' and so on, in a series of contestations with ostensibly 'external' histories), and also the site that *contains* a multiplicity of internal dissonant and dissident histories (that of the 'Highlands', say, against that of the 'Lowlands'; that of 'metropolitan' Glasgow or Edinburgh against that of the rural Grampians; and so on in a series of ostensibly internal conflicts and crises that shape the class and sometimes frankly sectarian or tribal structures of the modern nation).

Far from offering 'transparency' and immediacy (the perfect cohabitation of epistemology with ontology), mass culture is more mediated than ever; and one highly possible consequence is that we start to give up on a belief in any single and unified reality at all. Like the victims of mass culture that Adorno and Horkheimer saw us becoming, we give up on the real thing, having in our hands something even better than the real thing – even better in that it is administratively graspable, 'manageable': proof that the real thing exists. That 'proof' is always based upon a mythic, or, more generally, simply an 'imagined', version of the *essence* of the thing whose existence is supposedly proved; and such a proof allows for an administering of the real thing (a taxonomy of its components, an analysis of its intrinsic structure, a description of its *form*, such as that I gave above in my characterisation of Scotland as riven by internal and external other histories), while the reality itself (the component parts that are taxonomised, the relation of its instrinsic structure to a world outside of it, a description of its *content*) escapes everything *except* its administration.[4] The question to be posed here is a simple one: in the devolved age (when, ostensibly at least, Scotland has regained some control over aspects of the *administration* of Scotland), is it the case that 'not Scotland is offered, but merely evidences that Scotland exists'? In short, do we have a Scotland – and by extension, an 'England' or indeed any other nation-state – *in theory*, 'merely'?[5]

In what follows, I shall explore the question of the realisation or self-articulation of Scotland. What I aim to show is that while Scotland exists, it does so in what I shall call a mode of theoretical potentiality. I shall thus contend that arguments about whether we should regard Scotland in 'essentialist' terms, or 'Scotlands' as constructions, or Scotland as a deconstruction of nationhood, and so on, are all arguments that, while interesting, are strangely beside at least one central and key point. The real issue is whether we prioritise *Scotland* (in which case we see it simply as a theoretical possibility rather than as a material fact) or, on the other hand, the *existence* of Scotland (in which case we see it as material fact, devoid of further ontological possibilities, and thus, paradoxically denied the very history that its supposed existence claims in the first place). Scotland as theoretical potentiality is no less 'real' than any of these other variant and conflicting definitions; and, indeed, I shall argue that it is *only* by regarding Scotland as just such a theoretical possibility that Scotland, rather than just the evidence that it exists, can be offered. At stake in this is the question of how (and, indeed, if) Scotland determines itself, of how Scotland might be an agent of its own history (and that of others), of an autonomy in modern Scotland.[6]

2 On cynicism; or, on going to the dogs

It has famously been argued, by George Saintsbury and many others, that, with *Waverley* in 1814, Walter Scott effectively 'invented' the historical novel, and gave it a form that would be imitated right across Europe.[7] However, this position is one that takes the optimistic view of 'history-as-such' that has come to be regarded as problematic, especially in relation to the question of the particularities, even the very essence, of Scotland's history. In his more nuanced and attenuated reading of Scott, Cairns Craig – making in passing a series of extremely acute observations – has astutely argued that the text of *Waverley* is the site in which there is a paradoxical *elision* of history, in that the question of history as a temporal structure cedes place to a question of geography, where the text sets up oppositions that are determined according to a place-logic:

> What Scott does in *Waverley* is to make a division in geography equivalent to a division in history: to cross the Highland boundary is effectively to step into the past.[8]

And, in an expert gloss on this that serves to explain the huge popularity and success of this kind of writing, Craig goes on:

> For Scott, history, geography and psychology form a triptych whose terms are mutually interchangeable . . . . his heroes can stand on both sides of a *historical* divide precisely because they can travel across a *geographical* boundary and in so doing experience the changes in history at a *psychological* level.[9]

The argument here is something akin to Moretti's description of the European form of the *Bildungsroman*.[10] In *The Way of the World*, Moretti argued that the *Bildungsroman*, while ostensibly dominated entirely by history, is actually shaped by a static version of society, informed by a vision of society as inimical to historical change. The central character of the *Bildungsroman* starts as an outsider of sorts in her or his social formation, usually on account of the fact that she or he is youthful and not fully versed in the ways of her or his society. It is precisely those ways – the norms that constitute a normative and value-laden *ideology* – that the character has to learn; and, in so learning them, and indeed in internalising them ('appropriating' them, 'owning' them, as we lecturers in managerialist business-studies would now say), the character finds that she or he can be fully inserted into the very heart of the society, legitimised and authorised by it now as an independent adult (an adulthood typically signified by a supposedly freely chosen marriage, based upon affective individualism, to one who was always already a fully legitimised member of the society's insider-class)[11] precisely in the same instant that, in circular fashion, they legitimise the society by an endorsement and espousal (literally) of its ideology.

Thus, historical development becomes, at most, a psychological question (the question of the individual growing into adulthood, accepting fatalistically that 'experience' shows their youthful aspirations to be idealistic, 'maturing');[12] and material history, those forces that are larger than any single individual, are rendered as if constant, eternal and immutable. In this way, ostensibly denying the possibility of critique of the society that it represents, the text of the *Bildungsroman* legitimises the very ideology that its central, youthful character had seemed to question on behalf of its reader. While that youth, and that reader, might have thought that it was possible to change the world by an engagement with it that would set history and all its open possibilities going, the text serves to defuse that possibility by effectively domesticating the possibility of historical revolt or criticism.

Craig's view differs from this slightly in seeing the central character – in this instance Edward Waverley – not as one entirely defeated by ideology, but rather as one who mediates between two worlds, the one historical and shaped by Enlightenment ideas of the possibility of progress (that is, the possibility of getting history going; 'progress' in this case represented by England, though England as a psychological state of affairs and not a place); the other a world entirely 'out of history' and shaped by its exclusion from the centres of power and force that shape historical being itself (thus effectively becoming an *object* of historical progress, and its potential victim; in this case, Scotland is, psychologically, such an 'object'-world). For Craig, thus, the character of Edward becomes, in some ways, a vehicle for the reader's own imaginings, both of the possibility of progress (in which the reader is the *agent* of history) and of the thwarting of any such idea (in which the reader is effectively paralysed, the passive recipient – the *patient* – of a history that is beyond her or his grasp).

For our present argument, this has a particular importance when Edward gets his first impressions of Scotland as a place, for here we have Scott mediating a kind of foundational view of Scotland for us, one that carries a particular weight of legitimacy and authority precisely because it is the view of the naïve, innocent, youthful outsider. It thus pretends to a condition of some 'objectivity' (the word usually means simply 'neutrality'; but here it should be charged with the idea that Scotland is purely the *object* of this imaginative view).

Having arrived at, and spent some time in, his military quarters in Dundee, Edward Waverley decides to get out and see something of Scotland during a requested leave of absence. In this visit to Bradwardine's village-home of Tully-Veolan, he is effectively making his first proper engagement with the ostensible 'reality' of Scotland. The place stands outside of the 'official' Scotland, the Scotland presented to the military officer class; and it is here, therefore, that Waverley gets his first opportunity of seeing 'real' Scottish people.[13]

The first image that we are offered of the Scots here is that of an impoverished, violent, savagely physical people. Their houses were 'miserable in the extreme, especially to an eye accustomed to the smiling neatness of English cottages'; they are buildings that straggle their way irregularly along unpaved streets, 'where children, almost in a primitive state of nakedness, lay sprawling'. The children lie exposed to the danger of being crushed by passing horses; and, even when the aged women of the place want to rescue the children from such danger, they do so in a fashion that shows savage force, as some 'watchful old grandam . . . snatching up her own charge from among the sunburnt loiterers, saluted him with a sound cuff, and transported him back to his dungeon, the little white-headed varlet screaming all the while'.[14]

Most important in this description, however, is the next characteristic. The place is a bedlam of confused noise; and these people live among dogs:

> Another part in this concert was sustained by the incessant yelping of a score of idle useless curs, which followed, snarling, barking, howling, and snapping at the horses' heels; a nuisance at that time so common in Scotland, that a French tourist who, like other travellers, longed to find a good and rational reason for everything he saw, has recorded, as one of his memorabilia of Caledonia, that the state maintained in each village a relay of curs, called *collies*, whose duty it was to chase the *chevaux de poste* . . . from one hamlet to another . . . [15]

First, here is Scotland as, literally, *cynical*: like ancient Diogenes of Sinope, follower of Antisthenes, called 'the cynic' after the ancient Greek for 'dog' (*kuon*) and reputed to live among the stray curs of Sinop (in modern-day Turkey), the Scot has gone to the dogs. The non-cynical outsider (the French tourist), in an effort to understand or contain this cynicism, rationalises it as part of a national communications service. Scott here legitimises the view of the outsider who sees Scottish *communications* – the basis of Scottish society as such – as grounded in, indeed dependent upon, a fundamentally inhospitable and anti-social cynicism. The consequence of this representation is not only a view of Scotland as cynical and inhospitable, but also a view of the people as incapable of forming a society: here, there is no such thing as society.[16]

This figure of the cynical 'dogged' Scot recurs in the narrative, on a day singled out for its 'rationality', in Chapter Thirteen ('A Day More Rational than the Last'). When Bradwardine takes Edward out hunting they are surrounded not only by the hunting-dogs but also by the 'gillie-wet-foots', the impoverished young lads who want to join the hunt, working as beaters alongside (we might even say beneath) the hunting dogs. On the hunt itself, Bradwardine and Edward, on horseback, *mediate* or live 'between' cynicism (the gillie-wet-foots) and killing (the hunt itself). Importantly, they live also between two discourses. The *language* of the gillie-wet-foots goes unrepresented here (all we are told is that their usual mode of greeting Davie Gellatley is 'daft Davie' except when they want to go on the hunt, when it's 'Maister Gellatley'), while the language of the hunt appears, and is a polyglot mixture including English, French and some Scottish: the Baron flays the dead animal '(which, he observed, was called by the French chasseurs *faire la curée*) with his own baronial *couteau de chasse*', and, when he tells in this same passage of his literary tastes there is a highly distinctive Scottish flavour.[17] In this polyglot language, we may be witnessing precisely the kind of 'comparative literature' to which I adverted in chapter five, above; crucially, it draws attention to the experienced flavour of the spoken word.

After the hunt, Bradwardine takes Edward on a circuitous route home, effectively offering a tour that yields many historical anecdotes (the details of which Scott does not reveal, thus allowing the terrain to be passed over in a kind of silence for the reader) about the villages through which they pass. Here, he gives each local habitation a specific local history which, because local, is restricted to the level of the anecdote; but Edward's romantic mind enlarges the anecdotes into tales that reveal more general *character*, becoming thereby *illustrative* and exemplary tales whose purchase goes well beyond the local and precise fact. It is this hunt and this trip home that cements a bond between Edward and Bradwardine who, though differing in almost every respect, nonetheless find their point of communion through the day's outing. Their communion depends upon that union of Bradwardine's recounting of history as a tale of bare but precise facts with Edward's romanticising glosses that adorn those facts and give them a more general applicability. It is here, in the hospitable discovery of the possibility of an intimacy between two who are radically opposed as characters, that one finds the alleged 'rationality' of the day (reason operating here as a combination of sense and sensibility).

We might call this, then, a form of 'cynical reason', in that the social intimacy that they establish is *grounded* in the dogs whose local condition they transcend (and whose noise or language they effectively silence), one through his command of different languages, the other through his luxuriating command of the language of romance. In this, in their union with each other, they transcend their local condition; and they do so by the processes or possibilities of that very translation or translatability that, as we saw earlier, is central to the possibilities of love and of the experience of alterity. That is, they say one thing, but they mean many things by it. That plurality of sense opens communication to the realm of *possibility*, characterising it as the site of multiple sense, multiple meaning, mutable history; but this is preferable to a view that reduces communication to a simple transfer of information (the postal service).

It is important that this cynicism, on which the openness of communication-as-possibility rests, remains itself largely inarticulate; or, rather, that it has its own modes of discourse. The cynicism becomes thus the *means* of communication and not the communication itself; the Scottish lads, and, with them, Davie Gellatley, become the *medium* through whom Edward and Bradwardine are able to establish their social being, their 'rational' society; it thus establishes the form but not the content of communication (and thus, by extension, the form and not the content of the substance of the possibilities of their being a Scottish people or nation). This cynicism, thus, though itself inarticulate nonetheless operates at the level of the linguistic: in itself, it is a reduction of language *either* to the mindless and incoherent barking of dogs *or* to the ostensibly senseless but actually oddly rational songs of Davie; but it is more important for what it facilitates than for what it is in itself.

Davie Gellatley becomes a key figure in this. Supposedly the son of a witch and brother of a now dead poet, Gellatley seems almost permanently to live among dogs: whenever we see him, his dogs are not far away. He is less fool than *fainéant*, deploying his reputation as simple-minded in order to allow him to get his own way, to do little work except that which he himself wants to do. In this, he is using his status as mere object – in what Baudrillard will much later identify as a 'fatal strategy' – in order to assert a subjectivity.[18] Further, hovering always as he does between folly and privileged insight (if not total knowledge), he is described explicitly in the terms that cast him as the original cynic. On the morning of the initial *creagh* on Tully-Veolan, Edward is trying to work out what is going on, and he comes upon Gellatley who 'was also seen in the group, idle as

Diogenes at Sinope, while his country men were preparing for a siege'.[19]

This version of Scotland as informed by cynicism or by cynical reason is important. Cynicism, distrustful of 'civilisation', which it sees as an artificial graft that harms our natural condition of independence, effectively advocates precisely a stepping 'out of history' (to misapply Craig's terms here). Cynicism (like Adorno and Horkheimer; and, in different ways, like Rousseau and Freud) is troubled by the subsuming of real material conditions of human society beneath the regularities and norms of a society that sees its realities in the administratively established rules and norms that give the society its existence. In *Waverley*'s 'more rational day', however, we see what can be founded upon such cynicism. It is important to note that we do not get a 'real' Scotland; rather, what we get is the establishment of the possibility of human communicability, friendship, or pleasure. Such friendship or allegiance rests not upon transparent communication of a message between two individuals (as in one version of the postal service); rather, it rests upon the fact that communication establishes itself merely as the *possibility of communication* and as the *communication of possibility*. The name that the text offers for this, in which language is the condition of translatability and of mutable uncertainty, is Scotland. Scotland is thus the site of *possibility*, and it is in this possibility that the cynic, out of history, can be brought back into history as the very ground of history's possibilities.

To be out of history in the way described by Craig is, however, to be cynical in a different way; in the end, it is a way that aligns us not with those who will make history (the Edwards, the Bradwardines) but rather with the cynic herself in her silencing. There is a structural limitation in this form – a weaker form – of the cynicism that I discuss here. Craig's argument, of course, is the twofold thesis that, first, Scotland is *constructed* as being out of history, by such as Scott; and second, that history – by which he means official history, the kind that gets written – happens elsewhere. Thus, Scotland's attempts at writing its own history fall, of necessity, into imagination, into fiction. This is cleverly argued by Craig;[20] yet the terms in which he makes the case are terms that oppose history to barbarism. The case rests on the assumption of at least a common if not a universal history, bracketed at one end by progress, modernity and the civilised future and, at the other end by regressive and barbaric imaginings or primitivism. It is exactly such a view of history that leads inexorably to the story that Craig tells (in this accurately representing Scott, let it be said) in which history is a neo-Hegelian tale of victors and victims; and, in this, if one is not a victor, the only position left to assume is that of victim. The position that Craig offers us is either that of the little boy in the streets of Tully-Veolan, surrounded by dogs and threatened constantly with being trampled, or the position of Davie Gellatley, the 'critic' as licensed or knowledgeable fool.[21] In short, the version of history assumed by Craig is one in which progress must be based upon a 'fatal strategy' (at best) grounded in a logic of victimhood. In this, there is little possibility of Scotland *ever* escaping such a condition, which becomes instead ingrained, leading to the weak sarcasms of a little Scotlandism.

My contention here is, rather, that the logic of cynicism offers a different way of considering the question – one in which we find a better or more useful opposition, this time between history on one hand and potentiality or theory on the other. In Craig's terms, the opposition that is established seems to be of necessity backward-looking, in that it thematises the division between progress and barbarism, between being the agent and being the victim of history, as an opposition grounded in 1707 and thus as an opposition between England and a supposedly autonomous Scotland. Such a ground is indeed available in Scott; and it is to that that we can now turn.

3 Scotland as possibility

Near the start of *Waverley*, there is a definition advanced of Scottish scholarship, as evidenced in the figure of the Baron of Bradwardine:

> He was of a very ancient family, and somewhat embarrassed fortune; a scholar, according to the scholarship of Scotchmen, that is, his learning was more diffuse than accurate, and he was rather a reader than a grammarian.[22]

Scott goes on to characterise Bradwardine at this point with a story that he claims, in one of his authorial notes, as being derived from historical fact. Bradwardine is bookish to the extent that he trades his freedom for the reading of Livy. Having escaped imprisonment, he ventured back towards his captors in an effort to pick up the copy of Livy that he had been reading. Scott's own note grounds this in non-fiction, in factual history:

> The attachment to this classic [Livy] was, it is said, actually displayed, in the manner mentioned in the text, by an unfortunate Jacobite in that unhappy period. He escaped from the jail in which he was confined for a hasty trial and certain condemnation, and was retaken as he hovered around the place in which he had been imprisoned, for which he could give no better reason than the hope of recovering his favourite *Titus Livius*. I am sorry to add, that the simplicity of such a character was found to form no apology for his guilt as a rebel, and that he was condemned and executed.[23]

Bradwardine, on the other hand, gets away with it, due to the fact that his guard, who recaptures him, is of a similarly bookish disposition, favouring Livy almost as much as Bradwardine; having found a kindred spirit, the guard pleads on Bradwardine's behalf, and so softens the charge against him, that he gets off scot-free.

We should remark here the oddity of Scott's note, however. The point of the note is to claim historical veracity for his tale, to claim that this element at least is drawn from the particularities of a specific historical fact. Yet, in the opening sentence of the note, there is that discomforting intercalation, 'it is said'. In other words, the testimony for the verity of this passage is not historical fact, but rather mere anecdote. It is not true, but possible; and it is precisely such possibility that Scott sees as the ground for the legitimisation of his tale. As Nietzsche would later have it, 'in the end the true world becomes a fable'.[24]

The truth becomes possibility. Why might this be important? It is important here because the text offers us, in its opening section after the historical backdrop and genealogy, another specific view of Scotland, this time based on an idea of Scottish learning or 'scholarship'; it is a version that is picked up some hundred and fifty years later by George Davie, in his characterisation of a Scottish educational system as one that subtends 'the democratic intellect'.[25] The argument of this is straightforward, if far-reaching and consequential. The contention is that, due to historical and political circumstance (the details of which need not detain us here, except to say that they relate to a colonial situation in the nineteenth century), a Scottish tradition of generalist education has given way to the supervention of an English mode in which early specialisation in specific disciplines narrows the critical range of the student, giving very specific if 'untransferable' knowledge without astute and flexible cleverness, as it were.

The Scottish tradition is more democratic, it is claimed, not just because of the empirical fact that Scotland had more universities, but also – and primarily – because the Scottish student was being trained philosophically in how to think abstractly, to find the general or *theoretical* case that lay behind the particular. Thus, while the English student might be able to translate a particular term from ancient Greek into nineteenth-century English, say, she or he would have no knowledge of a general semantics, of the historicity of meaning, of the problems of translation between cultures and so on. The English is practical, the Scottish abstract; the English solves problems in their particularity, the Scottish sees the general problem that shapes the particular; and so on. The Scottish mode, thus, is more democratic because it is more foundationalist, more *theoretical*, and it is in this way that its beneficiaries can participate fully and autonomously – *critically* – in their history.

This 'Scottish learning', which is characterised as being 'more diffuse than accurate', is what Davie will later identify as the 'generalist tradition' of education as practised in the Scottish universities; and, in Davie (as in Scott), it is set against the rather mechanical 'knowledge' of technical particularity. Let us here call it, simply, 'Scotland *as* theory'. Yet in *Waverley*, an odd inversion is at work. In the 'more rational day' of the hunt discussed above, it is Bradwardine, the Scot, who professes 'mere' or factual historical knowledge, so that the young Englishman, Waverley himself, can be represented as 'imaginative' and romantic. In all the anecdotes that Bradwardine relates, he restricts himself to the bare knowledge of the particular facts: 'the Baron, indeed, only cumbered his memory with matters of fact – the cold, dry, hard outlines which history delineates'.[26] On the other hand, Edward 'loved to fill up and round the sketch with the colouring of a warm and vivid imagination, which gives light and life to the actors and speakers in the drama of past ages'.[27]

What follows from my argument above, however, is that it is an error to read this in simple allegorical terms, the terms that would be given to us by the kind of 'place-logic' so ably described by Craig, Crawford, and, in a different context, Moretti. It is not the case that Edward is England, Bradwardine Scotland. Scotland is neither one nor another character at all, not even one or another location; rather, it is the site in which communication between these characters, locations, and histories is established as the site of theoretical possibility. By this, I do not mean to signal just that Scotland makes communication possible; but, more forcefully and more radically, that Scotland makes communication into the communication of possibility, and that it establishes communication as a rather uncertain communication-as-the-possibility-of-communication itself. With this mode of communication, Scotland is more *possibility* than it is *theory*. Scotland might thus be seen as analogous to the condition that Keats had in mind as the negative capability that allows for Shakespeare's plays to have their particular reality and vitality.

In this 'more rational day', we have not just the *means* of communication being represented, but also the *fact* of it (though it remains a fact devoid of precise detail); the result is not only society but also the indulgence of pleasure. In this, we see a resolution of the hypothetical conflict between particularity and generality, between 'English' and 'Scottish' (indeed, 'Scotland' is the name for such an 'irresolute resolution'); and, importantly, the figure who resolves theory into practice is womanly, first Rose and then Flora. 'Shortly after dinner,' we are told, 'the Baron, as if to show that his temperament was not entirely theoretical, proposed a visit to Rose's apartment, or, as he termed it, her *Troisième Etage*'.[28] There we find Rose, conversant in French and Italian, able to sing and to recite poetry. In this image of a European multilingual culture, we have the prefiguration of the more romantic shape of Flora Mac-Ivor, another woman who can exist in the social precisely by her capacities for translation.

Flora shares these same 'accomplishments' but, living in a more isolated situation, she has added to them her knowledge of the local customs and language too. However, the text suggests that there are at least two ways in which one can come to such an engagement with the local. Flora differs from her brother, Fergus:

> When settled in the lonely regions of Glennaquoich, she found that her resources in French, English, and Italian literature, were likely to be few and interrupted; and, in order to fill up the vacant time, she bestowed a part of it upon the music and poetical traditions of the Highlanders, and began really to feel the pleasure in the pursuit, which her brother, whose perceptions of literary merit were more blunt, rather affected for the sake of popularity than actually experienced.[29]

Fergus, to return to the terms that began this chapter and, indeed, this whole study, is concerned with the *existence* of Scotland; Flora (and Rose both before and after her) is the person concerned with *Scotland*. It is important here to note that Flora is interrupted in her translation of the Gaelic song in which Edward had heard his name mentioned.[30] The incompleteness leaves him in a state of irresolution and uncertainty still; but it is precisely such uncertainty that enables the condition of sociability – it is such uncertainty (or, better, openness to possibility) that is Scotland. Scotland here is the word for such irresolution, and Edward is left in a state of uncertainty; but he nonetheless remains in a state of *society*, for the text situates Edward uncertainly between Rose and Flora (between an 'English' flower and a more general floweriness); and that condition – the condition of possibility – is Scotland, for us every bit as much as for Waverley.

The question of the existence of Scotland, then, as Keats would have known, has something of the Hamlet about it: 'to be or not to be, that is the question'. The same might be said of any emergent nation-state – emergent now, or indeed at any time in history. When Bradley, lecturing in Glasgow University at the turn of the twentieth century, analysed the character of Hamlet, he found his presiding force to be a moral melancholy.[31] Certainly, he argued, this play, like *Julius Caesar*, is a tragedy of intellect (though he concedes that passion – his other kind of tragedy – is present here too). Yet Hamlet's prevarications have little to do with excessive 'theorising', according to Bradley (complicit in this with a logic of the fatal strategy that is victimhood), and everything to do with the melancholy into which he is thrown by the precipitate behaviour of his mother. In this, Hamlet is entirely the victim of circumstance; as a victim, it becomes unclear as to whether he can effect any serious agency, whether, simply, he can act.

This, however, is the point, especially regarding the existence of Scotland. It is in Hamlet's most famous soliloquy that we can see, by analogy, an address to the question of the existence of Scotland. My claim here is that Scotland is, in a peculiar sense, 'the undiscovered country'. In Hamlet's speech, that country is one that lies beyond death, and in the realm of the spectral or ghostly. However, it is not definitively a place to which there is only a one-way street or one-way ticket; to go there is to go to another place without the promise of return but most certainly, as the Ghost shows (and as Hamlet makes clear he understands in this most famous soliloquy), with the *possibility* of return. Moreover, the undiscovered country might not even be there anyway. Its mode of existence is, we might say, pure potentiality.

In this, I borrow the term 'potentiality' from Giorgio Agamben.[32] There are two kinds of potential, he argues, following Aristotle. The first is a potential that exhausts itself in kinetic realisation (the child with the potential to become an adult, say, who stops being a child as soon as she reaches maturity). The second is of a different order, and Agamben explains it through the examples of the writer or the architect. The architect has the potential to build, certainly; but she does not exhaust that potential in its realisation, when she builds a building. The potential remains, even after the fact. This kind of potential is not to be set against realisation; rather it is to be understood as a potential that is kept in existence *even when it is not being articulated*. Thus, this kind of potential for some state of affairs to come about depends, paradoxically, upon the maintenance of the potential for that same state of affairs *not* to come about. Potentiality is aligned with impotentiality; or, as Hamlet has it, 'to be or not to be?' This question is best understood as one that does not pose a choice between two mutually exclusive opposites, but rather as an inclusive state of affairs that conditions Hamlet's being as pure potentiality. As with Hamlet, so also with Scotland: devolved, not independent – and therefore always as *possibility*.

It is only among those who see themselves as empowered by their victimhood in a fatal strategy of an inverted autonomy that such a state of affairs provokes the moral melancholy described by Bradley during his time teaching in Glasgow. A genuine autonomy – one that is predicated upon the more important issue of freedom, and thus one that is political and not merely psychological – would be one that is not dependent on the master–slave dialectics of Hegel, and thus not dependent upon the logic of inverting one's own self-constructed inferiority. As we have seen, and as we see again in this example from Bradley, this is also fundamentally a question of reading, or of how we read.

To go beyond the master–slave with its intrinsic logic of victimhood and its corollary of focusing on an identity politics, or a politics of being, will require that we engage not only with alterity but rather with the possibility that identity can – potentially – be other than it is, or can enter into a politics of becoming. It is important not to overstate this case: an opening of the self to the potential for becoming other does not require, as of necessity, that I become an other identity. It does not require, for example, that I am identified as 'woman' when I read Janice Galloway or Jackie Kay (or, if I am interested in other national identities, Toni Morrison), say; but it does require that I see this not as possibility (for it is, in fact, impossible) but as potentiality: 'to be *or* not to be'. Everything is in that 'or', that prevaricating negative capability or undecidability. A free Scotland – the only Scotland worth considering – is the endless perpetuation of its own possibility. *Then* we would have Scotland, and not just formal proof of its existence. The English question is also, of course, the Scottish question, as it is the Irish or the French and so on.

PART IV

Looking Forward

CHAPTER **8**

On Critical Humility

In 1941–2, Wallace Stevens addressed an audience in Princeton, as part of a series of lectures by divers speakers on 'The Language of Poetry'. Towards the end of his lecture, entitled 'The Noble Rider and the Sound of Words', he offered an idea of the function of the poet:

> What is his function? Certainly it is not to lead people out of the confusion in which they find themselves. Nor is it, I think, to comfort them while they follow their readers to and fro. I think that his function is to make his imagination theirs and that he fulfils himself only as he sees his imagination become the light in the minds of others. His role, in short, is to help people to live their lives.[1]

This much is probably relatively uncontroversial. Written at the time when the United States was entering the Second War, the passage sustains the always ongoing argument in Stevens regarding the proximity of the imagination with reality, the intimacy of aesthetics with materiality. As he glosses the argument further, he turns to the question of the audience for poetry, for what Milton had thought of as the predicament in which he faced a requirement to write for a 'fit audience, though few'. Here is Stevens from the same lecture:

> Time and again it has been said that he [the poet] may not address himself to an elite. I think he may. There is not a poet whom we prize living today that does not address himself to an elite. The poet will continue to do this: to address himself to an elite even in a classless society . . . And that elite, if it responds, not out of complaisance, but because the poet has quickened it, because he has educed from it that for which it was searching in itself and in the life around it and which it had not yet quite found, will thereafter do for the poet what he cannot do for himself, that is to say, receive his poetry.[2]

It is clear that such an argument, concerned so visibly with the 'elite' condition of an audience, makes for less easily acceptable reading today. While it may be relatively uncontroversial (even if contestable) to advance the view that it is the function of the poet to help people to live their lives, it is certainly provocative (even if arguable) to advance the view that poetry is in some sense addressed primarily to an elite.

Yet it is important here to be precise: Stevens is not so much concerned simply with the idea that poetry is a rather exclusivist coterie activity, pursued among an 'elect' group; rather, he is more concerned with the *availability* of poetry, with how it might be *received*. That is to say, his focus most certainly is on the audience, but on the audience that is characterised precisely by the receptivity required to make poetry heard at all, the audience equipped with the sensorium needed to allow poetry to be read, 'received' as he puts it.

What might it mean to 'receive' poetry? The point that Stevens makes here is that the poet makes her or his own audience, 'quickens' an audience into being; but that she or he makes it in the abstract form of a receptivity, as if the task of the poet was to make poetry (her own poems, and also poetry as such) *available* to an audience, to allow an audience to avail of it and, in that availing, to become precisely the fit audience, though few, that is required to make the act that is poetry (an act of making, of *poiesis*) happen. The 'quickening' in question here means that the poet brings an audience into a potential being: that is to say, the audience for the poet is one that is endowed with the status of 'becoming an audience', and the poet, through the poetry, realises that becoming, bringing it into material being.[3] A poem, we might say, describes that state of affairs when we temporarily arrest an act of reading, now also an act of becoming, and take stock of where we stand in the public sphere, in that instant. It is the process of enacting the 'receipt' of poetry – for which we might now read all art, or all aesthetic activity – that rouses me into becoming an audience; my receptivity is central to the establishment of relatedness between poet and reader, and it is in that relatedness that we can 'live our lives' or become properly human.

As we near the end of this study, it is becoming increasingly clear that one of the key aspects of an English question pertains to how we read as well as to what we read. Further, it has often been taken as axiomatic that one 'problem' of the University as an institution is its alleged elitism. The reader, within the University English department, is alleged to be an elite reader, sure of her or his identity and equally sure of her or his socio-cultural standing. My previous chapters, however, have thrown such a Leavisian description into some question: I hope, of course, into my English question.

What I wish to explore now, at this final stage, is what, by contrasting reference to that earlier position, I shall call a 'critical humility', by which I mean to signal the kind of receptivity in the critic that Stevens sees here as being necessary to the survival of poetry, and with it the survival of humanity too. That receptivity can be characterised as a kind of 'passivity', or, much better, as a 'passion' (and the link I shall forge here – relating both words to the notions of waiting, suffering, undergoing – is more than etymological). The dominant critical ideologies of our day – Marxist, feminist, post-colonial, a politically-inflected deconstruction, ethical criticism, even the residua of reader-response criticisms – are all concerned with the *agency* of the critic. My argument will be that such an agency is possible only if it is grounded in the *passion* of the critic; and, further, that such passion (or even passivity) is the very ground of the humanity of the critic herself or himself.

In the first section of what follows, I examine the idea of the human as the laughing animal, and consider the relation of humour to the kind of humility that I am advocating. This leads me to a consideration, in the second part, of autonomy and its relation to a specific kind of failure – the failure not only to hear poetry but also the failure to achieve the freedom that is associated with modernist autonomy. Finally, the third section turns to explore the relation of this passionate humility to love, via a consideration of the idea of reading as a 'bearing witness' to passion; it argues for an understanding of the 'becoming-human animal' as the loving animal.

I The humility of our humour

In the wake of the Cuban missile crisis of 1962, some twenty years after Stevens's lecture referred to above, twenty years that marked a significant increase in the possibility of total human self-destruction, Kenneth Burke offered one of the first pieces of what has now come to be called 'nuclear criticism', when he advanced a 'definition of man'. In passing in the definition, he attended briefly to Aristotle's *Parts of Animals*, chapter 10, where Aristotle considers the well-rehearsed idea of the defining characteristic of man as 'the laughing animal' to be inadequate. In a footnote following this, Burke suggests that a cult of comedy is 'man's only hope', given the readiness with which a cult of tragedy is only too ready, as it seemed to Burke and others in 1963, to 'help out with the holocaust'.[4] Here, Burke is advocating a *cultivation*, even a *culture* of comedy; and he does so in the face of the enormity of the possibility of nuclear devastation. If the definition of man, as advanced here, is one that finds some solace in the idea of humanity as the animal that laughs, then that is also a definition that has a pragmatic and directive purpose, being more than merely descriptive. Its purpose is 'to help people to live their lives' in the very basic sense that its aim is to sustain life, to keep us living on: its aim is survival. Laughter, in this mode of thinking, is a promise of futurity, a deferral of death; and it is to this extent that laughter and the culture of comedy can become part of the definition of what it means to become more fully human. In this, the human is considered in a quasi-Heideggerian, quasi-Sartrean fashion: the human is a 'project', a throwing forward in time, even, eventually, a throwing forward towards death, but a death that is there always as potential ('to be or not to be'), and always therefore deferred. Death, in this view, is an asymptotic instant that can never be reached; it is, as Wittgenstein noted, 'not an event in life';[5] and poetry, established as a humanising activity insofar as it is intimately linked to a cult of comedy in these ways, helps sustain us precisely through an apotropaic warding-off of death, through a laughter that is evoked in the face of death itself, a death whose very possibility becomes, through this attitude, an impossibility.[6] Poetry, for the human who is human insofar as she or he laughs in this way, engages this paradoxical but oddly logical impossible possibility (or possible impossibility) of death.

When Hobbes considered laughter in both the *Elements of Law* and in *Leviathan*, of course, he saw it as an element in the interminable struggle between humans, a struggle to the death that, for Hobbes, is concerned not so much with the articulation of an autonomous being as with the simple possibility of staying alive. Laughter is nothing but 'sudden glory', arising, as Hobbes puts it, 'from the sudden conception of some eminency in ourselves, by comparison with the infirmities of others, or with our own formerly'.[7] Glossing this further, he goes on to describe sudden glory as 'the passion which maketh those *grimaces* called LAUGHTER'.[8]

The important thing to note here is that, in Hobbes, laughter is the result of a play of forces. It is not willed (and therefore not a sign of autonomy), even if it is, in the terms that Burke would use, 'motivated'.[9] However, it is motivated by something beyond itself, and is therefore neither entirely autonomous not entirely a marker of the autonomous freedom of the individual who laughs, even if it is a marker of her or his felt superiority over others. We could say that laughter is something that visits us, that inhabits us, that possesses us; and, for Hobbes, indeed, it is important that we actively resist any such total possession. Laughter, he claims, happens most to those who are least aware of their own shortcomings and who need to reassure themselves of their own superiority by concentrating intently on the infirmities of others in relation to whom they can feel superior: 'And therefore much laughter at the defects of others is a sign of pusillanimity'.[10] Laughter, then, is a force to be resisted if we are to become 'great minds', as Hobbes puts it, meaning minds that are capable of encountering alterity.

Hobbes is writing, of course, at a historical moment when the very word 'humour' is undergoing a semantic shift. On one hand, it is related directly to a discourse of medicine, in which 'the humours' determine, through the play of their mutual forces, the physical condition of the individual, their possibilities for staying alive; yet on the other, humour is also coming to mean what we now know as the condition provoking laughter, concerned thus with the relations between or among individuals and not, in the first instance, a purely physical matter.[11] Given also that Hobbes sees laughter as essentially *satirical*, in that it depends upon our hierarchised relations with others in our public sphere, laughter is now also open to regulation by law. Both medicine and law, founding University disciplines, are brought together here. Given further that laughter is occasioned by an economy of forces, we can say that laughter is, in one sense, at the very core of a possible University.

In seeing laughter in the way that he does, Hobbes allows us to realise that laughter is passionate, certainly; but it is passionate precisely insofar as its passion is determined by something else that pre-determines it: in a particular sense, it marks our passivity and helplessness. It is thus not a marker of human autonomy or freedom, not a marker of our capacity to become fully human. In being passionate in this sense, it draws attention precisely to our passivity or receptivity, rather than to our capacity for agency: it marks not so much *spontaneity* (an acting *sua sponte*) as *responsibility* (an acting, or re-acting, that responds to something that precedes it or even 'pre-vents' it).[12] In the case of Hobbes, the proper action to be undertaken in the face of the force of laughter that moves us to feel our superiority is, rather, the suppression of laughter. It is only in fighting back against the spirit of comedy, a spirit that is thus all the more vital and fundamental to our becoming human, that we can become properly human at all, according to this.

Interestingly, this overlaps with a fragment in which Derrida considers the nature of passion itself, and specifically the nature of a passion of/for literature. In *Demeure*, he outlines seven 'trajectories' of passion; and, in the seventh of these, he writes that:

> 'passion' implies the endurance of an indeterminate or undecidable limit where something, some X – for example, literature – must bear or tolerate everything, *suffer everything precisely because it is not itself*, because it has no essence but only functions. . . . The same exposition may be taken to be literary here, in one situation or according to given conventions, and non-literary there. This is the sign that literariness is not an intrinsic property of this or that discursive event. Even where it seems to *reside* [demeurer], literature remains an unstable function, and it depends on a precarious juridical status. Its passion consists in this – that it receives its determination from something other than itself.[13]

Literature cannot define itself as such; and it is precisely in this condition, this state of affairs in which its autonomy is heavily circumscribed, that it finds itself to be the site of passion, even of passivity. In short, literature requires us – its audience – to 'quicken' it into becoming literature as such. In the terms proposed by Stevens, it makes us, its 'impassioned' or passionate victims, into the elite that it requires for its (and our) survival.

Might we say the same of human becoming, or of our becoming human, as we say here of literature? If so, then we might describe laughter not merely as a response to something other than itself, implying that laughter is a responsibility of becoming human; but also we might describe it as a receptivity, a 'passivity' in the face of agency from elsewhere, from another determination of ourselves. We might accept, in short, that the modernist project of the establishment of human autonomy – in which the human determines her or his own history through the free assumption of an agency that shapes her or his ends – depends, paradoxically, precisely upon passion, upon the acknowledgement that we can be determined *as ourselves* by something – indeed, *only* by something – that is other than ourselves. Or, in short: autonomy is 'prevented' by heteronomy; action is similarly 'prevented' by passion; and freedom is conditioned not by our individualised assertion of a spontaneous agency but rather by that encounter with alterity in which we allow our other most fully to become free.

I am tempting us to move towards the acceptance of a paradoxical relation between elitism and passion in these terms, in which I am arguing that it is passion – passivity – that makes us into exactly the kind of elite required by Stevens as the audience, the possibilities of hearing, the site of receptivity, of and for poetry (and by extension, of all art). Passivity in these terms is consistent both with the establishment of this elite (with all its implications of superiority), and also with the establishment of the human as 'humble', as one who 'responds' or 'receives' (with all the implications of inferiority, and of belatedness). My claim is that it is this paradox that shapes the condition that we call autonomy, or, more importantly, the possibility of human freedom. Freedom in this sense is not determined by a simple agency or by an existentialist determination of the possibilities of human action (that is to say, it is not characterised by *choice* or by the *acte gratuit*); rather, freedom and autonomy are determined precisely through the fact that we are located always within a pre-existing set of human relations, a set that *determines* or even *predetermines* ('pre-vents') our possibilities for becoming human. That is to say, freedom, autonomy, the very possibility of our becoming human at all, are characterised by *passion* and *humility*.

In this, I am effectively advocating that we reconsider the relation between humour in the sense of comedy and laughter and the bodily 'humours' as they were conceived in early modern medicine. Poetry, after all, is, among other things, a therapeutic device: like all art, it 'attends' us, waits on us. It is like the doctor who is at once our servant and our master, always ahead of us in that she or he knows more about us than we know ourselves, being able to diagnose our condition (and therefore 'waiting' for us to catch up, to heal ourselves, to live our lives), yet also always behind us, at our beck and call, attendant on us (needing us to call it forth into being, needing us to call upon it).

Yet if poetry is seen as a kind of medicine in this sense, then it is reduced to something concerned with mere and basic physical survival: a therapeutic device for keeping the humours – the play of forces that determines our actions and even the very possibility and condition of our acting at all – balanced. In the terms offered recently by Agamben, it is concerned with *zoe*, with 'bare life'. Yet the terms with which I began, those offered by Stevens, are concerned not with 'bare life' but rather with what Agamben calls *bios*, the 'way of living'. *Zoe* is shared by all animate life; *bios* is something different. We have established that poetry is a means of establishing a mode of receptivity for the survival not only of humans but also of poetry itself. We need to look more closely now at the *biology* of such passivity or passion.[14]

2 Passions for failure

Passion, we may now say, is a condition of bare life, of living on. Yet this passion cannot be entirely intransitive: we are passionate in relation to something other than the self. For existentialist thought, this becomes the ground for suggesting that the human is human precisely to the extent that she or he 'exceeds' herself or himself. That move, especially as it exists in political existentialism, reiterates the ground of a Hegelian aesthetic. At the start of the *Aesthetics*, Hegel argues that the beauty offered by art is *higher* than that proffered by nature, on the grounds of a certain kind of superfluity or excessiveness. Natural beauty is simply there; but artistic beauty is the product of a spirit, contingent, arbitrary, not necessary:

> The beauty of art is beauty *born of the spirit and born again*, and the higher the spirit and its productions stand above nature and its phenomena, the higher too is the beauty of art above that of nature. Indeed, considered *formally* [i.e. no matter what it says], even a useless notion that enters a man's head is higher than any product of nature, because in such a notion spirituality and freedom are always present. Of course, considered in its *content*, the sun, for example, appears as an absolutely necessary factor [in the uni-

verse] while a false notion vanishes as *accidental* and transitory. But, taken by itself, a natural existent like the sun is indifferent, not free and self-conscious in itself . . . [15]

The important aspect of this is that Hegel here identifies the possibility of aesthetics with the establishment or enactment or realisation of a freedom; and that freedom is marked precisely by the fact that it is *not necessity*, that it is 'in excess' of the way things are given to us. On this basis, a relation can be established between autonomy and aesthetics; and the name that we give to that relation has been, traditionally, modernity.

However, I want to argue that this is moving too fast for our present purposes. If we have established that it is a basic, if (self-evidently) *sufficient* condition of human becoming that we live on, then what might we characterise as a further *necessary* condition of that status? The answer is given to us by a kind of tautology: the human is the animal that seeks happiness; alone among the animals, the human is conditioned by *eudaemonia*. This is totalising to the extent that it includes its ostensible opposite: if I claim that I want to be unhappy, then I am also thereby saying that it will make me happy to be unhappy. That is to say, as soon as we begin to characterise the human beyond the most basic level of *zoe*, into *bios*, then it is axiomatic that the *bios* be characterised by eudaemonia.

Teilhard de Chardin wrote about this, in his brief essay *Sur le bonheur* delivered primarily as two lectures in Beijing/Peking in December 1943 (at that time in Japanese, that is, 'enemy', control). He had worked in China, as a palaeontologist concerned with what he called 'the human phenomenon', since the mid-1920s, playing a major part in the discovery of the pre-human (the 'becoming-human') fossil dubbed 'Peking Man' there in 1929.[16] In his lectures, he starts from the basic presupposition that the human being is marked by this fundamental desire to be happy. What distinguishes the human in this is the fact that, as a reflective and a critical being, she or he is not tied to the *immediate* realisation of happiness. The capacity for reflection and for criticism leads to the condition in which the human has a perception of the possible and a perception of the future. The consequence of this is that, whereas other animals proceed directly towards their happiness, happiness becomes for humans much more problematical, introducing fears and hopes, or obstacles of one kind or another in the pursuit of happiness, the pursuit of the basic characteristic that will make me what I am, a human in the process of becoming.[17]

In the face of this, Teilhard distinguishes humanity into three types. For each of them, we can see an equivalent in the groups that he would be addressing, in occupied Beijing, at this time; and we can also see some possible equivalents in the world of twentieth-century theory and criticism. First, there are *les fatigués*, the exhausted ones: these are pessimists who take the view that it would be better never to have been born. In this category, we might find those made miserable in the war; we might also find thinkers such as Adorno or Cioran (on whom more below) or (but this is much more complicated) Beckett. Second, there are *les bons viveurs*: these, fixated on the intensity of the present moment, are the epicures and hedonists. This group might contain those benefiting commercially from the present Chinese predicament; but it might also include some of those later 1970s anti-psychiatrists who celebrated schizophrenia (Laing, Brown and others), or critics concerned with pleasure (Barthes, say) and thinkers associated with the intensities of desire (Lyotard, Deleuze, the authors of a magic realism). The third group identified by Teilhard is that he calls *les ardents*: for these, being is inexhaustible and it is always possible to be more than we are. These are always striving for more and more experience, hungry for life itself and for exceeding themselves. Such a group might include pragmatists such as Teilhard himself, but also those rather neo-Romantic critics who follow the aestheticist line of Hegel: teachers – and here we might draw attention specifically to literature teachers, teachers of the English question, in the institution of the University.

For each of these categories, Teilhard identifies a specific characteristic of happiness. For the first, there is the *bonheur de tranquillité*, the happiness of tranquillity; those in this group would advocate a withdrawal into the self, a diminishing of the self in a rather ascetic fashion. The *bons viveurs*, on the other hand, have the *bonheur de plaisir*, and these advocate that we profit from life and savour the moment. Finally, *les ardents* enjoy the *bonheur de croissance* or *bonheur de développement*, the happiness associated with the feeling that we are exceeding our previously greatest capacities, that we are growing and developing more and more, exponentially and indefinitely. For Teilhard, it is this last category who are truly human, for 'the human is human only insofar as she cultivates herself . . . To be is, first of all, to make and to find oneself': 'l'homme n'est Homme qu'à condition de se cultiver . . . Être, c'est d'abord se faire et se trouver'.[18]

These categories are interesting in that, for Teilhard, they are not really equal possibilities. The first two, in fact – bleak pessimism, bland optimism – are not really identified as the condition of being human at all; it is only in the third condition, that of a kind of neo-Romantic self-cultivation, in which the self is always about-to-be, in which it is 'living on', or, better, characterised by its *survival beyond itself*, that we become truly ourselves, that we become human at last.

Here, then, we are closer to seeing the relation between poetry and survival-as-*bios*; that is to say, we are closer to identifying poetry with the way of living that allows us to exceed our 'bare life' or our *zoe*. Yet there remain some questions here. That this is, for Teilhard, a passion, goes without saying; yet his third position exists precisely as a reaction against the predicament in which he and his audience find themselves: at war, in enemy hands, suffering and awaiting deliverance. Thus, we might say, his third condition, the *bonheur de croissance*, with its establishment of the possibility of self-cultivation, of self-development or of *culture* itself, is precisely based upon the pre-existing condition of pessimism, of having had to withdraw into the self and find a *bonheur de tranquillité*, that 'pre-vents' (comes before, or conditions) that self-cultivation. For Teilhard is lecturing on this precisely because the condition that he advocates is prevented; it is prevented by the feeling that it would have been better never to have been born, the feeling that his audience has regarding the war.

That is to say, the passion for culture here depends precisely upon the passivity that is forced upon the human as a potential victim, as one who faces death. This recalls Pascal, for whom 'all the malaise of humanity derives from one single thing, which is not being able to sit at peace in your room: 'tout le malheur des hommes vient d'une seule chose, qui est de ne savoir pas demeurer en repos dans une chambre'.[19] Unhappiness derives from the fact that we have not learnt the spirit of tranquillity. It is this spirit or condition that I am calling here a 'critical humility'.

It is a humility that comes from the sense of one's own total superfluity, the unnecessity of being, the arbitrariness and absurdity of making a mark, of speaking or expressing when there is nothing to express, and yet the necessity to express it.[20] That is to say, the redundancy here lies in our actually saying anything about a work of art: our task is first and foremost to receive – or, as I have been phrasing it throughout this study, to experience it. All agent-oriented criticism is thus, in a particular sense, grounded in a premature utopianism. More fundamentally, it is simply *premature*, and, to that extent, *prejudicial*, pre-judged: what we used to call 'ideological'.[21]

Cioran would take a very different view of the condition of becoming human from that advanced by Teilhard. In *The Trouble With Being Born*, Cioran argues that 'Unmaking, decreating, is the only task man may take upon himself if he aspires, as everything suggests, to distinguish himself from the Creator'.[22] For Cioran, that Sartrean existentialist notion that 'man is the being whose project is to be God',[23] is simply wrong-headed; here, he effectively reverses it. It is a consequence of this kind of thinking that *failure* is an absolute necessity: 'failure, always *essential*, reveals us to ourselves, permits us to see ourselves as God see us, whereas success distances us from what is most inward in ourselves and indeed in everything'.[24] To Teilhard's demand that we find ourselves, Cioran replies that such a finding is always the discovery of failure, the revelation of failure: the impossibility, as it were, of our ever finding ourselves or ever becoming fully ourselves, fully human. For those of us engaged in the business of aesthetic or cultural criticism, there follows from this logic what could be read as a kind of injunction: 'To look *without understanding* – that is paradise. Hell, then, would be the place where we understand, where we understand too much'.[25]

Putting this crudely, we might suggest that poetry is not there *for us*, that it is not there to be understood by us, to be centred on us, that we are superfluous to it, unnecessary to its survival. However, we can still – should still – engage with it, be there for it, make ourselves available to it in the sense that we should make ourselves available as a potential audience whose receptivity of it will allow it, and us, to be quickened into being, into our becoming human.[26] The humility that I advocate is simply this first response, the responsiveness that has the quality of firstness about it. It is indebted, obviously, to Beckett. To become human is to fail again, fail better.

3 Bearing witness

In short, the condition that I advocate here can be called one of 'bearing witness'. In *Demeure*, Derrida identifies the possibility of witnessing with living on, first in the form of 'an essential kind of generality: is the witness not always a survivor?' he asks. His response is interesting for our purposes here:

> This belongs to the structure of testimony. One testifies only when one has lived longer than what has come to pass. One can take examples as tragic or full of pathos as the survivors of the death camps. But what ties testimony to *survivance* remains a universal structure and covers the whole elementary field of experience. The witness is a survivor . . . the one who survives. This surviving speech must be as exemplarily irreplaceable as the instance of the instant from which it speaks, the instant of death as irreplaceable, as 'my death,' on the subject of which no one other than the dying person can testify. I am the only one who can testify to my death – on the condition that I survive it.[27]

We might think of poetry here as something that can be aligned with 'surviving speech', a verbal act that lives on beyond itself, courtesy of a witness, the audience, whose very passivity is the condition that enables it to be quickened into becoming. In short, the humility of the witness, receiving a 'surviving speech', is what makes possible the *act* of bearing witness in the first place; it is only through such an act that we can reach the condition of allowing a *survival*, a living on of poetry and of the humanity that receives it.

It has been a kind of commonplace of contemporary theoretical criticism that Derrida long ago dispensed with the notion that there might be an intimacy between the speaking voice and a self that could be somehow located in the speech-act. The subscription to a phonologocentrism was based, it was said, upon a metaphysics of presence that was untenable precisely to the extent that it was metaphysical. Yet it is the case that Derrida himself has remained haunted by this kind of question; and, in his later work, he relates the questions of 'where we speak from' to the absolute liminal point of death.

This takes its most obvious turn when he makes a long-postponed engagement with Blanchot, in *Demeure*. *Demeure* is, in my terms, a 'receiving' of *L'instant de ma mort*, a humble passivity before it, an attempt to hear and to bear witness to what it is that 'Blanchot' says/writes or makes available in the displaced description and narrative of his own facing of a firing squad, his own 'instant/instance of dying'. The narrative told by Blanchot is that of a young man who faces death, but who gets a reprieve from the execution of that dying, remaining nonetheless haunted forever by the 'instant/instance' of 'my death'.

The fundamental question from which Derrida begins to listen is the one that asks how intimate is the relation between Blanchot and this 'young man'. It is nowhere acknowledged in the text that we have that Blanchot himself is/was the man in the case; but Derrida holds also a letter, dated 20 July 1994, from Blanchot, whose words seem clearly to identify Blanchot with the young man in the case. This letter acts as a kind of testimony; the question before us now is whether there is a relation obtaining between testimony, bearing witness, or, as I'll call it here, 'confessing', and passion.

To confess is, in a peculiar sense, to identify oneself firmly with the I of one's narrative. 'I stole the ribbon' would be, in this case, to forge an identity between the I who speaks the sentence and a person who stole a ribbon at some other place and time. In this case, this composite I is but an effect of the narrative. Thus far, thus commonplace. However, what is of more interest for present purposes is that a confession is an act that demands to be heard, to be *received*: it demands the passivity of a recipient who will remain passive while the confession is being enunciated. Further, its reception must be such that it is accepted, and that it is accepted as truth. This combination, of reception and acceptance, is what we can call a passionate passivity, a passivity that is precisely impassioned in its receptivity. So: 'I stole the ribbon' requires an audience that humbly receives that confession, and, in so doing, acknowledges humbly the *absolute singularity* of the I who speaks it. This I can speak only on behalf of itself: if I stole the ribbon, then no-one else can have done so. The audience is required to bear witness to the irreplaceable singularity of the speaking I, and, in so doing, acknowledges the I's potentiality for death.

Again, it is Derrida who offers the necessary links here. In *Demeure*, he is at pains to indicate that testimony testifies to an absolute singularity. In testimony, he writes, 'you must believe me because I am irreplaceable'.[28] This is a clear echo of what he had written some four years previously, when, in *The Gift of Death*, he argues that it is death that marks out such an absolute singularity:

> Death is very much that which nobody else can undergo or confront in my place. My irreplaceability is therefore conferred, delivered, 'given,' one can say, by death. . . . It is from the site of death as the place of my irreplace-ability, that is, of my singularity, that I feel called to responsibility. In this sense only a mortal can be responsible.[29]

Responsibility here is given by the fact of facing death, even of (in my terms) *receiving* death, as a gift; as in the Cuban missile crisis above. Receptivity faces the death that is there in testimony; as in the case of Stevens's elite.

Passionate speaking allows us to acknowledge that the voice speaks us; but that it can only do so if it is 'responsible', if it is bearing witness and answering; and to answer, it must hear what is asked. What is asked, simply, is that the other be heard. Another word describing this situation is 'love'; and we might here venture a definition of becoming human in these terms given to us by Auden, writing, in 'September 1, 1939', of another instant constitutive of the promise of death: 'We must love one another or die'.

'We must love one another or die'. The becoming-human, then, is the loving animal. Teilhard's view of love is useful here to some extent. He considered love to be the 'most universal, formidable, and mysterious of cosmic energies', believing that, in a peculiar sense, 'love' uses humanity to further the end of the Universe's grand evolution towards its (theological) centre. It is where he 'humanises' the concept of love, seeing it as something specific to humanity and not just as an abstract play of forces, that he offers us an interesting commentary:

> 'L'Amour 'hominisé' se distingue de tout autre amour parce que le 'spectre' de sa chaude et pénétrante lumière s'est merveilleusement enrichi. Non plus seulement l'attrait unique et périodique, en vue de la fécondité materielle; mais une possibilité, sans limite et sans repos, de contact par l'esprit plus

que par le corps: antennas infiniment nombreuses et subtiles, qui se cherchent parmi les délicates nuances de l'âme; attrait de sensibilisation et d'achèvement réciproques, où la préoccupation de sauver l'espèce se fond graduellement dans l'ivresse plus vaste de consommer, à deux, le Monde.[30]

Here, love is concerned with the survival of the species, with living on; but as more than 'bare life'. Love is that in which we must acknowledge the absolute singularity of the lover and of the loved: in a very specific sense, it is unique on every occasion, non-transferrable, an absolute singularity of an event. The nature of this event is that it transforms passion and passivity (being loved) precisely into action and agency (loving). The lover, as we know from Derrida's work on the politics of friendship, is always 'in advance' of the loved:[31] love in this sense is also, like death, a question of responsibility, of the possibility of answering to an occasion, of (in the terms that are germane specifically to this argument) hearing and being a passive/passionate recipient for poetry. In such passive reception, we can quicken the life of poetry and of the human through the love (the 'I like this poem') that is the consequence of a critical humility.

Without which, what is the point of going on?

CHAPTER 9

Clandestine English

In 2004, the *Cambridge Quarterly* launched a debate around the topic of 'the English Literature degree'. Specifically, it invited responses to a piece by Felicity Rosslyn called 'Literature for the Masses', in which Rosslyn considered the lengthy distance travelled between one kind of 'origin' of English studies (Cambridge at the turn of the twentieth century) and the state of affairs in the supposed mass-system of the early twenty-first century. On one hand, there have been huge successes: the numbers of students for this 'most humane of humanities' as Rosslyn refers to it (alluding to Leavis) increases seemingly exponentially. The student cohort, however, has changed in its levels and modes of preparedness 'now that we have democratised our admissions procedures to the point where there is an institutional place somewhere for virtually anyone who wants it'.[1]

The piece is extremely interesting for the ways in which it characterises the English degree, its students, and a striving for purpose among both teachers and students. Vitally for my present argument, Rosslyn points out that 'we could admit that it [our discipline of English] was content-free without greatly damaging our case, for the important part of what we do so obviously turns on the process of doing it' (8). Now, at one level, it is precisely this kind of evacuation of content from the degree that I have argued to be troubling. However, as we read Rosslyn's piece, it turns out that what we do, essentially, is not entirely content-free; but the content in question is the content of an action. Essentially, at the core of the actual classroom situations she describes, one major outcome is the building of trust among people: one seminar she describes, for a typical example, as 'at the most basic level . . . a display of trust. A few students have trusted one another, and trusted me, enough to say things they genuinely mean' (4). At some level, as Rosslyn describes her own role, she starts to approximate to that condition of *le maître ignorant* described by Rancière: essentially, she becomes a kind of catalyst or focal point around which social and cultural relatedness takes place. What these examples go to show is that we might properly think of our subject as being determined not so much simply by the monumental content of 'the histories of literatures' for which I have argued earlier, but also as being partly determined by the fact that it makes positive things – such as the establishment of a social order built on trust – possible, and makes them happen or come about.

The piece is deserving of more sustained engagement, and in this concluding chapter, I shall return more directly to the very particular specificities of our 'English question', as I take a stand in relation to the current state of affairs. At the centre of Rosslyn's concern, she captures well the discrepancy and distance between what our English QAA-governed 'benchmarks' suggest that we do in English university teaching and the actual facts of the typical reality. Tellingly, she phrases this in a fashion designed to bring back to mind another debate from near the start of the last century. In offering a 'quick description of three ordinary groups in an ordinary week' (8), Rosslyn recalls Virginia Woolf, in that phrase redolent of echoes for those who are 'inside', or for the audience 'fitted' by their substantive engagement with literature. Woolf's despairing plea was for an attention to the inner life against what she saw as the near tyrannical systematisation of 'the novel' and she asked that we '[e]xamine for a moment an ordinary mind on an ordinary day'. Admitting that she was being vague, Woolf there nonetheless asserted that 'the thing we seek' in modern fiction, whether we call it 'life or spirit, truth or reality, this, the essential thing, has moved off, and refuses to be contained any longer in such ill-fitting vestments as we provide'.[2]

The most remarkable thing about Woolf's language and imagery in these celebrated pages on her essay on 'Modern Fiction' is that it is organised almost entirely around an opposition between freedom and autonomy for the writer (which she values) and what she sees as imprisonment, coercion, unscrupulous tyranny and constraint (which she rejects). In Rosslyn's echo of this essay, she is touching a live nerve for those of us involved precisely in the teaching of Woolf and the other figures of the history of English and its associated literatures. When Rosslyn notes that 'much of the value of an English degree derives from things that could never be mentioned in the prospectus' (8), she is, whether by design or not, inviting a comparison in our own time between an institution that is shaped by tyranny on one hand (the QAA and its bureaucratised and managerialist audit-culture in the place of Wells, Bennett, Galsworthy as it were) and freedom, the life of the mind, the 'luminous halo . . . this varying, this unknown and uncircumscribed spirit' (106), however vaguely expressed, on the other.

For some time now, broadly since the inception and growth in importance of the QAA and its surveillance-oriented monitoring culture, it has been clear that there exist not simply two tendencies within the university sector, but actually two universities within each separate institution. The first of these is what might be termed the 'official university', beloved of government agencies and newspapers and that new constituency called 'customers' or 'stakeholders'. This is the university that describes itself in terms of mission statements, research reports, more or less colourful prospectuses and websites, excellence in teaching standards (and who would advertise and boast of anything else?),[3] and so on. It is this institution that inhabits a position in the various, often totally inconsistent, immediately obsolescent league tables that shape what passes, lamentably, for a source of alleged information on the quality of British university education and, within that, of separate identifiable English departments.

There exists, however, another university within the official one. Let us call it the 'clandestine university', the one that is occluded behind the journalistic ease and flash of prospectus and league table, the one that knows itself to be operating somewhat in a subversive fashion in that it refuses to prioritise the official workings of the university and sees its task, instead, as being to get on with what the university fundamentally exists to advance: that Woolfian 'unknown and uncircumscribed spirit'. This clandestine university, interested in the pursuit of the 'unknown' and in the search for the limits of our knowledge, has no truck with teaching as 'knowledge transfer', and is identified precisely with *unknowability*, with teaching and research as a combined *search* for knowledge That quest or questioning is conducted here as, in Seamus Deane's pregnant phrase, a 'reading in the dark'; it is not impressed by claims for various forms of so-called 'transparency'.

It may seem extravagant to describe this as 'clandestine', with its conno-tations of samizdat production and dangerous dissent. However, the relation of the academic to her or his institution has now changed some-what from the structures that pertained when I, for one, entered the profession. Twenty years ago, a colleague who expressed sceptical criticism of the work of her or his department did so in the spirit of dialogue and debate, in which all colleagues searched for the better argument. Dialogue and debate were taken as a mark of serious and substantive solidarity with our discipline and its priorities. Of course, personal and professional rela-tions may have become strained, and even embittered. However, the important point is that the very stakes of such critique are profoundly different today.

Today, by contrast with that past, we need to be clandestine, for many of us are now in the ridiculous – even dangerous – position where we might fear that anything we say can be taken down and held against us: the offi-cial university requires or demands a culture of compliance. Now, any negative-sounding remark we make is seen as potential treachery against the corporate identity and brand, and is therefore dangerous. No doubt that is one reason why, when the editors of the *Cambridge Quarterly* invited the debate around Rosslyn's piece, it agreed to accept that any articles published might – very unusually – be published anonymously: the editors, like many potential contributors to the debate, are aware of what is at stake.

In the earlier state of affairs, dialogue indicated that solidarities with the discipline were profound. In our present condition, the profundity of such allegiances has been systematically attacked. The culture of compliance leaves us with a condition in which the first allegiance to be pledged is, paradoxically, to silence; and, if that silence is to be broken, it is to be broken only by the sound of a branded agreement with a corporate identity. That, clearly, is purely superficial, because brands change with the coming-and-going of Vice-Chancellors or PR departments.

More importantly still, the silence is one that goes well beyond individual institutions and disciplines and extends across the entire tertiary education project. To dissent from the current dominant ideology of the 'instrumentalist' degree, from the wilful mistaking of homogenisation for democratisation, from the merely economistic version of the University, and from the platitudes of 'modernisation' that govern these things, is to mark oneself out as a fly in the smoothing ointment, and, worse, as a fly whose buzzing is simply disregarded – silenced – on the grounds that it is not a legitimate part of the branding operation that puts the misleading label on the ointment jar. The voice of the critic within, as it were, is no longer taken to be in any form or function *representative*; for the culture requires that voices be managed and not represented. The possibility of friendship – or of Rosslyn's trust – is essentially damaged; and if such a possibility is to persist, it cannot do so in the terms given us by our surveillance-oriented structures.

Both universities – official and clandestine – organise themselves around structures of trust in authority. The official university places its trust in abstract and general systems that may have no purchase on truth or reality but that obey a transparent, if tyrannical, logic (those clear and distinct ideas given by the ordinal numbers in a league table; those algorithmically deduced sums of money disbursed by HEFCE (the Higher Education Funding Council for England, that one-time non-politicised funding council for UK universities). The clandestine university places its trust in human beings working together, engaged in risk-taking argument and dialogue. These, clearly, give two entirely different inflections to the nature of the University institution. More importantly for present purposes, both offer entirely distinct versions of freedom.

Our freedoms are not naturally occurring and are, of course, regulated by authorities. As I argued at the start of this study, the authorities in question used to be those of medicine, law and economics. I also proposed that, at the very core of these authorities – insofar as they are authorities that can be legitimised in the public domain – is a certain poetry or rhetoric. My claim and argument is that the very institution that should be forging the greatest kinds of intellectual – and other – freedoms, the institution that is the University, is being placed in a position where, thanks to essentially inhumane governmental directive and ideology, it actually imposes constrains on poetry or literature, by which I mean that it imposes constraints on what is thinkable, on the imagination and, by extension, on our possibilities for imagining a future that might be otherwise than the present. The question is how we got here; or why we have not attended properly to Woolf's argumentation and position in 'Modern Fiction'.

The argument is important for those of us engaged in English, not simply as part of a clichéd jeremiad about contemporary conditions, nor as part of an already much-rehearsed argument about the place of English within a massified tertiary education sector. Its importance lies more firmly in terms of the question concerning the relation of English to *freedom*, which was, after all, Woolf's primary concern – and which should remain ours.

The freedom I have in mind here is not that framed by the specific parameters of 'academic freedom', as outlined by Jaspers in 1946, when academic freedom was explicitly related to relations between the academy, or 'official' science and knowledge and the State (in a hoped-for post-Nazi Europe); rather, what I want to attend to is the deployment of English as part of a more general emancipation, in which reading contributes to an ever-increasing general freedom.[4] This freedom is essentially characterised by the exploration of the unknown: it is not strictly a search for knowledge, for it accepts that knowledge, by definition, is always subject to change. Rather, then, it is a search for the *limits* of knowledge, and hence is typified by a drive towards unknowability. It is a common pursuit, certainly; but the object of the pursuit is necessarily unclear, always to-be-discovered through the process of the pursuit. The obvious corollary here is that the very 'commonality' of the pursuit, its establishment of community as such, is always about-to-come. The community that shares the pursuit is not already established or already given (as, for examples, a class or 'raced' or gendered community), for such an already known and acknowledged identity would of necessity narrow and identify the parameters within which what passes for truth is accepted. The identity of such a community would be consolidated, consoled even, and certainly confirmed by the pursuit and discovery of what it secretly already knows: its own intrinsic value. Instead, then, we are seeking here what Agamben thinks of as a 'coming community'; the very search is itself constitutive of the communality of the pursuit.

This does not assume an already established identity for the reader (as being, say, 'gay', 'of colour', 'gendered' for examples); rather, it takes as its task the *production* of a new and ever-changing community: an identity as alterity, a being as becoming, a knowing as learning.

In this state of affairs, we might look historically at the ways in which we have related the 'life of the mind' (perhaps a key concern of a University) to the practical activities that seem to establish or to enact our freedom as such: the ways in which we have related consciousness to history, theory to practice, the academy and its intellectuals to society and its workers. There have been various metaphors that have governed our conception of this. To Hobbes, for example, the totality of society could be productively imaged as a body, governed by a head; the analogy is with a head of state governing several and diverse corporate affairs in such a way as to regulate and unify those affairs. That imagery is taken from similar poetic tropes dating back at least to Spenser and Charles d'Orléans, and behind that to medieval and classical allegory. Later, we start to think of the social in terms or rather organic metaphors, derived essentially from the language of agriculture. Thus, we have 'fields' of study, 'areas' of inquiry, giving us relative degrees of 'cultivation', with a 'fertility' or 'fecundity' of ideas contributing to economic 'growth' or 'development'. This – essentially a continuation and furthering of the metaphor of 'the body-politic' – persists even through the industrial revolution; but it starts to undergo a shift as that revolution itself offers new possibilities for new governing metaphors. Then, the social as machine, regulated in terms of input and output and efficiency, comes to replace the organism. We edge towards something close to where we are now, in the well-described 'administered society' in which, rather than having a body (work) governed by a head (intellect) or a history governed by consciousness, we have essentially a self-regulating and autonomous *system* driving the whole. It is important to note that, in this, what is being governed now is effectively *unreflective* work and *unconscious* history. In the metaphor of systematisation, we lose the very idea of autonomous control of our own history: the body works as a totality, not as something governed by conscious motivation, or by self-critical drives or desires.

Importantly, however, another metaphor has been conjoined with this to give us the specific flavour of our contemporary condition. In 1984, during the infamous miners' strike which Mrs Thatcher explicitly saw in terms of a class warfare, she and her partners in the National Coal Board, especially Ian McGregor, indulged in a somewhat despicable rhetoric whose key phrase was 'the *rights* of managers to manage' (my emphasis). If there was anything in that rhetoric that relates to freedom, it was this: a freedom for managers to restrict and control or regulate the freedoms of those whom they managed. The whole of the systematic structure of society was now to be governed itself by a model based on 'business' and its codes of *management*. Thus, the social and all our human interactions should now be seen in business terms, as a series of 'investments' that we might make (in education, for example) in the interests of efficient productivity (not growth in any organic sense, but simply the production of money, especially for ourselves as individuals, given that 'There is no society; there are only individuals and their families', as Thatcher put it). With this modification of the systems metaphor, we now find that we do in fact have a motivating force for history after all: not our consciousness, but our managers. However, there is now this important difference (different even from Thatcher's time – if possible, worse): managers are themselves *part of* the system, and are therefore not responsible for anything they do, since it is the system as such that is autonomous. This gives us that condition in which we now find ourselves: a structure of power without responsibility.

Managerialism, as I indicated in an earlier chapter, is the very antithesis of managing. Managing requires decisions, human and humane interventions, risks and responsibilities. Managerialism is designed to ensure that no-one can ever be held personally accountable for anything, even in the midst of an ever-growing talk of accountabilities and an ever increasing litigation culture. Managerialism works by what we might call the 'delegation of blame' through the prioritisation of processes over actualities; so that when, for example, we have an inquiry into any ostensibly damaging action in the public sphere, the enquiry can no longer be into actual decisions but only the processes and systems that governed the troubling actions. (On a larger scale than my present concern, of course, that is the story of various inquiries into the Iraq War and the British government's position on British participation.)

This, with the concomitant effect in cultural ideology that places the 'Business School' rather than philosophy, say, at the centre of our university institutions, has a major impact on the relations between teaching, research and freedom, especially within English studies.

For an analysis of this, we might usefully turn to Benjamin's most frequently (and often trivially) cited essay, 'The Work of Art in the Age of Mechanical Reproduction'. Put very briefly, part of the weight of that article derives from two combined observations. First, the work of art prior to mechanical reproduction is, as it were, replete with its historical locatedness; but, in reproduced condition, what we get is an evacuation of the historical specifics that shape and inform the work 'as such'. The consequence of this is that we start to consider work in terms of its aesthetic form, forgetting or failing to see that the form itself depended upon a content that we once knew as historical specificity. Secondly, Benjamin relates this to a wider political phenomenon in which the social legitimises itself in purely formal fashion, emptied of any content. Thus, for example, where people – 'the masses' – 'have a right to change property relations', he points out that Fascism 'sees its salvation in giving these masses not their right, but instead a chance to express themselves'.[5]

From this, we might, for present and shorthand purposes, suggest a general principle that institutions in which legitimacy is gained by formal method, rather than by attending to the specifics of content, are fundamentally aligned with an ideology that is not interested in freedom but rather in constraint. In (polemical) short: the QAA (by this point, I am using this abbreviation to cover a whole culture of managerialist surveillance – but I also mean the QAA in its own specificity as well) is an incipiently 'fascist' mechanism which, in pretending to offer all sorts of 'assurances', in fact operates to assure only one thing: the impossibility of a fundamental gaining of freedom, considered as the freedom of an uncircumscribed spirit seeking participation in a coming community. Instead of this, QAA reduces freedom to the merest notion of a 'freedom of choice', in which prospective students (who, by definition, *cannot know in advance* what they want) are 'enabled' to choose between competing institutions and programmes (their choice being based on already existing and already given – i.e., not to be changed – identities). QAA and all its governmentally-driven works are shaped by the freedom of the consumer (actually an enslavement, of course), not the freedom of the citizen.

It is this latter freedom, the freedom to become a citizen, that the clandestine university organises itself around; and it is fundamentally at odds with the consumerist 'freedom' of the customer as celebrated by the official institution and by a Murdoch- or Fox-frightened government.

As is well known, the QAA was/is never interested in the actual content of teaching: it simply measures formal procedures. If my published schedule said that I would be discussing Racine, say, in week 6, then I had to make sure that when the inspectors arrived in week 6, my seminar was indeed focused on Racine. The fact that students might have become so engrossed in Molière the week previously that they wished to defer discussion of Racine to further their engagement in thinking about comedy would only redound negatively on our QAA result. What the QAA has contributed to is the growing tendency within our contemporary culture more generally to legitimise and to even evaluate activity on grounds that have effectively been hollowed out of any content, any meaning. And yet, formally, we have more validation and procedures for legitimisation than ever before. 'Light touch' is to audit as computers are to paper: it promises less, but needs and generates more.

One can see this at every level within English teaching. In the 'official' university, English has no content whatsoever (QAA does not care *what* we teach at all), and has been reduced to a set of instrumentalist 'skills' (sometimes called 'learning outcomes'). The great and abiding paradox of our time, however, is how university English has been too often complicit with precisely this tendency. Ominously coterminous with the rise and demise of Thatcher, 'English' became a site of contention in the universities, thanks to a ferment of debate around what was conveniently called 'theory', where the focus of interest lay more or less explicitly in questions of legitimisation, valuation, and power. Those of us who were centrally involved in these 'debates' (debates where the opponents didn't really speak to each other too much) felt rather passionately that we were contributing to general emancipatory movements. However, the net result of the struggle is somewhat ambiguous. On one hand, we are now able to welcome fully into our areas of concern texts that have been recuperated, re-quickened to pressing life, brought into view from their occluded positions. On the other hand, and at the same time, the forms of attention that are given to these texts have become too often homogenised, stratified, reduced to purely formal exercises in tracing the play and effects of power along lines of class, 'race', gender and so on. I do not mean to deny the importance of these issues, for they are among the most pressing for those of us concerned with freedom. However, a genuine interest in freedom would not reduce the singularity of a specific woman, say, to a representation of woman-as-such in a critical exercise. That is, it would not generalise or 'theorise' from the historical specifics of a fully particularised case to a more general state of affairs in which the specific is brought into line with a formal template.

When some university teachers argued that it was more important to teach students *how* to read than it was to give guidance in *what* to read, they were, often despite themselves, becoming complicit with the evacuation of content from the university degree, and reducing English to a set of skills (this time allegedly theoretically informed skills; but skills nonetheless).[6] The same process is happening on a larger scale nationally, of course; and it would not be too rash a prediction to suggest that in the not too distant future we will find that we have a governmental 'Department for Skills', with the education erased from its brief almost entirely. After all, for the last two decades or more, British governments at least have been reluctant to let education stand with its own dedicated portfolio, preferring to link it either to work, to skills (as the work of the artisan becomes more important than that of the industrialist) or, most recently, to childcare (in the 'Every Child Matters' brief).[7]

Students pay for their education now, of course (as, in fact, they always have done through progressive taxation, even in earlier grant-giving days); what they are buying is a certain freedom, but it is the vacuous (and, in the end unethical) freedom of the consumer, a freedom that has no content other than the contents of one's wallet. If we would save the freedom of the citizen from those government agencies that serve to curtail it, we need to re-pack English with content. What this means, of course, is the explicit denial that there is anything such as 'knowledge-transfer' in our practices. Reading is precisely the *search* for knowledge in the first place. Further, it requires the explicit denial of any project that sees English and the university as things that operate in the service of business, the economy, or the wider community's identity. Reading is precisely the *search* for what the meaning of community might be or might become; it is the making of a community, not the serving of some already stable and identified community ('the English', the 'middle (or any other) classes', 'GB plc', 'employers' and so on).

In this way, the 'ordinary' becomes what it also has become in a proper exercise of reading: the extraordinary, that breaking of the boundaries of what is accepted or acceptable and that we more commonly know under the name and sign of freedom. Thankfully, such freedoms are still available, but only in our clandestine activities.

Let me return to an opening gesture. English occupies a special place for the elucidation of this freedom, and it was Vico who set up essentially a similar kind of opposition to that which I am describing here. Fundamentally, in his *Orations*, he set the ancient eloquence tradition of Aristotle against the new Cartesian systematisation of modern *method* (which we would call 'process' or system) that, in its clear and distinct ideas (or 'transparency'), would grant us the forms of truth (as in abstractions such as mathematics) without the necessity of any content: $2 + 2 = 4$, certainly; but it is a different matter entirely if we seek to add two men to two women, say, as in some typical comedies by Shakespeare. For Vico, eloquence occupied a regulating terrain between what he thought of as *sapientia* (the wisdom of a self-knowledge, but a self-knowledge that is not psychological, biographical or even much interested in introspection) and *prudential* (the kind of acting that would lead to *civility*, to the possibilities of our living together in a community).[8]

To pack English with content is to rehabilitate eloquence, to think of our pedagogical task as being somewhat akin to that of the poets: acting as curators of the language and of its possibilities. And the poets, of course, are the most clandestine figures of all: whoever knows what it is that they might mean? It is in the content of their work – in literature – that we may find what we seek: the capacity to emancipate an otherwise circumscribed spirit, Prospero's difficult farewell to Ariel, the future. That, of course, is genuinely historical and potentially critical – even dangerous; and for that reason, the clandestine University – with its teachers who try to *teach* in complete disregard of prescriptive mediocrity-generating, limiting benchmarks; with its researchers who carry out research, sometimes without the hypothesised outcomes but generating instead the joy and potential of surprise, and so without a primary eye on the crude quantifiers of RAE and the like – has been forced into its present position. Thankfully, it survives.

If we are concerned, as we ought to be, for the kinds of freedom celebrated by Woolf at the start of the last century, then we might begin to demonstrate that concern by fighting to regain some of our institutional freedoms, to recover the content of English to give ourselves the English Question. Otherwise, we find ourselves in the position of a treacherous clerisy, betraying the very idea and principles of a University education in English – and, even more importantly, betraying our students and our citizens.

And then, we might be in a position to start to consider what it might mean to pose the English Question, what it might mean to reinstate trust, friendship and the possibilities of freedom.

Notes

1 The English Question

1 It may be useful here to offer, as a context for the work of Leavis but also for the present study, the famous comment by Adorno, that 'To write poetry after Auschwitz is barbaric' (see Adorno, *Prisms*, trans. Samuel and Shierry Weber; MIT Press, Cambridge, MA, 1983), 34. It is not just the 'after-Auschwitz', however; we are also 'after Hiroshima' and, more recently, after 9/11. What is the place and importance of English in relation to questions of freedom after these trauma? For a preliminary consideration of this larger question in the present context, see also Adorno's 'Education after Auschwitz' in his *Critical Models* (trans. Henry W. Pickford; Columbia University Press, New York, 1998), 191–204.

2 The war to which this refers is not the Iraq war; rather, I mean to suggest that we have never properly moved on from the legacy of 1945. For a fuller exploration of this, see, for example, the work of Giorgio Agamben with its shocking suggestion that the concentration camps of the Second World War remain with us and that the war haunts us in the figure of the ever-present refugee. I comment on this in more detail in my *Aesthetic Democracy* (Stanford University Press, Stanford, 2006), 89–110.

3 Stefan Collini's perceptive insight that what is at stake here is essentially a fundamental inability to deal properly with the legacy of the Industrial Revolution in England is surely correct. See his introduction to his edition of C. P. Snow, *The Two Cultures* (Cambridge University Press, 1993).

4 To push my joking Snow White analogy further, of course, these scientists would be akin to the labouring seven dwarfs, heigh-ho-ing off to their various labours, happy or grumpy, bashfully modest or absent-mindedly dopey and so on. The point of the joke is really to suggest that the Disney story is also a story about the relation of science to prosperity, and more importantly the competing powers of grafting labour by 'small' bourgeois people against aristocratic love in these matters. The paradox is that it is Snow who is on the side of labour, while Leavis looks to 'mediate' labour and love.

5 This is not the place to look at the detail here; but it is worth looking at exactly what it is that Leavis prized in writers such as George Eliot or Conrad or Lawrence, say, and to see it in terms of a regulation of sense and sensibility. Interestingly, there is a suggestion, in some of his work, that there are clear political corollaries of his preferences, as in his attention to issues of Judaism in *Daniel Deronda* or his attitudes to 'the Levantine' that appear in his thoughts on doctoral research in Cambridge.

6   This word has become a rather cant term in contemporary political discourse. It has been evacuated of any actual meaning, and is used rhetorically simply to win an argument, for who would be against 'modernisation'? By using it here, I am trying to restore some of its semantic content: to indicate that it has something to do with progress and advancement, with being *avant-garde* – and, crucially for this book, that in this sense, it is tied firmly to the form and function of the University institution.

7   I am borrowing the term 'pagan' here from Jean-François Lyotard's work, in which the pagan is she or he who is from the 'pagus' (in French, *pays*): it has the sense of the person who is on the margins of an established social order, one from the 'surrounding' environment: a peasant, in the most positive sense of the term (but for me, without any Maoist overtones). See also Murray G. Ross, *The University* (McGraw-Hill, 1979).

8   It would be interesting here to compare the kind of analysis of the rhetoric of irony put forward by Paul de Man in his famous 'Rhetoric of Temporality' essay. In that essay, he makes a fundamental move that is key to his entire literary and critical philosophy. In an examination of Baudelaire's essay 'De l'essence du rire', he is able to set up a quasi-normative state of affairs in which matters of consciousness can be aware of historical and material realities, but, through the very fact of self-consciousness (or *dédoublement*, as he calls it), are caught in a predicament whereby the consciousness spirals ever further away from the historical, even as it becomes more aware of it. For the full argument on this, see my *After Theory* (revised and expanded edn; Edinburgh University Press, Edinburgh, 1996), 119–41.

9   R. D. Anderson, *Universities and Elites* (Cambridge University Press, 1995), 17.

10 The most immediate result of this is apparent in virtually every social formation that has a principle of 'selection' in its schooling: from the madness that is the 'eleven-plus' to the bureaucratic nightmare that is the baccalaureat, it is mathematics that determines who gets 'selected' and who is rejected. English has no central place in this, even in the Anglophone world.

11 For the idea of 'cultural capital', see, for example, Pierre Bourdieu, *Distinction* (1979; trans. Richard Nice; Routledge, 1984) or John Guillory, *Cultural Capital* (University of Chicago Press, Chicago, 1993). See also the moment in Shakespeare's *The Tempest* (1: ii) when Ferdinand meets Miranda and hears her speak. He is shocked to hear 'My language! Heavens! / I am the best of them that speak this speech, / Were I but where 'tis spoken.'

12 James Shapiro, in discussion with Trevor Nunn. Programme notes for RSC production of *King Lear*, Stratford-on-Avon, March 2007.

13 Francis Bacon, *The Advancement of Learning*, ed. Arthur Johnston (Clarendon Press, Oxford, 1974; repr. 1980), 4.

14 On this issue of aestheticism, the object of criticism is not the aesthete as such, but rather the aesthete who is *self-regarding*: i.e., the person who considers it more important to be seen to be or to show oneself of as 'a person of taste' than simply to exercise taste and judgement. For fuller arguments

on this kind of position generally, though not with regard to Bacon, see, for examples, Pierre Bourdieu, *Distinction*; Giorgio Agamben, *L'Uomo senza contenuto* (Rizzoli, Milano, 1970; repr. 1974); John Joughin and Simon Malpas, eds., *The New Aestheticism* (Manchester University Press, Manchester, 2003); and Thomas Docherty, *Aesthetic Democracy* (Stanford University Press, Stanford, 2006).

15 Samuel Johnson, *Lives of the English Poets: A Selection* (Dent, 1975), 11.

16 G. W. F. Hegel, *Introductory Lectures on Aesthetics*, ed. Michael Inwood (trans. Bernard Bosanquet; Penguin, 1993), 4. For a fuller commentary on this, see my *Criticism and Modernity*.

17 John Milton, 'Comus', lines 662–5, in *Poems*, ed. B. A. Wright (Dent, 1956; repr. 1976), 67

18 There is, in fact, a third possibility: 'I am not free now, but I can be free and will be free in the future'. This is freedom-as-possibility, to which my present argument is sympathetic, but which is difficult to attain under the terms of the mind–body dualism that shapes our construction of the institution.

19 Richard Rorty, *Achieving Our Country* (Harvard University Press, Cambridge, MA, 1998), 14.

20 It was, of course, the utter vacuity of the ever-present notion of 'excellence' that was a central target in Bill Readings's posthumously published study of *The University in Ruins* (Harvard University Press, Cambridge, MA, 1996).

21 On this distinction between the legal and the legitimate, see, for example, Jürgen Habermas, *Legitimation Crisis* (1973; trans. Thomas McCarthy; Heinemann, 1976).

22 Jacques Rancière, *Le maître ignorant* (Fayard, Paris, 1987), 22 (my translation).

23 An alternative source for this kind of thinking might be found in Pope's 'Essay on Criticism' which might productively be read as, among other things, a poem that argues for sovereignty as the establishment of freedom against a rule-bound administration. See especially lines 150–62.

24 John Carey's work over the last two decades seems to be increasingly indebted to a certain journalism. Essentially, he has turned to defend what might be called the 'middle-brow', and legitimises this by a claim that suggests he is defending the 'ordinary' reader against the snobbish and elitist 'intellectual'. He fails to see that reading is that process that renders the ordinary extraordinary; and thereby reveals the extraordinariness of the very readers that he (patronisingly) characterises as 'ordinary'.

25 A. N. Whitehead, *The Aims of Education* (1932; repr. Ernest Benn, 1959), 138–9.

26 'Information' is *like* knowledge, but with the content of the knowledge – all its efficacy – removed: it is like decaffeinated coffee, alcohol-free lager and so on.

27 Rainer Maria Rilke, 'Archaic Torso of Apollo'. In relation to this, we might also compare the arguments advanced by Ortega y Gasset in his 1930 'Misión de la universidad', in *Obras* completas, tomo IV (Alianza Editorial, Revista de

Occidente, Madrid, 1983), or in Julien Benda, *La Trahison des clercs* (1927; repr. Bernard Grasset, Paris, 1975).

28 It could be worse, of course. One might consider the costs of maintaining the QAA and all its works; and one might add in the massive drain on scarce resources caused by the utterly decadent growth of auditing work, and its intrinsic support of managerialism over management, within the University sector as a whole. See also John Stuart Mill, *Utilitarianism* (Dent, 1993); and Strohl, 'The postmodern university revisited', *London Review of Education*, 4: 2 (2006), 133–48.

29 Marx, *The Eighteenth Brumaire of Louis Bonaparte* (Foreign Languages Press, Peking, 1978), 13.

2 The Fate of Culture: *Die Welt ist Alles*

1 Though the readership is thus divided, into those who know and those who don't, my text here tries almost immediately to reunite them by identifying the source. It might be more precise still to identify a third group, one that would have recognised Wittgenstein had he been quoted in English translation, but who hear only an echo of the English phrase with which they are familiar, 'The world is everything that is the case', in the original German. See Ludwig Wittgenstein, *Tractatus Logico-Philosophicus* (German text with English trans. by C. K. Ogden; Routledge, 1922; repr. 1992).

2 Frank Kermode, *The Genesis of Secrecy* (Harvard University Press, Cambridge, MA, 1979), 2.

3 A yet more crude way of thinking this is that offered by governments: should we 'widen access' so that those usually 'outside', those usually 'excluded', can now be included, brought inside? In what follows, I shall have more to say on how we might understand the issue of 'public access'.

4 See Jean-François Lyotard, *The Postmodern Condition* (trans. Geoff Bennington and Brian Massumi; Manchester University Press, 1984). It is always worth recalling that this text was initially presented as a report on knowledge formation commissioned by the Conseil des Universités of the government of Québec. It is perhaps most productively seen as a contribution not to 'the postmodern debate' but rather to the condition of contemporary education in a post-colonial environment.

5 Margaret Hodge, then minister for higher education in the British government, in an answer to the parliamentary select committee on education, January 2002.

6 It is worth noting in passing that the British public appears to be happy to fund a national health service or a police service directly through taxation, even though it is the case that most individuals would probably hope that they never require the service provided: most, axiomatically, would not wish to be the victims of illness or of crime, but accept that, although not all individuals benefit from these services *as individuals*, nonetheless they benefit from them as members of a society. The same does not appear to be the case with

education, which politicians have successfully translated into a game of personal rewards, personal benefits, higher pay for specific individuals – and this against the manifest evidence that while the effect of gaining a BA, say, is positive in wage terms, that of gaining the MA is neutral, and that of gaining a PhD is negative.

7 Note that I am not deploying the notion of 'dwelling' here in the sense ascribed to it by Heidegger.

8 See Bill Readings, *The University in Ruins* (Harvard University Press, Cambridge, MA, 1996). For a fuller engagement with this issue than I can provide here, see my *Criticism and Modernity: Aesthetics, Literature and Nations in Europe and its Academies* (Oxford University Press, 1999), especially chs. 6–7, pp. 163–245.

9 Readings, *University*, 2.

10 Wim Wenders, *Im Lauf der Zeit* (1976); Lyotard, *Postmodern Condition*, 76.

11 Readings, *University*, 90.

12 Here, then, the world is not 'everything that is the case' but rather 'everything insofar as it signifies'. Wittgenstein followed his opening gambit in the *Tractatus* with another: 'Ein Satz kann nur sagen, wie ein Ding ist, nicht was es ist' (proposition 3.221) – 'A proposition can only say *how* a thing is, not *what* it is'. Wittgenstein thus offers here a legitimation of the activity of Cultural Studies; yet it remains to ask whether the proper purpose of the study of culture would be to say 'what' a thing is, not just 'how' it is, to see its quiddity and not just its mode of operation or function.

13 Readings, *University*, 99.

14 Ibid., 102.

15 Victimhood here applies also to the individuals supposedly at the centre of this (absent) 'culture': white Eurocentric colonialist males (one could add to the description, but the gist is clear). It is worthy of note that even critics such as Allan Bloom could present themselves – *had* to present themselves – as 'outsiders', victims of some feminist/lesbian/black/Hispanic (add the further adjectives) conspiracy against the 'culture' of which he was a product.

16 Readings, *University*, 113.

17 Geoffrey H. Hartman, *The Fateful Question of Culture* (Columbia University Press, New York, 1997), 26.

18 T. S. Eliot, 'Tradition and the Individual Talent', in *Selected Essays* (1932; repr. 2nd edn, Faber and Faber, 1980), 16. In citing Eliot here, it should not be assumed that I endorse the entirety of his commentary on culture or tradition. There is much in his *Notes towards the Definition of Culture* (Faber and Faber, 1948), such as the argument for the necessity of maintaining class distinctions, for one example, with which I would take issue. Centrally, however, I would argue against the conception of culture as the kind of archival body of texts that Eliot seems to take it to be in that book. However, his comments on the dead in the 'Tradition' essay are apposite here.

19 Matthew Arnold, *Culture and Anarchy*, ed. J. Dover Wilson (Cambridge University Press, 1971), *passim*.

20 On the 'leisure-merchants' and how they are anathema to culture as such, see André Gorz, *Farewell to the Working Class* (trans. Michael Sonenscher; Pluto Press, 1982) and *Critique of Economic Reason* (trans. Gillian Handyside and Chris Turner; Verso, 1989).

21 See Immanuel Kant, *The Critique of Pure Reason* (2nd edn, 1787; trans. J. M. D. Meiklejohn; Dent, 1934), esp. 28–32.

22 Emmanuel Levinas, *La mort et le temps* (Editions de l'Herne, Paris, 1991), 13. For a fuller argumentation of the relation of literature to death, see my essay 'Deconstruction not reading politics', in Martin McQuillan, ed., *Deconstruction Reading Politics* (Clinamen, Manchester, 2007), and the fuller version of the case in my *Aesthetic Democracy* (Stanford University Press, 2006).

23 See, in relation to this, Jean Baudrillard, *Pour une critique de l'économie politique du signe* (Gallimard, Paris, 1972) and, yet more pointedly, his *L'Echange symbolique et la mort* (Gallimard, Paris, 1976).

24 See Maurice Blanchot, *The Work of Fire* (1949; trans. Charlotte Mandell; Stanford University Press, Stanford, 1995), 313.

3 On Reading

1 Bernhard Schlink, *The Reader* (trans. Carol Brown Janeway; Phoenix, 1997), 186. Who has not felt the same as this, watching a child learn to read? It is worth noting also that the translator here, in making the German text available to me, has effectively been *my* reader, 'reading' the book to me in her act of translation/writing. Such translation creates 'a strange combination of distance and immediacy' (ibid., 117); and such a combination will be central to my argument below.

2 For a poignant example of this, see chapter 16 of Charles Dickens, *Bleak House*; and cf. the commentary on this in Valentine Cunningham, 'Reading now and then', in Brian Cox, ed., *Literacy is not enough* (Manchester University Press, 1998), 9–11.

3 For an explanation of 'situatedness', see two recent books by David Simpson, *Situatedness* (Duke University Press, 2002) and *The Academic Postmodern* (University of Chicago Press, 1995). In the political context, the opposition here is that between the subject considered as consumer and as citizen; for an explanation of the stakes of this in relation to democracy, see Larry Siedentop, *Democracy in Europe* (Penguin, 2000).

4 John Milton, *Paradise Lost*, Bk. VII, ll. 30–33; see also David Trotter, *The Making of the Reader* (Macmillan, 1984). I shall turn to the question of Modernist art in more specific detail when I discuss 'The Aesthetic Event' below.

5 See Frank Kermode, *The Genesis of Secrecy* (Harvard University Press, Cambridge, MA, 1979). 'Widening participation' in University education is a stated aim of British government policy since 1998, directed at bringing

into such education individuals from social groups and classes where it has not been the norm or the expectation. Those 'outside' are to be called 'inside'; but, as Kermode's 1979 analysis shows, and as Milton would have believed, this is no simple piece of social engineering solved by an administrative or bureaucratic procedure.

6 Harold Bloom, *A Map of Misreading* (Oxford University Press, 1975), 3; Paul de Man, *Allegories of Reading* (Yale University Press, 1979), 58; J. Hillis Miller, *The Ethics of Reading* (Columbia University Press, 1987), 3.

7 Eric Bolton, 'Introduction; why books matter', in Cox, ed., *Literacy*, 2.

8 I. A. Richards, *How to Read a Page* (Routledge and Kegan Paul, 1943), 10.

9 Jane Austen, *Emma* (1816; repr. Penguin, 1966), 58, 77.

10 Matthew Arnold, *Culture and Anarchy* (1869; repr. Cambridge University Press, 1971), 6–7.

11 For fuller details of the controversy, see James Winter, *Robert Lowe* (University of Toronto Press, Toronto, 1976), esp. 159–94; and cf. A. Patchett Martin, *Life and Letters of Robert Lowe, Viscount Sherbrooke*, vol. II (Longman, Green & Co, 1893), 210–35. In recent times, the equivalent would have been to take the side of a French philosopher who became a minister for education, such as Luc Ferry, against an English northern radical who became a British Secretary of State for education, David Blunkett. The former's ideas were influenced by a general philosophy of education and of human being, the latter's were influenced by Ron Dearing, formerly of that great information-transfer organisation, the Post Office.

12 The terms 'culture merchants' and 'leisure merchants' are borrowed from the work of Adorno and of Gorz. See, especially, André Gorz, *Farewell to the Working Class* (1980; trans. Michael Sonenscher; Pluto, 1982).

13 Plato's arguments pertinent here are from *Republic*, especially Bks II, III, X; and cf. George Steiner, *Language and Silence* (Penguin, 1969), 29.

14 See George Steiner, *No Passion Spent* (Faber and Faber, 1996), 3–5; cf. Italo Calvino's great novel about the reader, *If on a winter's night a traveller* (1979; trans. William Weaver, Picador, 1982), 10–11, and also his *Why Read the Classics?* (1991; trans. Martin McLaughlin; Vintage, 2000), 9: 'reading the classics is always better than not reading them'.

15 See Steiner, '"Critic"/"Reader"', repr. in Philip Davis, ed., *Real Voices on Reading* (Macmillan, 1997).

16 Roland Barthes, *Image-Music-Text* (trans. Stephen Heath; Fontana, 1977), 148.

17 Barthes, *The Rustle of Language* (1984; trans. Richard Howard; Blackwell, Oxford, 1986), 41. This in turn generates the sense of reading as *délire* in Lecercle and Deleuze.

18 Marcel Proust, *A la recherche du temps perdu*, ed. J.-Y. Tadié *et al.* (Pléiade; Gallimard, Paris, 1987), I: 601.

19 Fredric Jameson, *The Political Unconscious* (Methuen, 1981), 9. A recent comic version of this same predicament is in Umberto Eco, *Baudolino* (2000;

trans. William Weaver; Secker & Warburg, 2002), 89–91.
20   Alberto Manguel, *A History of Reading* (Flamingo, 1997), 93.
21   Steiner, *Language and Silence*, 26.
22   T. S. Eliot, 'Tradition and the Individual Talent', in *Selected Essays* (Faber and Faber, 1932; repr. 1980), 15.
23   Maurice Blanchot, *The Work of Fire* (1949; trans. Charlotte Mandell; Stanford University Press, Stanford, 1995), 337. Cf. Blanchot and Derrida, *The Instant of my Death* and *Demeure* (1994, 1998; trans. Elizabeth Rottenberg; Stanford University Press, Stanford, 2000).

4   The Question concerning Literature

1   It is worth noting, at the outset, the difference between two questions: 'What is literature?', which invites a rather open response ('this' is literature, or 'that' is; and so on); and 'Literature is what?', which invites a closed response, a strict definition. It is this latter question that has usually been addressed by a criticism that wants to 'explode' the boundaries or category of the literary.
2   For a fuller consideration of these questions in some historical detail, see, respectively, Bill Readings, *The University in Ruins* (Harvard University Press, Cambridge, MA, 1996); and Thomas Docherty, *Criticism and Modernity: Aesthetics, Literature and Nations in Europe and its Academies* (Oxford University Press, 1999).
3   Terry Eagleton, *Literary Theory* (Blackwell, Oxford, 1983), 1. Subsequent page references in parentheses in text. Note, in passing, that these other ostensibly 'non-literary' texts could not be called 'factual' at all; they are all grounded in imaginings, in 'essaying' or assaying ideas.
4   William Cowper, 'The Task' in *The Poetical Works of William Cowper* (John Kendrick, 1852), 251.
5   For how this is understood in the American academy, see Richard Rorty, *Achieving our Country* (Harvard University Press, Cambridge, MA, 1998), where Rorty points out that the 'excluded' in this situation is itself a category that excludes those who are the 'wrong' types of victims in society (i.e., those for whom a fully-fledged 'theoretical' understanding of their victimhood has not yet been formulated in the academy – such as the unemployed). In many cases, argues Rorty, as we saw in the previous chapter, the cultural left's futile attempts to philosophize one's way into political relevance are a symptom of what happens when a Left retreats from activism and adopts a spectatorial approach to the problems of its country. 'Disengagement from practice produces theoretical hallucinations' (94). In relation to this, see also Martha C. Nussbaum, *Cultivating Humanity: A classical defense of reform in liberal education* (Harvard University Press, Cambridge, MA, 1997), which I discuss in more detail below.
6   Catherine Belsey, 'All texts are our province', *The Time Higher Education Supplement*, 30 January 1998.
7   Martha C. Nussbaum, *Cultivating Humanity* (Harvard University Press,

Cambridge, MA, 1997), 98; subsequent page references in parentheses in the text.

8 It is worth noting how this notion of a 'deliberative democracy', one based on verbal deliberation, persists within the thought of those Marxists such as Habermas whose work took a 'linguistic turn', according to which the primacy of rational argument or *Diskurs* can determine the possibilities of the establishment of a democratic – rational – state of affairs. Additionally, it is worth indicating that the ethics of this position can fundamentally be related to a neo-Christian theology, in that 'those outside' were also precisely the people who represent a problem-case for the Christian understanding of parables. In relation to this, see Frank Kermode, *The Genesis of Secrecy* (Harvard University Press, Cambridge, MA, 1979), itself dedicated to 'those outside'.

9 Karl Marx, *The Eighteenth Brumaire of Louis Bonaparte* (Foreign Language Press, Peking, 1978), 50–1.

10 Hans-Georg Gadamer, *Praise of Theory* (trans. Chris Dawson; Yale University Press, 1998), 123; subsequent page references are in parentheses in the text.

11 Reading, *University in Ruins*, 65.

12 This, clearly, is a different position from that advanced by Rorty, say, in *Achieving our Country*. There, Rorty points out how, following some of the reforms in education that are sneered at by the Right as merely 'politically correct', the change in the way that (educated) Americans treat one another is enormous, and for the better (though he concedes, of course, that it is still possible to be sexist, homophobic, racist, misogynistic and so on; but it is not quite so easy to be these things as it was some forty years ago). This change, he argues, 'is largely due to the hundreds of thousands of teachers who have done their best to make their students understand the humiliation which previous generations of Americans have inflicted on their fellow citizens. By assigning Toni Morrison's *Beloved* instead of George Eliot's *Silas Marner* in high school literature classes . . . these teachers have made it harder for their students to be sadistic than it was for those students' parents' (81). I agree with this; but this is not yet a sufficient reason for assigning Morrison. My view, simply, is that we assign Morrison because *Beloved* is literature; and we know it to be literature precisely *because* of its edifying effects.

13 Alain Badiou, *Petit manuel d'inesthétique* (Seuil, Paris, 1998), 21; trans. mine. Subsequent page references in parentheses in text (all translations by present writer).

5 For a Literature that is Without and Beyond Compare

1 The reference here is to Massimo Cacciari, *Posthumous People* (trans. Rodger Friedman; Stanford University Press, 1996).

2 I owe this salutary reminder to my colleague, Jeremy Treglown: private discussion.

3 Franco Moretti, 'Conjectures on World Literature', *New Left Review* (new series), 1 (2000), 66.

4 Jonathan Swift, *A Tale of a Tub*, in Louis A. Landa, ed., *Jonathan Swift: Gulliver's Travels and Other Writings* (Oxford University Press, 1976), 310.

5 Michel Serres, *Eclaircissements: entretiens avec Bruno Latour* (1992; repr. Flammarion, Paris, 1994), 76.

6 Lest this be thought of as a slight aimed at Spivak, recall that the most vigorous debates in this arena take place within the pages of *New Left Review*. My contention is that it is difficult, even for those critical of globalisation on the left, to avoid this complicity.

7 The sense of 'event' here is that given by Alain Badiou. See, especially, his *L'Etre et l'événement* (Seuil, Paris, 1988). For a more simple articulation of what is at stake, see his *Conditions* (Seuil, Paris, 1992). I give my own gloss on this in my recent book, *Aesthetic Democracy* (Stanford University Press, Stanford, 2006).

8 Moretti, 'Conjectures on World Literature', 55.

9 For a fuller argumentation of my position here, see my chapter 'On Critical Humility', below.

10 George Steiner, *No Passion Spent* (Faber and Faber, 1996), 150.

11 Ibid., 142.

12 This, of course, tries now to effect a kind of continuity between my argument above, 'On Reading' and our present predicaments.

13 Here, a word on 'globalisation'. As Bill Readings has pointed out, globalisation is not experienced in the same way in Dakar as it is in Washington. In many cases, what is at issue is not globalisation but Americanisation. See Bill Readings, *The University in Ruins* (Harvard University Press, Cambridge, MA, 1997).

14 Giorgio Agamben, *Homo Sacer* (trans. Daniel Heller-Roazen; Stanford University Press, Stanford, 1998), 131.

15 Gayatri Spivak, *Death of a Discipline* (Columbia University Press, New York, 2003), 3, 4.

16 Erich Auerbach, *Mimesis* (trans. Willard R. Trask; Princeton University Press, 1968), 552. Cf. Edward Said, *The World, the Text, the Critic* (Faber and Faber, 1984), 5–9; and for my own commentary on this, see my *After Theory* (revised 2nd edition; Edinburgh University Press, Edinburgh, 1996), 144–7.

17 Moretti, 'Conjectures on World Literature', 67.

18 In stating it this way, that is, in terms of the regulation of uniformity and diversity, I am alluding to the aesthetic principles outlined by Frances Hutcheson in his 1725 *Inquiry Concerning Beauty, Order, Harmony, Design*, repr. In Hutcheson, *Philosophical Writings*, ed. R. S. Downie (Everyman, 1994). This fundamentally aestheticist drive, with which I am happy to concur, foregrounds beauty; but in what follows, I shall give a specific inflection to this, in an attempt to infuse the aesthetic with an ethics, which will result in an attention to 'love' as being central to Comparative Literary studies. For more on the aestheticist basis of this, see my *Criticism and Modernity* (Oxford University Press, Oxford, 1999).

19   Jean-François Lyotard, 'Answering the Question: What is Postmodernism',
     repr. in Thomas Docherty, ed., *Postmodernism: A Reader* (Columbia University
     Press, 1993), 46.
20   Alain Badiou, *Conditions* (Seuil, Paris, 1992), 258. For a fuller explanation of
     the stakes of the argument here in a wider theoretical context, see my *Alterities*
     (Oxford University Press, 1996), 203–5.

6 Newman: The University and Universalism

1   The title and epigram for this chapter both come from John Henry Newman,
    Discourses on University Education, in Newman, *Prose and Poetry*, ed. Geoffrey
    Tillotson (Rupert Hart-Davis, London, 1957), 360 and 357 respectively.
    Those whom Newman describes as 'dazzled by phenomena, instead of
    perceiving things' are the immature, who are immature precisely because they
    have had an inadequate education.
2   I use the term 'militant' here to describe Newman's stance. This is unusual.
    Roy Foster, in *Modern Ireland 1600–1972* (Penguin, 1989), 395, describes
    Newman, with some validity, as an 'armchair nationalist', even though
    Newman did see his term and mission in Ireland in the quasi-military terms
    of a campaign. Further, however, the sense I have in mind when I use the
    term 'militant' here in given more fully by Alain Badiou in his *Saint Paul –
    la fondation de l'universalisme* (PUF, Paris, 1997), where Paul is seen as 'un
    penseur-poète de 'l'événement, en même temps que celui qui pratique et
    énonce des traits invariants de ce qu'on peut appeler la figure militante' (2).
    See later in the present chapter for the relation of Newman to this figure.
3   Richard Rorty, 'Le cosmopolitanisme sans émancipation: en réponse à Jean-
    François Lyotard', *Critique*, 41 (May, 1985), 570. See my comments on this
    position in my *After Theory* (2nd revised edn; Edinburgh University Press,
    Edinburgh, 1996), 63–4; and see also Jacques Derrida, *Cosmopolites de tous les
    pays, encore un effort!* (Galilée, Paris, 1997), trans. as 'On Cosmopolitanism' in
    Derrida, *On Cosmopolitanism and Forgiveness* (trans. Mark Dooley and Michael
    Hughes; Routledge, 2001).
4   This notion of self-fulfilment has its contemporary counterpart in Rorty,
    Achieving our Country (Harvard University Press, Cambridge, MA, 1998),
    where the idea of fulfilling oneself is tantamount to becoming a good
    American. See later in the present chapter for how Newman's position radi-
    cally differs from this, in being 'globalist' rather than nationalist.
5   In this respect, Soros's position is one that is tacitly accepted even by left-
    leaning or liberal Irish thought. See, for example, Mary Robinson's
    'Opinion' piece, 'Globalisation has to take human rights into account', *The
    Irish Times* (22 January 2002). There, she argues that 'What is emerging is
    the need for globalisation as an economic process to be subject to moral and
    ethical considerations and to respect international legal standards and prin-
    ciples'. Robinson, unlike Soros in this respect, argues for the necessity of
    linking the realms of global business with those of morality; Soros, as we

shall see here, takes a more austere line, separating the two realms.

6   George Soros, *Open Society: Reforming Global Capitalism* (Little, Brown & Co., New York, 2000), xi.

7   Ibid., xii.

8   Terry Eagleton, *Nationalism: Irony and Commitment* (Field Day Pamphlet, no. 13; Field Day Theatre Company, Derry, 1988), 6; repr. in Seamus Deane, ed., *Nationalism, Colonialism and Literature* (University of Minnesota Press, Minneapolis, 1990), where the passage cited appears on pp. 24–5.

9   Ibid., 6; Deane, ed., 25.

10 Newman occasionally identifies one of these islands as 'England', which is not, of course, an island at all. He is in good company in this error: Shakespeare also famously allows John of Gaunt in *Richard II* to describe England as 'this scept'red isle . . . .bound in with the triumphant sea'.

11 Newman, *Discourses on University Education*, 359.

12 The provenance of this film, and its production, is important here. Doyle is a former Dublin schoolteacher, who had worked in the less privileged or wealthy parts of the city. Parker is an English director who is shy of any forms of intellectualism in his films or in the discussion of cinema generally. The screenplay of the film was by Doyle and two other writers, Dick Clements and Ian La Fresnais, whose forte was the populist television comedy form. In all of this, the question of education is being set against populism; and this opposition – essentially a revisiting of the Renaissance opposition between 'scientia' and 'opinio' – is one that is frequently used to legitimise global capitalism in our times, when 'opinion' (as seen most forcefully in market-choices, supposedly freely made) is held to be more valid than abstract 'knowledge' (which becomes a specialist matter for intellectuals only, allegedly divorced from the real or material world).

13 Erich Auerbach, *Mimesis* (trans. Willard R. Trask; Princeton University Press, New Jersey, 1968), 552. This passage is extraordinarily poignant, and relevant here, given the circumstances of its composition. Auerbach pleads here for an argument from literature that will defeat Nazism. See my more detailed comments on this in my *After Theory*, 144.

14 For an interesting exploration of this link in a different context, see Lyn Innes, *The Devil's Own Mirror* (Three Continents Press, Washington, 1990).

15 Seamus Deane, 'Civilians and Barbarians', in Deane *et al.*, *Ireland's Field Day* (Hutchinson, 1985), 33.

16 It is important to be fair to Rorty in this. Rorty's politics are profoundly aware of the disadvantaged in society; and, in *Achieving our Country*, he rightly takes to task that criticism that believes it can simply change the world from within the discourses of the academy. An earlier generation of leftist intellectuals, he points out there, were more genuinely politically engaged. It is an error (and here I am in total agreement with Rorty) to read one's politics – and more especially one's political efficacy – straight off from one's philosophy.

17   Bill Readings, *The University in Ruins* (Harvard University Press, Cambridge, MA, 1996), 2.

18   And, for the New Historicists remaining among us, herewith an originating anecdote for this chapter. While teaching in Trinity College Dublin between 1990–95, I used to take my morning coffee in Bewley's in Dublin's Grafton Street. This 'Oriental' tea-house, whose interiors evoked fin-de-siècle Vienna coffee-houses, was staffed almost exclusively by Northside Dublin women. On my return to Dublin in 1998, it was noticeable that the interior had lost its traditional feel, being replaced by homogenising ('universal') plastic; and the staff were almost exclusively students and young people not from Dublin but from the margins of Europe. The question is not just 'where did the Dublin women go?' but also where did the entire infrastructure that they supported – and that supported them – go?

19   See John Milton, 'Paradise Lost', Bk. 12, line 646, in Milton, *Poems*, ed. B.A. Wright (Dent, London, 1956), 388; and John Donne, 'The Sun Rising', in Donne, *The Complete English Poems*, ed. A. J. Smith (Penguin, 1973), 80. I have written in detail about the Donne phenomenon in my *John Donne, Undone* (Methuen, 1986). More important in this present context is that two of the founding principles of the modern University – the regulation of bodies and of number/economies – are explicitly correlated in this poem.

20   In this respect, a comparison is available with John of Gaunt's idea of England. As I indicated above, Gaunt erroneously takes England for an island. To claim Ireland as an island is, of necessity at the time of my writing this, a political gesture akin to that made by Auerbach in his analysis of Woolf. An island is precisely what Ireland is still struggling to become – but to become again, for it once was. When Newman was writing, long prior to Partition, its boundaries were clearer, paradoxically, than now. See also my essay called 'The Place's Fault', in Ondrey Pilnij and Clare Wallace, eds., *Global Ireland* (Literaria Pragensia, Prague, 2006), where I argue that a nation, to be a nation, must fundamentally be incomplete, fissured in some way.

21   Marcel Proust, *A la recherché du temps perdu*, ed., in four volumes, Jean-Yves Tadie *et al.* (Pleiade; Gallimard, Paris, 1987), vol. 1: 8.

22   Ibid., 1: 43–4.

23   For the relations of Joyce to Svevo at this time, see, of course, Richard Ellmann, *James Joyce* (revised edn; Oxford University Press, Oxford, 1982), 271. See also Jean-François Lyotard, *Heidegger and 'the Jews'* (trans. Andreas Michael and Mark Roberts; University of Minnesota Press, Minneapolis, 1990).

24   Newman, *Discourses on University Education*, 355.

25   Saint Augustine, *Confessions* (trans. R. S. Pine-Coffin; Penguin, Harmondsworth, 1961), 222.

26   Jorge Luis Borges, 'Funes the Memorius', in *Labyrinths* (Penguin, Harmondsworth, 1970), 94.

27   Ibid., 105.

28 Ibid., 102. The first ellipsis in the passage here appears also in the original. 1824 is the date of the Act that establishes free trade between Britain and Ireland in manufactured items. I have not yet been able to ascertain that Borges knew of that; though it would be important and significant if he did.

29 Cf. Lyotard, *Heidegger and 'the jews'*, 5, on this phenomenon in relation to the 'French' and the French literary tradition.

30 Dare one suggest that this is akin to the Marxist academic who gives us to believe that the world can be changed by the brilliant rhetoric of his writings?

31 Borges, *Labyrinths*, 99.

32 Paul, 1 Cor. 15: 21–2.

33 1 Cor. 15: 2.

34 Newman, *Discourses on University Education*, 378.

35 Ibid., 379.

36 Ibid.

37 Ibid., 380. In relation to this, see also Auerbach, *Mimesis*, ch. 3 (esp. pp. 68–76), on the relations of parataxis to figural style and to modernity in Augustine.

38 Newman, *Discourses on University Education*, 380. The reference to 'Protestant Berlin' is to Humboldt's University of Berlin.

39 Ibid., 382–3.

40 Ibid., 383

41 For an illuminating explanation of the stakes of the confrontation between Peter and Paul, see Alain Badiou, *Saint Paul*, 23–4.

42 Badiou, *Saint Paul*, 47.

43 Ibid.

44 Ibid., 48.

45 Ibid.

46 James Joyce, 'Grace', in *The Essential James Joyce*, ed. Harry Levin (Penguin, Harmondsworth, 1963), 476.

47 Badiou, *Saint Paul*, 81.

48 See my earlier chapters and comments on Readings; and, for the fuller and more detailed historical account of the relation of the University in Europe to the emerging modern nation states, see my *Criticism and Modernity: Aesthetics, Literature and Nations in Europe and its Academics* (Oxford University Press, 1999), esp. ch. 7, pp. 205–45.

7 The Existence of Scotland

1 Theodor Adorno and Max Horkheimer, *Dialectic of Enlightenment* (1944; trans. John Cumming; Verso, 1979), 148.

2 See especially Fredric Jameson, *Postmodernism* (Verso, 1991), 10–16.

3 Gianni Vattimo, *The Transparent Society* (1989; trans. David Webb; Polity Press, Cambridge, 1992); see especially the opening chapter.

4 If there is one founding element of Frankfurt School philosophy, I would venture to put it in these terms: the Frankfurt School analysed the problem-

atic of cultural history as the demise of content in the face of the rise of form. The issue here is whether we have the form of Scotland (thus evidence that it exists) devoid of content (thus no material existence).

5 'Merely' here means not simply 'only', but also 'purely'; it this has a positive inflection rather than the negative that the word often implies.

6 For an excellent meditation on the question of such autonomy, from an entirely different point of view, see Lindsay Paterson, *The Autonomy of Modern Scotland* (Edinburgh University Press, Edinburgh, 1994).

7 For a sense of the impact of this on world literature, see the catalogue of names advanced by Andrew Hook as the followers of this new form of historical novel in his 'Introduction' to his Penguin Classics edition of Sir Walter Scott, *Waverley* (1972; repr. Penguin, 1985), 10.

8 Cairns Craig, *Out of History* (Polygon, Edinburgh, 1996), 70.

9 Ibid., 70–1.

10 See Franco Moretti, *The Way of the World* (trans. Albert Sbraggia; Verso, 1987). In relation to Scott's *Waverley* and how space becomes time 'only in the proximity of the internal border' in historical novels, see his *Atlas of the European Novel: 1800–1900* (Verso, 1999), 38ff.

11 On 'affective individualism' as the ground of a supposed free autonomy in the making of marriage-allegiances, see Lawrence Stone, *The Family, Sex and Marriage in England 1500–1800* (1977; repr. Penguin 1982).

12 For a fuller consideration of the question of 'experience', its relation to history and to material practice in the sphere of the aesthetic, see my *Aesthetic Democracy* (Stanford University Press, 2006), especially the chapter entitled 'Aesthetics and the Demise of Experience'. Key figures in the question of experience are Benjamin, Agamben, Leavis.

13 The trope here is that which will be adopted by E. M. Forster as a guiding principle for both *Where Angels Fear to Tread* (1905) and *A Room with a View* (1908). In both these novels, Forster sets up an opposition between an 'official' Italy and 'real' Italians, between the country and its inhabitants, such that reality is to be found in the inhabitants and not in the official country itself. The trope becomes of more obviously pressing political importance when he deploys it in *A Passage to India* in 1924; but the political issues that shape that twentieth-century novel of colonialism are present fully in *Waverley* too.

14 Scott, *Waverley*, 74.

15 Ibid.

16 Famously, both Margaret Thatcher and, in a rather different way, Jean Baudrillard, both questioned the existence of society. Thatcher's view (so roundly rejected in contemporary Scotland, of course) was precisely akin to the view proffered here via Scott, paradoxically. It might be worth adding that 'society' as I use the term here refers also to 'official' society, the *haut-monde*.

17 Scott, *Waverley*, 107–8. See also Robert Crawford, *Devolving English Literature* (Oxford University Press, Oxford, 1992), 124–31 on this multilingualism.

18 See Jean Baudrillard, *De la seduction* (Denoel, Paris, 1979), where he first advocated a 'fatal strategy' for feminism, advising women that the road to power lay, counter-intuitively, in 'going over to the side of the objects'; and cf. his *Les Strategies fatales* (Grasset, Paris, 1983), where he generalised this hypothesis more widely.

19 Scott, *Waverley*, 123. Gellatley, it might be said in passing, owes much to the character of Thersites in Shakespeare's *Troilus and Cressida*, though with the bitterness of spirit withdrawn.

20 See especially *Out of History*, 67–72.

21 That position is one that became favoured under the influence of Bakhtin in recent times. For a useful consideration of the position, see Terry Eagleton's essay, 'The Critic as Clown', in his *Against the Grain* (Verso, 1986), where he relates it to pastoralism.

22 Scott, *Waverley*, 65–6.

23 Ibid., 495.

24 See Friedrich Nietzsche, *Twilight of the Idols* (trans. R. J. Hollingdale; Penguin, 1968).

25 See George Davie, *The Democratic Intellect* (1961; repr. Edinburgh University Press, Edinburgh, 1982). For a fuller account of the stakes of the argument than I shall advance here, see my *Criticism and Modernity: Aesthetics, Literature and Nations in Europe and its Academies* (Oxford University Press, 1999), esp. section three.

26 Scott, *Waverley*, 109.

27 Ibid.

28 Ibid.

29 Ibid., 169

30 It will be remembered, in passing, that it is actually the arrival of Fergus's dog that arrests the translation.

31 See A. C. Bradley, *Shakespearean Tragedy* (1904; repr. 2nd edn., Macmillan, 1976), 86ff.

32 Giorgio Agamben, *Potentialities* (trans. Daniel Heller-Roazen; Stanford University Press, Stanford, 1999). For a fuller account of Agamben, dealing with the trajectory of his oeuvre as a whole, see my 'Potential European Democracy' in *Paragraph* (2002), special issue on Agamben, ed. Brian Dillon; and of my argument on Agamben in *Aesthetic Democracy*.

8 On Critical Humility

1 Wallace Stevens, *The Necessary Angel* (Vintage Books, New York, n.d.), page 29

2 Ibid., 29–30.

3 I use the word 'potential' here, as in my previous chapters, in the rather strict sense that it is given in the work of Giorgio Agamben. For a full clarification, see Agamben, *Potentialities* (trans. Daniel Heller-Roazen; Stanford University Press, Stanford, 1999).

4   Kenneth Burke, *Language as Symbolic Action* (University of California Press, Berkeley and Los Angeles, 1966), 20, n. 2.

5   Ludwig Wittgenstein, *Tractatus Logico-Philosophicus* (bilingual edn, trans. C. K. Ogden; Routledge, London, 1992), 184/185: prop. 6.4311

6   On this apotropaism as a modern phenomenon, see Hans Blumenberg, *The Legitimacy of the Modern Age* (trans. Robert M. Wallace; MIT Press, Cambridge, MA, 1983), esp. ch. 2.

7   Thomas Hobbes, *Elements of Law*, published under the title *Human Nature and De Corpore Politico*, ed. J. C. A. Gaskin (Oxford University Press, Oxford 1994), 43–4.

8   Hobbes, *Leviathan*, ed. Edwin Curley (Hackett, Indianapolis, 1994), 32.

9   In the work of Kenneth Burke, 'motives' play a central operational part. For a useful introduction to this, see Steven Bygrave, *Kenneth Burke: Rhetoric and Ideology* (Routledge, London, 1993).

10   Hobbes, *Leviathan*, 32.

11   For a fuller tracing of the effects of this on European culture, see my *Criticism and Modernity: Aesthetics, Literature and Nations in Europe and its Academies* (Oxford University Press, Oxford, 1999), esp. ch 2, 'Love as the European Humour'.

12   The notion of 'prevention' I have in mind here is one to be found in the poetry of George Herbert. Herbert frequently complains that he has been 'prevented' from doing as he might by God, in the sense that God has always done it first. He is thus denied authority and autonomy precisely in the very moment when he most fervently tries to assert it; and it is this condition of belatedness – in which his entire life is prevented by God's – that Herbert paradoxically finds his subject for poetry. For a fuller explanation, see my *On Modern Authority* (Harvester-Wheatsheaf, Brighton, 1987).

13   Jacques Derrida, *Demeure*, in Maurice Blanchot, *The Instant of my Death* and Jacques Derrida, *Demeure* (trans. Elizabeth Rottenberg; Stanford University Press, Stanford, 2000), 28.

14   For the distinction between zoe and bios here outlined, see Giorgio Agamben, *Homo Sacer* (trans. Daniel Heller-Roazen; Stanford University Press, Stanford, 1998).

15   G. W. F. Hegel, *Aesthetics*, vol. 1 (trans. T. M. Knox; Oxford University Press, Oxford, 1975), 2. This should recall my opening chapter where I related this to the fact rather than to this potentiality for freedom.

16   On the sinanthrope as 'prehominians', see Pierre Teilhard de Chardin, *The Human Phenomenon* (1955; trans. Sarah Appleton-Weber; Sussex Academic Press, Brighton, 1999).

17   Teilhard de Chardin, *Sur le Bonheur / Sur l'Amour* (Seuil, Paris, 1997), 9–10.

18   Ibid., 21.

19   Blaise Pascal, *Pensées* in *Oeuvres complètes* (Seuil, Paris, 1963), 516; liasse VIII, fragment 136 (Lafuma edition: corresponds to fragment 139 in Brunschvicg edition).

20   Here, I am alluding in passing not only to the Pascal fragment from the *Pensées* just cited, but also to the preceding fragment (135; 469 in Brunschvicg): 'Je sens que je puis n'avoir point été . . . donc je ne suis pas un être nécessaire', but also, more obviously, to Beckett's famous dialogues with Georges Duthuit. Interestingly, Teilhard also has a relevant comment here. Twice in two pages of *The Human Phenomenon*, discussing the 'original forms' in the 'birth of thought' , he writes: 'Man came silently into the world'.

21   On this, see Paul de Man, *The Resistance to Theory* (Manchester University Press, Manchester, 1986), 11, where he puts it thus: 'What we call ideology is precisely the confusion of linguistic with natural reality, of reference with phenomenalism'. My gloss suggests that ideology is the too-rapid and unreflective – prejudiced – move from reference to phenomenalism in these terms. A fuller exploration of the politics in question here might be found in Norberto Bobbio, *In Praise of Meekness* (Polity, Cambridge, 2000), esp. ch. 1.

22   E. M. Cioran, *The Trouble with Being Born* (trans. Richard Howard; Quartet Books, London, 1993), 6.

23   Jean-Paul Sartre, *Being and Nothingness* (trans. Hazel Barnes; Philosophical Library, New York, 1956), 566.

24   Cioran, *The Trouble with Being Born*, 17.

25   Ibid., 28. In our fully administered and managed University system, Hell is that 'transparency' in which there is no possibility of surprise; it is that place – that class – shaped by the auditory mechanisms and the monitoring systems of QAA and all its Beelzebub-like self-vauntings.

26   It should be noted in passing that the consequence of this kind of humility is very definitely not a self-loathing. As Cioran writes, 'he who hates himself is not humble', *The Trouble with Being Born*, 26. Such hatred is already a premature agency or action, not passionate enough.

27   Derrida, *Demeure*, 45

28   Ibid., 33

29   Jacques Derrida, *The Gift of Death* (trans. David Wills; University of Chicago Press, Chicago, 1995), 41.

30   Teilhard de Chardin, *Sur le Bonheur / Sur l'Amour*, 52–3.

31   See Jacques Derrida, *Politiques de l'amitié* (Galilée, Paris, 1994), 27–8; and see my commentary on this in my *Criticism and Modernity*, 62–7.

9 Clandestine English

1   Felicity Rosslyn, 'Literature for the Masses: the English Literature Degree in 2004', *Cambridge Quarterly*, 33:1 (2004), 1; 2. The piece takes the by now almost standard position that the 'rise of English', as Eagleton called it in his influential *Literary Theory* (Blackwell, Oxford, 1983) was a rather domestic affair. My own view, as I hope is now clear, is that such a view is essentially too parochial, not 'comparativist' enough, and that it fails to account for both the condition of vernaculars generally and the condition of English as a globalising language. For a fuller argumentation of the emergence of English, see

my *Criticism and Modernity*, especially chapter 7. See also Robert Scholes, *The Rise and Fall of English* (Yale University Press, New Haven, 1998).

2   Virginia Woolf, 'Modern Fiction', in *Collected Essays*, vol. II (Hogarth Press, 1966), 106.

3   Those semantic vacuities of our contemporary claims for 'excellence' are, of course, at the centre of Bill Readings's coruscating commentary in *The University in Ruins* (Harvard University Press, Cambridge, MA, 1996).

4   The parenthesis in this sentence is important. I allude to the 'hoped-for' post-Nazi Europe; and my anxiety, maked by the parenthesis, is that, although we are certainly *post*-Nazi, we are also nonetheless equally certainly post-*Nazi*. That is to say, I believe that we need to question how far Europe – and not only Europe – has moved away from the carceral ideology that we usually believe we defeated in 1945. Two key thinkers here are Agamben and Badiou, whose work I consider in this regard in more detail in my *Criticism and Modernity*.

5   Walter Benjamin, *Illuminations*, ed. Hannah Arendt (trans Harry Zohn; Fontana, 1973), 243.

6   At the start of my career, I attended an LTP ('Literature Teaching Politics') conference during which Terry Hawkes, a major scholar of Shakespeare and seventeenth-century literature, attacked what he called 'the myth of wide reading', arguing that it was better to read a small number of things well than to have saturated oneself in swathes of literature. I have always felt uneasy about that; but it has probably become much more of a mainstream view than my own, which envies the massive erudition of older critics such as Ernst Robert Curtius or Erich Auerbach or George Steiner and so on. Taking a line deriving now from Rancière, I would claim that wide reading – *even* if done in some belle-lettristic fashion – yields enormous dividends in the interests of freedom.

7   I initially wrote this passage in 2004. Interestingly, on 28 June 2007, Gordon Brown as the new British prime Minister, closed the Department for Education and Skills, and replaced it with two offices: 'Department for Children, Schools, and Families', and the 'Department for Innovation, Universities, and Skills'. Education has in fact disappeared; and the logic of the Blair–Brown project has been carried to its conclusion.

8   The best simple introduction to this in detail is in the introduction to Giambattista Vico, *On Humanistic Education*, ed. Giorgio A. Pinton (trans. Giorgio A. Pinton and Arthur W. Shippee; Cornell University Press, Ithaca, 1993).

Index